The Schools We Deserve

THE
SCHOOLS
WE DESERVE

Reflections on the Educational

Crises of Our Times

DIANE RAVITCH

Basic Books, Inc., Publishers

NEW YORK

Library of Congress Cataloging in Publication Data

Ravitch, Diane.

The schools we deserve.

Bibliographic references.

Includes index.

1. Education—United States—Aims and objectives.
2. Education—Standards—United States.   3. Education—
Humanistic—United States.   4. Education and state—
United States.   5. Minorities—Education—United States.
6. School integration—United States.   I. Title.
LA209.2.R38   1985   370′.973   84–45303
ISBN   0–465–07236–4 (cloth)
ISBN   0–465–07235–6 (paper)

For Joseph and Michael

CONTENTS

PREFACE   ix

Introduction   3

1. Forgetting the Questions: The Problem of Educational Reform   27

2. The Schools We Deserve   45

3. The Continuing Crisis: Fashions in Education   58

4. Bring Literature and History Back to Elementary Schools   75

5. American Education: Has the Pendulum Swung Once Too Often?   80

6. Scapegoating the Teachers   90

7. The Meaning of the New Coleman Report   100

8. From History to Social Studies: Dilemmas and Problems   112

9. Curriculum in Crisis: Connections Between Past and Present   133

10. Is Education Really a Federal Issue? 151

11. 60s Education, 70s Benefits 157

12. The Case of Tuition Tax Credits 161

13. The Uses and Misuses of Tests 172

14. On the History of Minority Group Education 182
in the United States

15. Integration, Segregation, Pluralism 208

16. Desegregation: Varieties of Meaning 226

17. Color-Blind or Color-Conscious? 249

18. Politicization and the Schools: The Case of 260
Bilingual Education

19. A Good School 275

20. On Thinking About the Future 295

21. Prospects 309

NOTES 317

ACKNOWLEDGMENTS 323

INDEX 325

PREFACE

THE essays in this collection were written during the past decade. Some of them represent fragments of work that later became part of a book; as such, they permitted me to think out loud about a problem that later— in the book— shrunk to only a few paragraphs or a sentence. Some of them overlap because they are different attempts to think through similar questions, such as the three essays on curriculum history and the four essays on the issue of race and education. All of them owe a great deal to the many people who heard me out as I was trying to think through some issue that intrigued me. As ever, my husband, Richard, was patient, supportive, and understanding. My friends endured more than one would normally expect of good friends: they kept listening. For their friendship and colleagueship, I want to express my deep appreciation to Chester Finn, Jr., Rita Kramer, Abigail Thernstrom, Patricia Graham, and Michael Timpane. I owe special thanks to Mary F. Butz, who taught me to see many of the things I care about from the teacher's perspective. In this work, as in everything else I have written, I continue to be in the debt of Lawrence A. Cremin, who indelibly influenced my understanding of American education. I am grateful to Martin Kessler of Basic Books, who saw this volume through to completion. The book is lovingly dedicated to my wonderful, handsome, witty, intelligent sons, Joseph and Michael, without whom none of this would be worthwhile.

DIANE RAVITCH

The Schools We Deserve

Introduction

IN the mid-1980s, the condition of the nation's schools became a major issue. It is not often that the schools gain the attention of the public for any sustained period of time. Some educators reacted angrily or defensively to the sudden scrutiny of the institution for which they were responsible, treating the unaccustomed concern for the schools as unwarranted attacks on them. Others realized that the time might be right to initiate some long-overdue reforms in the way schools function and to build public support for better education.

Usually, education is taken for granted as a public service that is available on an "as is" basis. People who do not have children are only dimly aware of what happens in schools; people who do have young children frequently care little about what happens beyond their own school.

Occasionally, a series of events or a set of conditions causes public attention to focus on the nation's schools not as a given but as a problem. Such a situation occurred after the Russians' launching of Sputnik in the late 1950s, when the media, the Congress, and the public concluded that America had fallen behind in the race for scientific and technical superiority in space because of inadequacies in the teaching of science, mathematics, and foreign languages. Since then, one transient shortcoming after another briefly captured the public's interest, but not until 1983–84 was there another full-blown sense of crisis. Then it was the report of the National Commission on Excellence in Education that sounded the claxon, swiftly followed by other declarations of alarm about the state of American education.

As a result of the attention generated by the many national reports, school reform moved to the top of the political agenda across the nation. Legislatures, school boards, and governors in nearly all the states took steps to improve public schools. Taxes were raised to increase teachers' salaries and provide better funding; a number of states adopted merit pay plans or career ladder programs to provide incentives for superior teachers; some districts adopted tests for incoming teachers in order to screen out unqualified candidates; high school graduation requirements were raised; many state universities reimposed entrance requirements, abandoned in the late 1960s, not only to improve the quality of their freshman class but also to encourage high schools to buttress graduation requirements.

For the first time since Sputnik, school improvement had a broad constituency. There was a significant difference, however. The target group for post-Sputnik school reformers had been the gifted, but the school reformers of the early 1980s expressed their critique in broadly democratic terms: Why shouldn't all children get the best education we can afford to provide? The future of school reform depends on whether the reformers maintain this commendable democratic ideology, whether they forge an indissoluble link between quality and equality in their aspirations for the schools. It will not be easy to sustain the momentum for school reform; it never has been. It is difficult to keep public interest concentrated on problems that are so complicated and that respond so sluggishly to reformers' efforts.

These periodic swings of the educational pendulum, from one pedagogical extreme to another, from public apathy to intense concern, are puzzling to many Americans. They are even more baffling to foreigners, who find it difficult to understand an educational tradition that seems consciously antitraditional, pragmatic, and experimental. I gained new perspective on some of the issues when I undertook to explain what was happening here to foreign educators. In the spring of 1984, I traveled across Yugoslavia, lecturing to university students and faculty members about American education. They were manifestly eager to learn more about the current educational issues and trends in our country, and I tried to convey to them some sense of the ongoing national debate about the quality and direction of our schools. I told them about the series of reports that had emanated from private and public blue-ribbon commissions in the early 1980s calling for increased academic rigor and higher standards. I described the criticism directed with special urgency at our high schools, because of declining enrollments in such subjects as mathematics, science, and foreign languages. I tried to explain how complicated it is to reform a national school "system" that is not actually a system at all, but rather nearly 16,000 decentralized school districts.

I learned a great deal from the questions that my audiences asked and from their responses to my presentations. They could not fathom why we permitted students not to learn a foreign language or why our requirements for the study of science and mathematics were so low. Our self-criticism about science and mathematics education was especially puzzling to them, since they saw the United States as the most scientifically and technologically advanced nation in the world. Librarians at the American cultural centers in Yugoslavia told me that the most popular publications were those about science and that young people followed the progress of our space shuttle program with a rapt attention that American teenagers had long since lost. Because of their admiration for American scientific achievements, Yugoslav educators found the laxity and permissiveness of our educational practices incomprehensible. How could a great country allow some children to grow up ignorant of major areas of knowledge, they asked? Since I shared their incredulity, I could not defend the educational policies and assumptions that made certain studies—like foreign languages and advanced science and mathematics—optional for most American children.

In contrast to my embarrassment about aspects of our precollegiate practices, I developed an enormous sense of pride as I explained the apparent chaos called American higher education. Viewed as a system, it is a mess: Anyone can go to college; and anyone, at any age, can return at any time to take courses, develop new skills, or change occupations. What we have, I realized, is a system (or nonsystem) in which there is no last chance, in which everyone has as many chances as he chooses to take, in which education is available at relatively low cost to be acquired by the consumer as he wishes. How do the colleges know which courses to offer, Yugoslav educators wondered? Is there a government agency that plans what the colleges should offer in anticipation of the needs of the economy? No, I explained, higher education adds and drops courses in direct response to student demand. The student-consumers tell the colleges what they want by their patterns of enrollment, and most colleges adapt quickly to perceived needs. Of course, if higher education responds only to market trends, this is good news for computer programmers and not very good news for professors of Renaissance art, but a sensible combination of market sensitivity and academic integrity is undoubtedly more efficient and more dynamic than a system in which higher education is planned by a government bureaucracy. It came as something of a shock to me to realize that higher education in America may be one of our strongest bastions of free enterprise, with both its good and bad features.

Something else that I observed in these meetings gave me a renewed respect for American education. As a lecturer, I found that it was exceedingly difficult to elicit questions from the audience. At the end of each talk, I invited queries and invariably felt disappointed when no hands were raised. An interpreter told me that it was generally believed that asking questions of a lecturer was disrespectful; it signified criticism. Once I understood this, I began each lecture with a statement about the importance that Americans place on the value of dialogue and discussion. An American speaker, I told them, expected and wanted questions from the audience. If, after this careful preparation, there were still few questions, I implored them to "pretend to be Americans for just a few minutes," and that was usually enough to get a lively discussion going. As I reflected on the problem of getting a good exchange started, it occurred to me that most American teachers stress questions and answers, even in primary school reading classes. I thought about classrooms I have visited in which teachers routinely asked, "Why do you think that?" "Does anyone know the answer?" "What happened next?" Even in the most didactic settings, American teachers want responsive students; they want, at the least, assurance that the students are paying attention and are fully engaged. That this is indeed the case was brought home to me only days after my return from Yugoslavia, when I spoke before an audience at Western Michigan University in Kalamazoo; hardly had I finished when the arms were flailing in the air, challenging statements that I had made. This instinctive encouragement of debate and discussion and inquiry, I thought, excused a great deal about American education. Whatever students learn or fail to learn, they do learn to ask questions; to measure what they hear against their own judgment and experience; and to believe that their opinion counts for something, even in the presence of a so-called expert.

This is not an unalloyed blessing. A friend who teaches at MIT told me about a college freshman who said that he had heard that the U.S. government had three different branches, but had also heard that this was only an opinion. Other professors complain about students who arrive at college with strong convictions but not enough knowledge to argue persuasively for their beliefs. Having opinions without knowledge is not of much value; not knowing the difference between them is a positive indicator of ignorance.

As I reflected on my travels in Yugoslavia, it seemed to me that we Americans too often sell our schools short. With all their faults—and many are spelled out in the essays in this book—they nonetheless have extraordinary accomplishments to their credit. For most of our history, penniless immigrants have streamed through our port cities; their transition from poverty and illiteracy into the vast American middle class owes much to the public schools. The children of the European immigrants who arrived during the nineteenth and early twentieth centuries learned the common language of the U.S., the common culture, and a sense of belonging in the public schools. Sometimes crudely, but almost invariably with remarkable success, the public schools made them Americans and taught them the language and ideas with which they could later demand equality and justice. Few nations have opened their doors so widely or offered citizenship so freely as has the United States. In recent years, after the liberalization of the immigration laws, the nation has again experienced a dramatic wave of newcomers, this time consisting of persons from the Orient, Latin America, and elsewhere who had voted with their feet for economic and political freedom. Once again, the burden of teaching them how to become Americans fell on the schools. Other countries, including many whose borders are closed or who deny citizenship even to the children of aliens born on their soil, take cheap shots at us as we struggle to educate children from diverse cultures. In willingly accepting this responsibility, our schools have occasionally made mistakes, but usually with good intentions; we owe no apologies to those who take no such risks.

For more than a century, the United States has led the world in popular education, and the investment has been a good one. Our nation's commitment to free schooling has contributed to our high standard of living, to general respect for our democratic ideals, to the maintenance of our free institutions, and to our continuing openness to social and technological change. Increased levels of educational attainment appear to promote social and economic progress by improving people's intelligence and skills. There is a vast literature on the relationship between education and economic advancement, which I will not attempt to summarize here. Some economists have argued that equalizing education is not an efficient way of equalizing incomes, and I agree: The Internal Revenue Service does a far better job of redistributing income than the schools could ever do, and does so much more quickly. Even so, increasing educational attainment is still a good investment in human resources over the long run. As I was writing this essay, I received a new study by James P. Smith of the Rand Corporation, who offers a statistical demonstration to buttress his conclusion that "during this century, America has undergone an evolutionary process, spawned in large part in its schools, that permanently altered and improved the relative economic position of black Americans." The narrowing of the educational gap between blacks and whites, Smith argues, contributed powerfully to upgrading the quality and quantity of skills that blacks brought to the labor market, and as the "human capital" of blacks increased, so did their earnings.'

The public schools, it should be noted, did more than increase human capital. They did more than assimilate the children of diverse immigrant groups. They taught the ideology of democracy, even when they did not practice democracy. At the segregated public school that I attended in Houston, Texas, we learned year after year that America was the land of freedom, democracy, equal rights, and opportunity. We were told time and again that our nation embodied the unfolding of the human struggle for dignity and a just society. We studied the Declaration of Independence and the Constitution with care and celebrated the democratic ideals of our beloved nation. We embraced what Gunnar Myrdal called "the American creed," even though our school and our city violated it daily. We learned the principles of justice in an unjust setting. I think that this tension, this conflict between cherished rhetoric and everyday reality, helps to explain the possibility of change in the South after the *Brown* decision of 1954. Even though it has become fashionable in some circles to say that the *Brown* decision changed very little, anyone who lived in the South in 1954 knows that the change in the status of blacks since then has been substantial, and in many places dramatic. The schools helped to make peaceful change possible. This was so, first, because educated people were less likely to resort to force or violence, having learned in school that disputes should be settled by law and reason; and second, because over a long period of time the schools taught the very principles of justice on which the civil rights movement rested its case.

While I believe that the rising level of educational attainment across the population has been a positive good, I would not claim that high levels of literacy automatically sustain free institutions; there are too many totalitarian countries with highly literate populations for such a claim to ring true. John Dewey warned in the 1930s that an efficient school system could easily become the instrument of a totalitarian regime; good schools are a necessary but not a sufficient condition for the creation of a democratic social order. A free society requires not only universal schooling but also a free press, free trade unions, and a strong democratic polity. Awkward as it is for some of our more strident critics to acknowledge, the United States does have universal schooling, a free press, free trade unions, and vigorous democratic institutions. As a nation we are not without faults, but none of them goes unremarked. Our readiness to criticize ourselves is part of the glory of our educational tradition, which at its best teaches us to think for ourselves and to ask questions.[2]

I know that my positive perspective on the value of education is not universally shared, but I have also observed that skepticism about schooling is most pronounced among those with the most education. I was reminded of this irony in May 1984, when attending my older son's graduation from Amherst College. There, at the Phi Beta Kappa initiation ceremony, the featured speaker denounced education in general and liberal education in particular. A

Third World woman and professor of political science, she told a story about a village in India that had no school, where poverty, illiteracy, and backwardness were age-old. Government officials came one day, she said, with an offer to educate the children. After much discussion, the women in the village prevailed by defeating the offer. They knew, said the professor, that educating their children would disrupt their community life and would alienate the children from their families. The professor thought that this was a profoundly wise decision on the part of the village women. She asserted that illiterates make the best political activists and that educated people become tools of the dominant social order. Liberal education is especially iniquitous, she claimed, because it puts a premium on such "selfish" values as excellence and individual achievement, values that lead people to the reactionary conclusion that their accomplishments belong to them as individuals rather than as members of social groups.

Having written a critical analysis of radical revisionist interpretations of American education some years earlier, I found what she had to say to be trite, hypocritical, and wrong. If education was so pernicious, why was she teaching? If liberal education socialized the talented young to become docile cogs in the machine of the oppressive state, why was she teaching in an eminent liberal arts institution? Why was she ruining my day? It has been my observation that those who denounce literacy never stop exercising their own considerable skills of literacy and never deny their own children these powerful tools. Happily, the overwhelming majority of Americans have never succumbed to the fallacies that certain elites entertain; they understand full well that education offers a valuable path to opportunity, and that this path can be traveled only by those who use the schools to become literate.

From the mid-1960s until the late 1970s, radical attacks

on the schools were commonplace; the bookstores teemed with intemperate denunciations of the schools. Some claimed, like the speaker at Amherst, that the purpose of the schools was to turn American children into complacent servants of a corrupt society; or that the schools were prisons where children were condemned to serve time; or that the very structure of the school crushed children's hearts and minds by imposing other people's ideas on them. But who was listening to these calumnies? Consider the gap between elite and mass opinion in the late 1960s. At that time, policymakers in government, foundations, and universities agreed that the schools were in a deep crisis, and this consensus led to a nearly frenzied search for changes that were "structural" or "comprehensive" or "radical." But in 1969 the Gallup Poll, in its first survey of attitudes toward the public schools, found that the general public held them in high esteem; three out of four people said that they would be pleased if their child became a teacher. The elites and the public never did get together in their diagnosis of the ills of the schools; as public regard for the schools slipped in succeeding years, lack of discipline was named as the leading problem in the Gallup Poll every year save one. But discipline was not a priority item on the agenda of the policymaking elites.

The long period in which the schools were treated contemptuously and in which academic effort was derided had corrosive effects. Certainly, it must have discouraged entry into the teaching profession by those who were aware of the hostility of elite opinion; it must also have demoralized those who continued to teach despite the low esteem of the schools among policymaking elites. I believe that scorn for academic effort contributed to several injurious practices: the lowering of college entrance and high school graduation requirements; grade inflation; automatic promotion; absenteeism; and an overall slackening of the

13

academic "press" that spurs children to learn, to aspire, and to achieve. As such practices spread, every measure of academic achievement declined. Enrollments in foreign languages and advanced courses also fell.

The slackening of graduation requirements facilitated the phenomenon of "tracking" in American schools. Tracking has always had its proponents, and they range across the ideological spectrum. Conservatives traditionally defended tracking on the ground that it was inefficient to give an academic education to all children; progressives defended it as an appropriate pedagogical response to the differing needs and abilities of children. Whatever the rationale, the results were the same. By the early 1980s, only 35 to 38 percent of secondary school students were enrolled in an academic track—an abysmally low rate, especially since far more than that percentage proceed into postsecondary education. Tracking differs from ability grouping. Usually, ability grouping is practiced in order to help students reach similar goals (though not the same level of achievement) over different periods of time. But tracking places children in wholly separate curricular tracks ("academic," "vocational," and "general") in which the ultimate goals are widely divergent. Children in the academic track are considered college bound; children in the vocational track are trained for a specific occupation; and those in the general track get an assortment of courses that are neither academic nor vocational.

Tracking is wasteful of children's minds; it unnecessarily narrows their educational experiences. As the reader will discover on more than one occasion, I strongly believe that all children who are capable of learning should receive a broad liberal education during their years in school. All should study literature, history, science, mathematics, a foreign language, and the arts. In the ideal school, there would be no curricular tracking. All children would be expected to learn the major disciplines of knowledge; some would learn faster, some slower, but all would share in the riches of our cultural and scientific heritage; all would have a good start in understanding the physical universe that we inhabit; all would gain the political and historical knowledge to participate effectively in the democratic process; and all would master the literacy that empowers people to read, write, think, and make judgments.

Students should meet some reasonable standard of accomplishment in the major realms of knowledge. In recent years, the high school diploma has come to represent very little; in some districts, it has been handed out as a recognition of years spent in school, not of proficiency. I think that we should view a high school diploma as we do a driver's license: It should be awarded only when the student has mastered the skills and knowledge that the high school teaches. Some will take longer to achieve mastery than others, but all must be expected to meet certain goals of learning. We do not give driver's licenses to those who cannot drive, even when they mean well and even when they have mitigating reasons for their incapacity; we withhold the driver's license because we know that the incompetent driver would be a danger to himself and to others. If we took learning as seriously as driving, the high school diploma would be of far more value to those who hold it. If we put as much emphasis on learning as we do on athletics—or perhaps even half as much—and if the analogous goal was fitness for all, then the condition of our schools would not be a national problem.

If we do not take decisive steps to improve the curriculum and the academic program for all children, the pressure for increased differentiation will mount. In recent months, I have heard several reputable educators seriously propose that we undertake to provide differentiated schools and diplomas; they believe that the comprehensive high school and single diploma have tended to degrade the academic track. They suggest that we set up more elite high schools, limited to those who pass a stiff entrance examination, or that we award diplomas that recognize different levels of achievement. What they suggest, in effect, is that we make our implicit practices explicit for the benefit of the talented minority on whose future leadership we depend.

I don't agree with this assessment. I too am critical of the comprehensive high school and worry about dilution and fragmentation in the academic program. But where others call for more differentiation, I believe that what is needed is a strengthening of the academic program for all children. I would like to see all children meet real standards of achievement in history, literature, science, mathematics, and foreign language. It is difficult for me to understand how a publicly supported school can justify providing one group of children with the equivalent of a prep school experience, another group with training for a trade, and a third group with preparation for nothing at all. I argue here not for a homogeneous curriculum, nor for indifference to the special problems that burden some children's learning, but for a sense of commitment to intellectual development as a proper goal for all children, not just the gifted.

I recognize that there is a small minority of adolescents who are utterly hostile to formal education; some of them are now in alternative programs, and others have dropped out altogether. Some of these youths may do well in work-study programs or in therapeutic groups or even in telic settings modeled after the Depression-era Civilian Conservation Corps. But we should not reorient the entire school program around the special needs of the intensely alienated, particularly since we still are uncertain about how to educate those who do not wish to learn. We will surely continue to try new approaches as well as old approaches, but it is no failing to acknowledge that the schools cannot provide a remedy for every problem of our society nor for every troubled young person.

Although I would not enlist in the ranks of supporters of vocational education, I know that it has value as a motivational tool for some children and that in the hands of gifted teachers, even vocational studies can become vehicles for teaching reading, writing, arithmetic, and logical thinking. But I question the practice of permitting young people to major in a vocational subject like carpentry or meat cutting. We know that the schools have had a difficult time employing teachers for the skilled trades (since teachers' salaries are often less than those of electricians or carpenters); we know that the schools seldom can afford the up-to-date equipment that is found in the workplace. And we know that many employers run their own training programs designed to impart job-related skills. But there is a deeper problem with training for a specific trade or vocation. As the economy shifts from smokestack industries to technical and knowledge-based industries, it becomes clear that the nature of work is changing; we cannot predict with any accuracy what kinds of job skills will be needed ten or fifteen years from now. In the face of this near-certain uncertainty, the best preparation that any young person can bring into the workplace is a general education, a sense of responsibility, and the capacity to keep on learning.

I think that those who wrote the national education reports of the early 1980s shared this perspective; I have to surmise it because vocational education is scarcely mentioned in any of the reports. Their unifying theme is the need for a common basic curriculum for all children. The various reports (and at this point I have lost track of how many there were) have been roundly criticized on one ground or another: for being overly critical of the performance of the schools; for emphasizing standardized test scores too much; for relying on faulty international comparisons; for stressing the nation's economic needs too heavily; for ignoring the problems of minority youth; for putting too much emphasis on higher standards and academic rigor; for blaming the schools for society's problems; and so on. I was delighted to see the explosion of report writing, even though I did not agree with all the particulars of every report. I thought this response to the long slide of American education was overdue, and it helped to generate a healthy public interest in the problems of the schools. Whatever the flaws of the reports, this much must be said for them: All of them treated the schools seriously as constructive institutions; all of them believed that the schools have a positive, valuable, and important role to play in American society. Not one of them echoed the derision and despair that were so fashionable a decade earlier. Not all of their prescriptions were sound, but they were grounded in an assertion of faith in the potential beneficence of schooling.

In writing books on educational history, I have attempted to remove myself from the narrative as much as possible. I do not write about the past in order to divine guideposts for the future or policy counsel for the present. A few reviewers of my last book complained about the absence from its pages of a set of policy prescriptions, but this absence was intentional. In contrast, a collection such as this one is necessarily tilted toward prescriptions, opinions, and proposals. Most of these essays were written for journals of opinion. Some are obviously polemical; most were written with the intent to persuade the reader or at least to make the reader critically reexamine the conventional wisdom. It should by now be abundantly clear that I believe in the value of good education. When the schools are attacked by those who scorn literacy or try to bend the schools to narrow political ends, then I rise to their defense. When the schools seem to lose sight of their mission to abolish ignorance, then I become a critic.[3]

I try to be a responsible critic, because I believe in the school as a potential instrument of enlightenment. I want to see it strengthened in the performance of its functions, and my criticism is intended not to undermine but to build. I never lose sight of the fact that I am neither a school teacher nor an administrator, and that I am therefore in a precarious position as an outsider. I have profound respect for the teachers who work every day "in the trenches," as many of them say. I do not delude myself into thinking that I could do a better job than they do; I know that I could not. I have never believed that a ship can be navigated by someone who stays on shore.

Yet this is what many of our educational policies attempt to do. The history of education in the United States during most of this century has been characterized by a widening rift between those who make policy and those who engage in educational practice, and by the subordination of practitioners to policymakers; teachers are seldom invited to make policy or to shape the curricula that they will have to implement. Yet teachers have had to bear the burden of one reform after another, imposed upon them by zealous policymakers who do not live with the consequences of their brainstorms. Typically, educational reform movements have taken teachers for granted and treated them as classroom furniture rather than as thinking, possibly disputatious human beings. In one era after another, the same story has been repeated: The policymakers in the government and the university identify the problems and devise new solutions, with little regard for the views of teachers. When the new policy reaches the classroom, the beleaguered teachers react less than enthusiastically to the new course of study, the new curriculum, the new standardized test, and the new textbook; what they had hoped for was a period of stability and the resources and time to write their own curriculum or their own test. It is not simply low salaries that prevent teaching from being a respected profession. Until teachers exercise the prerogatives and responsibilities of professionals—exerting some control over entry into the profession, taking part in the evaluation of members of the profession, playing a responsible role in the design of curricula and programs—in short, until teachers enjoy autonomy and collegiality, teaching will continue to be a job rather than a profession. Nor will teaching be a respected profession until inferior teacher education programs are eliminated; all teachers should have a baccalaureate degree in an academic subject or combination of subjects, followed by serious professional training. All educators should be educated.

In preparing this collection, I reviewed everything I had written about schools over the past sixteen years. Many pieces were excluded because they seemed too topical or dated to merit reprinting; some were about educational programs or policies that no longer exist. One such article was the first I ever published on the subject of schooling— a review of successful programs of compensatory education. Rereading it, I was struck by the conceptual similarity between what I had written in 1968 and what I was writing in the middle 1980s. The article contended that compensatory education should not be viewed as a quick fix to reverse the educational deficits of culturally disadvantaged children; that good compensatory education programs did not consist of special methods tailored to poor, black children; that the best of these programs would be "as exciting to a middle-class child as to a lower-class child"; and that "compensatory education at its best is simply quality education." I argued that compensatory programs failed because they were wrongly understood as an array of remedial techniques rather than as high-quality education. I concluded that "the kind of education that is desirable for all children is absolutely necessary for the lower-class child." Although there was considerable support in the educational world for the idea that poor and minority children needed a special curriculum that was written specifically for them, I expressed unqualified opposition to this view. I continue to believe that a pluralistic society must have a pluralistic approach to education, not curricula specifically written for particular racial or ethnic groups. I believed then, as I do now, that the means of education may vary considerably, depending on the needs of the child, the skills of the teacher, and the state of pedagogical knowledge, but that the goals of education must be fundamentally the same for all children, regardless of their heritage or circumstance.[4]

This is not to say that intellectual development is the sole purpose of the schools. Schools must do many things for children that lie outside direct instruction but that are necessary to make instruction possible. If children come to school hungry, then they must be fed or they will not be able to learn. If they need glasses or a hearing aid, the school must direct them to proper treatment. If children have emotional difficulties, school personnel must help them obtain professional guidance. If children are victims of parental neglect or abuse, school personnel must be trained to deal appropriately with the situation. Horace Mann, Henry Barnard, and other founders of the common school movement could not possibly have imagined the social situation of the schools in the 1980s; could not have imagined the condition of the family, the divorce rate, the rise of child abuse, the widespread neglect of young children by their parents; could not have imagined the spread of addictive drugs to young children barely in their teens; could not have imagined the soporific and powerful effect of television, which distracts children from the normal growing-up processes of childhood, taking as many as six hours a day from their life, their play, and their studies. How could they have foreseen the social disintegration that would force upon the school the roles of parent, minister, policeman, social worker, psychiatrist, and babysitter?

I do not suggest that the school can reduce the number of its functions, but I believe that it must establish priorities among them. While providing the social services that are necessary to keep children available for learning, the school must not forget that these services are supplementary to its central purpose, which is the development of children's knowledge and character. A school that attended only to its students' intellectual development without regard to their character would be seriously defective. Nineteenth-century public schools took very seriously their responsibility for character formation; schools in the late twentieth century scarcely know how to think about the problem. Recognizing that parents and the public expect the schools to teach values and good character, some schools have responded by offering courses in "values clarification" and what is called moral education. Such courses are almost uniformly disappointing. In a public school setting, the need to avoid indoctrination encourages a relativistic, value-free approach to the teaching of values, thus producing the opposite of what was demanded in the first instance by a public hungry for simple verities. The answer to demands for character development in the school lies not in the creation of new courses but in recognizing that the school already has its own powerful resources, in both the formal and the implicit curriculum. Science, properly taught, teaches children the values that are imbedded in scientific inquiry: honesty, openmindedness, critical thinking, and the capacity to withhold judgment in the absence of evidence. Literature gives students the opportunity to see how men and women in different times and places have responded to moral dilemmas and to understand the connections between intentions and consequences, ideas and actions; not only is literature a potent vehicle for questions of personal and social values, it contains within its scope rich possibilities for exploring psychological and sociological issues. No less than literature, history provides limitless prospects for the study of values and ethics. It is a living laboratory in which to consider the relations among ideas, actions, and consequences; it offers the opportunity to discuss and debate decisions made by individuals in light of what they knew at the time, what they hoped for, and what happened as a result. As humanistic studies, literature and history inevitably evoke questions of value and inspire questioning about the nature of the good society, the moral attributes of a good life, and the qualities of character that awaken our admiration or elicit our contempt. This formal curriculum, having within it the story of human experience over the ages, as it happened and as it was imagined, should not be underestimated; its methods, its ideas, and its questions are likely to remain with students for the rest of their lives.

The implicit curriculum of the school is also an important agency for the teaching of values and character. The rules of the school affect character by establishing what is permitted, encouraged, or forbidden; adults in the school affect character by the example of their behavior in dealing with students and with their colleagues; the social climate of the school sends clear messages to children about the kinds of values that are prized by students and adults; educational policies affect character by actively, purposefully cultivating certain values and disparaging others. Values like responsibility, honesty, fairness, independence, kindness, courtesy, diligence, persistence, and self-discipline are not taught by role-playing games; they are taught by the life that is actually lived in the school: by the interactions between adults and children, by the examples that adults set, and by the expectations that are created for students in performing their daily tasks. What the schools should not do is preach to students; since they won't listen anyway, it is better to leave the rhetorical exhortations to others.

Important as character development is, it is not a unique function of the school. The home is a far more potent shaper of individual character. The function for which the school is uniquely responsible is the development of the child's mind. If children do not learn mathematics or science or history or a foreign language in school, they probably never will. Each of the major disciplines represents not only an intrinsically valuable body of knowledge but also a different way of understanding the world. If children do not read the great works of world literature in school, they may never make the effort on their own. If they do not learn the joys of poetry as students, they may never know the difference between a sonnet and a commercial jingle. If they never study Western European history, they will never know where we got the ideals by which we judge ourselves. If they never study American history, they will never comprehend what is worth preserving in our system of government. If they are ignorant of the historical development of other societies, the events of the world they inhabit will make little sense. If they manage to avoid the study of science and mathematics, they will be incapable of understanding either the natural world or the man-made changes that shape the age they live in. If they never learn a foreign language, they will lose a precious opportunity to communicate with another culture, whether through its literature or through conversation and use.

We cannot say that it is "useful" to read poetry or to solve a quadratic equation or to know why the Constitution was written as it was or to understand a chemical formula. But why should knowledge and understanding be subjected to a strict criterion of utility? When we teach children ideas, facts, and skills that are new to them, we cannot predict what doors will be opened for them, whether the new learning will fire their imagination, broaden their outlook, engage their curiosity, suggest career possibilities, inspire them to learn more, or simply leave them bored. If utility were our only curricular guide, little more would be required in schools than the basic skills, health education, and vocational training; these are the only indisputably useful subjects, at least in the short run. But utility and value should not be confused. It is not accidental that parents who can afford the best education for their children choose programs of broad liberal education. They select not for utility but for value, knowing that what is most immediately useful may be least valuable in the long run.

Efforts to improve the quality of schooling for all children ought not depend on a manufactured sense of crisis; the formal education of the young ought to receive our constant concern, not merely intermittent interest. We should not need the prod of national reports to alert us to the conditions that demoralize teachers and deprive children of a rich and powerful education. Yet we know from past experience that concern for the schools has been crisis-driven. Inevitably, the present crisis in education will fade, as its predecessors did. When public attention turns to other, more gripping problems, the momentum for school reform will falter, but life in the schools will go on. What then will remain of this moment? If school reformers continue to press for strengthening the quality of American education at every level—for higher standards of learning, meatier curricular offerings, better textbooks, improvements in the preparation and selection of teachers, higher teachers' salaries, and a clear set of purposes—then the moment will not be lost. But if the movement for school reform becomes internally fragmented by special interest pleading, by politicization, or by simplistic thinking, then it will soon squander its force and disappear, to be remembered only as a lost opportunity for educational improvement. The success of school reform will require a coherent consensus among the public and professionals about the value and definition of good education. If the consensus that seemed to emerge in the early 1980s should dissipate, we can anticipate an intensification of demands for public subsidy for nonpublic schools and of attacks on the education profession. In 1951, Robert Hutchins posed a challenge to American education that remains pertinent; he wrote, "Perhaps the greatest idea that America has given the world is the idea of education for all. The world is entitled to know whether this idea means that everybody can be educated, or only that everybody must go to school."[5] As Hutchins implied, quantity is not enough. We expect more of our schools, and we should. The quality of schools tends to reflect the degree of public interest and support invested in them. Whatever happens in the future, we can expect to have the schools we deserve.

1

Forgetting the Questions:
The Problem of
Educational Reform

(1981)

IT WOULD be difficult to find a sustained period of time in our history when Americans felt satisfied with the achievements of their schools. From the early nineteenth century on, it has been commonplace to find a fairly consistent recitation of complaints about the low state of learning, the poor training of teachers, the insufficient funding of education, the inadequacies of school buildings, and the apathy of the public. The temptation exists to attribute the concerns of the 1980s to this strain of despair about the historic gap between aspiration and reality, this sense that schools have always and will always fall short of their mission. But it would be wrong to do so, not only because it would encourage unwarranted complacency but because the educational problems of the present are fundamentally different from those of the past.

One important difference is that so much of the past agenda of educational reformers has been largely fulfilled. In one sense, the educational enterprise is the victim of its own successes, since new problems have arisen from the long-sought solutions to earlier problems. Idealistic reformers, eager to improve the schools and to extend their promise to all children, sought the appropriate lever of change. If only teachers had college degrees and pedagogical training; if only teachers would band together to form a powerful teachers' union; if only there were federal aid to schools; if only all children were admitted to school regardless of race or national origin; if only all students of high ability were admitted to college; if only colleges could accommodate everyone who wanted to attend; if only students had more choices and fewer requirements in their course work; if only schools were open to educational experimentation; if only there were a federal department of education . . . The "if only" list could be extended, but the point should be clear by now. All these "if onlies" have been put into effect, some entirely and others at least partially, and rarely have the results been equal to the hopes invested.

In reality, many present complaints are reactions to hard-won reforms of the past. Though the educational preparation of teachers is more extensive than ever, at least when measured by degrees and years of formal schooling, the education of teachers is still a subject of intense criticism. The realization has dawned in many quarters that a credential from a state university or a school of education is no guarantee that its bearer knows how to teach or what to teach, loves teaching or loves learning. Nor are today's critics delighted by the undeniable power of teachers' unions. True, the unions have used their political clout to improve teachers' salaries and to win vastly enlarged federal education expenditures, but unionization has not produced the educational changes that some of its advocates had anticipated. Similarly, the sense of achievement that should have followed the removal of racial barriers to higher education quickly gave way to concerns about social stratification, vocationalization, and declining quality. The reforms of the 1960s were effective, though not in the way that reformers had hoped. Now everyone who wants to go to college can go to some college, though not necessarily that of his first choice. By 1980, at least one-third of all institutions of higher education admitted everyone who applied, more than one-half accepted most or all of those who met their qualifications, and less than 10 percent were "competitive," that is, accepted only a portion of qualified applicants. As college enrollments decline, the number of competitive colleges will grow fewer. Curricular reforms have broken down the coherence of the liberal arts curriculum, both in high school and college, so that students have a wide degree of choice and few requirements. And a federal department of education has at last been established, though with what benefits or burdens for schools and children it is too soon to say.

Yet having won so many victories, some of truly historic dimension, American education is still embattled, still struggling to win public support and approval, and, perhaps worse, still struggling to find its own clear sense of purpose. Paradoxically, the achievements of the recent past seem to have exhausted the usually ready stock of prescriptions for school reform and to have raised once again the most basic questions of educational purpose.

Like other major institutions in our society, the schools are continually judged by today's demands and today's performance, and no credit is extended by clients or critics for yesterday's victories. Which is as it should be. School criticism, as I noted earlier, is nothing new. Behind any criticism, however, are assumptions about what schools should and can do, and criticisms have shifted as assumptions about the goals and potentialities of schools have changed. Since the early nineteenth century, the tenor of school criticism has been essentially optimistic; no matter how despairing the critic, his working assumption has been that schools are valuable institutions, that they have within them the power to facilitate social, moral, and political regeneration, and that more money, or more public concern, or better teachers could extend the promise of schooling to everyone. If more people had more schooling, critics have contended, and if schools were amply financed and well staffed, there would be enormous benefit to the individual, the society, the economy, and the body politic. With relatively little dissent, Americans have believed in schooling—not because of a love of the hickory stick and the three Rs, or (as some latter-day critics would have it) because of the schools' ability to make children docile workers, but because Americans are deeply committed to self-improvement and the school is an institutionalized expression of that commitment.

Participation in formal schooling has grown sharply in recent decades. The proportion of seventeen-year-olds who graduated from high school grew from about 50 percent in 1940 to about 75 percent in the late 1960s. Similarly, the proportion of young people who entered college climbed from about 16 percent in 1940 to about 45 percent in 1968, at which time it leveled off. In no other country in the world does participation in formal schooling last as long, for so many people, as in the United States. To understand why this broad democratization of educational participation occurred, as well as why the 1980s began on a note of disillusionment, it is useful to consider some of the expectations we have attached to formal schooling.

Until well into the twentieth century, only a small

minority of Americans attended college. College was not only expensive but exclusive. Many, perhaps most, colleges maintained quotas for some groups (like Jews and Catholics) and excluded others altogether (blacks). After World War II, more than 2 million veterans attended college, crowding and sometimes overwhelming America's campuses. The GI Bill launched the world's first experiment in universal access to higher education. While most veterans did not use their benefits to attend college, the experience of those who did benefited the individuals, the institutions, and the economy. In light of the success and popularity of the GI program, the conviction that college should be a right rather than a privilege gained broad support.

While demand for expanded access to higher education grew steadily in the states and nation, other political forces combined to advance the role of education as a weapon against poverty. The notion that knowledge is power was certainly not novel, nor was the very American belief that schooling is an antidote to crime, poverty, and vice. The school promoters of the early nineteenth century repeatedly argued that schooling would give people the means to improve themselves and thereby break the cycle of poverty. During the early 1960s, this traditional rhetoric was given new life by scholars and policymakers. Educational programs burgeoned as an integral part of the federal government's war on poverty. Jacob Riis had written in 1892, "the more kindergartens, the fewer prisons"; in 1965 Lyndon Johnson predicted that the lives of children in the Head Start summer program would be spent "productively and rewardingly rather than wasted in tax-supported institutions or in welfare-supported lethargy." The hope of eliminating poverty and inequality provided the major rationale not only for Operation Head Start but for general federal aid to education as well.

By the time the period of educational expansion reached

a high tide in the middle 1960s, much was expected by a variety of publics. It was hoped that more education would:

- Reduce inequality among individuals and groups by eliminating illiteracy and cultural deprivation.
- Improve the economy and economic opportunity by raising the number of intelligent and skilled individuals.
- Spread the capacity for personal fulfillment by developing talents, skills, and creative energies.
- Prove to be an uplifting and civilizing influence in the nation's cultural life by broadly diffusing the fruits of liberal education.
- Reduce alienation and mistrust while building a new sense of community among people of similar education and similar values.
- Reduce prejudice and misunderstanding by fostering contact among diverse groups.
- Improve the quality of civic and political life.

These hopes and expectations were a heavy burden for the schools to bear. Perhaps predictably, they did not accomplish all that was asked of them. Most of the problems that were laid at the schools' doors remained just as problematic years later (and some critics would argue that the provision of more schooling had produced the opposite effect in every instance). Poverty and inequality did not disappear; their roots were elsewhere, and the schools were not able to cure deep-seated social and economic ills. While the disadvantaged received more schooling, so did the advantaged. Many poor youths entered the middle class by using educational opportunity, but others remained as poor as their parents. The value of a high school diploma declined not only because its possession became nearly universal but also, and most important, because high school graduates were not necessarily literate—mainly because of the well-intended effort to keep as many youths in school for as long as possible and to deny no one a diploma, regardless of his educational development. Society's investment in education probably did spur economic development, but it did not prevent the emergence of skepticism about the desirability of economic growth; in fact, it was precisely among the educated (and the advantaged) that economic growth became suspect because of its association with the bureaucratization, centralization, and depersonalization of modern economic life. It is impossible to gauge the effects of increased schooling on popular culture or high culture. Television, which invariably seeks the largest possible audience, undoubtedly has more power to shape popular culture than schools do (a mixed blessing, since television disperses both sitcom pap and major cultural events to mass audiences). Participation in popular culture and high culture has surely been broadened, yet it is arguable whether the quality of either has been elevated during recent decades. Nor is it possible to demonstrate that increased educational participation has eliminated distrust between groups or contributed to a new sense of community. On the contrary, educational institutions have become settings for expression of militant particularism along racial, religious, ethnic, sexual, cultural, and linguistic lines. Very likely the differences among groups have been accentuated in the past twenty years. But again, it would be difficult to hold the schools directly responsible for these trends. More likely, it appears, the schools are the stage on which such issues are acted out rather than the cause of their appearance. Nor can the schools claim to have improved the quality of political life, since political participation has waned along with public regard for political institutions. But once again, it was not the schools that were responsible for the apparent ebbing of civic commitment and the surge of political apathy, nor could they even serve as a counterforce against such attitudes. The same attitudes of distrust, skepticism, hostility, and apathy eroded the schools' own status in the social order. The same confusions that pervaded the social atmosphere also pervaded the schools. If they failed to teach citizenship, it was at least in part because teachers and parents were confused about what a good citizen was and whether "citizenship" could be taught without imposing a partisan interpretation. In short, a society that is confused and contentious cannot look to its schools to straighten things out, for the schools will reflect the same confusion and contention.

In retrospect, it was folly to have expected the schools to transform society or to mold a new kind of person. The schools are by nature limited institutions, not total institutions. They do not have full power over their students' lives (even total institutions, like prisons, have discovered the difficulty of shaping or reshaping the lives and minds of those they fully control). Schools are not fully independent in their dealings with students; they are interrelated with, and dependent on, families, churches, the media, peer groups, and other agencies of influence. Nor can schools be considered as if they were machines, all operating in the same predictable manner. Teachers vary, administrators vary, students vary, communities vary, and therefore schools vary. The schools, being complex human institutions composed of actors with different goals, different interests, and different capacities, cannot be treated as if they were all interchangeable.

As it became clear that more schooling would not provide any magical solutions, the utopian hopes once focused on the schools dissipated. Having briefly been the repository of grand and even grandiose dreams of human betterment, the schools became a scapegoat for all the wide-ranging problems they had failed to solve. Having revealed that they were but fallible instruments of social change and that any change they promoted would only be incremental, the schools became the object of rage and scorn. They were portrayed as intractable, bureaucratic, even malevolent barriers to social change. But just as it was unrealistic to believe that the schools had the power to remake society by molding those who passed through their doors, it was equally unrealistic to assert that they were powerless, meaningless, superfluous institutions with no purpose other than the care and feeding of their own employees.

Nonetheless, when the dream of a school-led social revolution faded, school criticism shifted in tone. The voices of liberal critics—those who believed that men and women of goodwill might work together to improve schools by using this program or that curriculum—diminished to mere whispers. They were drowned out by critics who believed that only radical changes in teaching or in governing schools could "save" them; by those who believed that the public schools were beyond redemption and ought to be replaced by "free" schools; and by those who advocated the abolition of compulsory schooling and the "de-schooling" of society. For a time in the late 1960s and early 1970s, bookstore shelves fairly bulged with apocalyptic predictions about the imminent demise of schooling. One book, playing on the then current phrase "God is dead," was titled *School Is Dead.* While some of the writing of this period contained sharp and telling portraits of insensitive teachers and uncaring bureaucrats, others gave vent to undisguised anti-intellectualism in their attacks on academic standards, discipline, science, and rationality. In the larger culture—and, alas, especially in academic institutions—a great revival seemed to sweep the land, casting aside "old" doctrines of deferred gratification, structured learning, and professionalism while espousing mysticism, Eastern religions, the occult, astrology, and whatever else promised to touch the spontaneous, untrained inner spirit.

These trends had curricular and programmatic consequences. In colleges, students demanded, and usually won, the abolition of course requirements, the adoption of pass-fail grading, the de-emphasis of competition and testing, and extensive choice in selecting their own programs of study. As requirements for admission to college were relaxed, high schools soon succumbed to many of the same pressures that had changed the colleges: Course requirements were eased, new courses proliferated, academic standards dropped, homework diminished, and adults generally relinquished their authority to direct student learning. At all levels, both in college and high school, educational administrators reduced, to the extent possible, the schools' role as *in loco parentis.* To some extent, this period of student assertiveness and adult retreat was the educational side of the movement against the war in Vietnam, which provoked youthful revolt against authority in many parts of the society and the culture. But even after the war ended, there remained a lingering hostility to science, technology, and reason—as though these were the root causes of the hated war.

As the 1980s opened, it appeared that this wave of anti-intellectualism had spent itself, for complaints about the schools suggested entirely different concerns. The well-publicized decline in Scholastic Aptitude Test (SAT) scores created a context for worrying about a national deterioration in the quality of education. Not that the SAT scores were important in themselves, but they provided a sense of a pattern in the carpet that had not previously been discernible. For several years college officials had reported a steady increase in the number of freshmen who read poorly and wrote atrociously; the phenomenon of remedial reading and remedial writing classes spread throughout higher education, even to elite institutions. The apparent explanation, at first, was that so many new students from poor families had begun to attend college, but analysis of the SAT drop showed that the score decline continued long after the socioeconomic profile of the college-going population had stabilized. Bits and pieces of evidence from other sources began to fit together. Other standardized measures of academic ability reported score declines paralleling the SATs. National newsmagazines discovered a writing crisis and a literacy crisis. Educational malpractice suits were filed by disgruntled parents because their children had received a high school diploma in spite of being "functionally illiterate." The Council for Basic Education, a lonely voice for liberal education since its founding in 1958, found itself back in the educational mainstream, while still a lonely voice for liberal education. Demands for minimum competency tests seemed to spring up spontaneously in almost every state, though no national organization existed to promote or coordinate the movement. As concern for educational standards spread in the middle 1970s, demands for testing grew—not only minimum competency tests for high school graduation but tests at critical checkpoints in the lower grades and tests for would-be teachers. Reaction against these demands was not long in coming. The assault upon standardized testing was led by consumer activist Ralph Nader and the National Education Association. Nader released a lengthy attack on the credibility of the SAT, the most widely used college admission test, and lobbied successfully in New York State and elsewhere for passage of a "truth-in-testing" law.

While it did generate controversy, the dispute over testing was superficial, for tests were neither a cause of nor a remedy for the underlying malaise in American education. Nearly all the educational controversies of the 1970s—

whether over bilingualism or sex education or testing or open admissions or busing—dealt with some aspect of the educational process that was of great importance to some constituency, but none directly raised these questions: What does it mean to be an educated person? What knowledge is of most worth? Are the graduates of our schools educated people?

The very absence of such questioning suggests a failure in educational thinking. Educators and, most especially, educational policymakers have fallen into the habit of analyzing school issues almost entirely in sociological and economic terms. In recent years it has been customary to think of schooling as a quantifiable economic good to be distributed in accordance with principles of equity or in response to political demands. The sociological-economic perspective has come to dominate educational discussion and has informed public policy. Without doubt it has contributed to necessary changes in patterns of schooling, by redirecting resources in a fair manner and by opening up access to educational opportunities. But the functionalist perspective became dysfunctional when it crowded sub-stantive educational concerns off the policymakers' agenda, when the desire to keep students in school was unaccom-panied by interest in what they would learn while they stayed in school. What I am suggesting here is not a conflict between the functionalist perspective and the educational perspective, but the danger of analyzing the schools through only one of the two prisms. There has been a fairly persistent tendency, I would argue, to neglect the role of schools as educational institutions, to treat them as sociological cookie cutters without regard to the content of their educational program. When I consider why this is so, I conclude that there are several possible explanations.

First, the sociological perspective has become dominant because it relies on quantifiable data that are accessible. It is far easier to gain information about years of educational attainment and socioeconomic status than it is to ascertain the conditions of learning in any given school. Educators cannot agree on how to assess the educational climate or even on what should be learned. Thus it becomes irresistible to deal with, perhaps even become the captive of, data that are both available and measurable.

Second, the sociological perspective is a useful adjunct to the concept of the school as a tool of social reform. By measuring which groups are in school and how their social background relates to their choice of occupation, we can attempt to monitor how educational resources are allocated and whether schooling is contributing to social progress. While it is neither new nor unusual to regard the school as a lever of social reform, it is unusual and perhaps unwise to see the school *solely* as a tool of social reform and *solely* as a resource to be redistributed. One consequence is that the school's diploma is confused with the learning that it is supposed to represent. In recent years, policymakers have sought to equalize educational attainment (years-of-schooling) without regard to the quality of education. This is like putting people on a diet of 1,800 calories a day without caring whether they are consuming junk food or nutritious food. Years-of-schooling, or a diploma, has been treated as an end in itself. Thus we have seen courts require school districts to present a diploma to students who could not meet minimum state standards of literacy, as if it were the diploma itself they needed rather than the learning that the diploma is supposed to signify. When school reformers in the nineteenth century advocated universal education as a way of improving society, they meant a broad diffusion of knowledge and wisdom, not a broad diffusion of diplomas.

Third, educational analysts have relied on the sociological perspective because it is easier to raise the level of educational attainment than it is to raise the level of educational quality. Staying in school, not dropping out, and getting a diploma represents a clear, unambiguous goal that everyone can understand without quarrel. As soon as school officials begin to define what should be taught and learned during those years, disagreements arise, which are best settled by making the schools all things for all people.

For these reasons and others, educational policymakers have tended to view schooling as an instrument to achieve some other goal, only rarely as an end in itself. To the extent that they do so, they rob schooling of the very attributes that give it power. If a young man or woman has a high school diploma but can scarcely read or write, then the diploma is worthless. When a diploma, either at the high school or college level, represents a certificate of time served but not of the systematic development of intelligence and skill, then it is difficult to know why it should have any inherent value. And of course it does not.

An educational critique of schooling should have as its starting point, I believe, the idea that the essential purpose of schooling is to develop the powers of intelligence: thinking, knowing, reflecting, observing, imagining, appreciating, questioning, and judging. Beyond that, schooling has many additional purposes, both for the student and for society. Educational literature teems with lists of the many ways in which schools should meet individual and social needs. But the schools' first purpose is to encourage and guide each person in the cultivation of intelligence and the development of talents, interests, and abilities. Schools do many other things as well: They may provide food, social services, psychological services, medical care, and career guidance. But no matter how well or how poorly they fulfill these functions, the schools must be judged in the first instance by how well they do those things that only they can do. We expect the schools to teach children command of the fundamental skills that are needed to continue learning—in particular, the ability to read, write, compute, speak, and listen. Once they have command of these skills, they should progress through a curriculum designed to enlarge their powers. Such a curriculum would contain, for every student, history and social studies, language and literature, mathematics, science, and the arts. Students need to learn these skills and disciplines in school because, except for those rare individuals who can educate themselves without a teacher, they are unlikely to have another chance to do so.

The schools are responsible both for preserving a sense of the past and for providing the ability to think about, and function in, the present and the future. More than any other educational agency, they ought to have an intelligent understanding of the inexorable connection between past, present, and future. Certainly there is disagreement about the meaning of the past and how it relates to the present and the future, and awareness of such disagreement is often invoked to justify educational aimlessness. But much of what seems to be dissension is a chimera; democratic debate ought not to be confused with chaos, nor should pluralistic politics be confused with anarchy. Education proceeds from widely shared values, and we do, in fact, have widely shared values. We may not agree about how democracy is to be achieved and about whether we have too much or too little of it, but few would question the idea that each person has the right as a citizen to participate in the shaping of public issues. We believe in the idea of self-government and in the greatest possible involvement of citizens as voters, as volunteers in community organizations, as members of interest groups, and as spokesmen for different views. While we may differ over particular educational issues, there is general support for the idea that schooling is a necessary mechanism for achieving society's goals: to prepare the younger generation to be thoughtful citizens; to enable each person to appreciate and contribute to the culture; to sharpen the intellectual and aesthetic sensibilities for lifelong enjoyment; to develop readiness for the educational, occupational, and professional choices that each person will confront; to kindle a sense of responsibility for others and a sense of integrity; to teach children how to lead and how to follow; and to acquaint young people with the best models of achievement in every field while encouraging them to strive to realize their own potential.

If these are widely shared educational aims, and I believe they are, then none of them should be left to chance. The curriculum should be designed so that every student has the fullest opportunity to develop his powers, intelligence, interests, talent, and understanding. Every student needs to know how to form and articulate his own opinions. To do so, he must learn how to read critically, how to evaluate arguments, how to weigh evidence, and how to reach judgments on his own. Every student, to understand the world in which he will be a participant, should be knowledgeable about history; should master some other language as well as his own; should discover the pleasures of literature, especially its power to reach across time and cultures and to awaken our sense of universality; should study science and technology, both as a citizen who will be asked to comprehend complex issues and as an individual who must live with constant change. Since we believe that everyone should be equally concerned about the problems of our society, then we must believe that everyone, every student, should be schooled in a way that meets his need to know history, science, mathematics, language, the arts, literature, and so on. And yet it is not simply on the grounds of utility, relevance, and political value that the case for liberal education rests. We do not *need* to know how to read Shakespeare; we can be good citizens without any knowledge of Athenian civilization, even though our concept of citizenship is based on the very period of which we are ignorant. We must concern ourselves with the survival of history, philosophy, literature, and those other humanistic disciplines that may lack immediate utility because without them ours would be an intellectually impoverished and spiritually illiterate civilization.

To some people, all this is so self-evident that it ought not be necessary to plead for the value of an education of substance and content. Yet it is necessary, because of the widespread disarray in high school and college curricula. In the face of changes that have occurred in the past decade or so, many educators seem unable to remember how to justify or defend or champion liberal education. The proposition that all students should be subject to curricular requirements that define the essentials of a good education has become controversial, rather than a starting point in defining the nature of a good curriculum.

Confronted with conflicting demands from those who want reduced requirements and those who want curricular substance, many schools have resolved the dilemma by reducing requirements while expanding electives. Thus students may take "history" courses to meet their minimal graduation requirement, but these so-called history courses may be little more than classes in current events or pop sociology. Or they may meet their English requirement by reading popular fiction, mystery stories, or science fiction. There is no harm in what is included; from the perspective of a liberal education, what is unfortunate is the wide body of knowledge that is excluded when course proliferation and lax requirements are joined together. Professors regularly encounter students who are ignorant of anything that happened before the Civil War as well as anything that happened, or was written, outside the

United States. They may have *heard* of Plato and Aristotle in a survey course, but they have never read anything written by either and have only a dim notion (usually wrong) of what they "stood for." Mention Dickens, Tolstoy, Conrad, or Melville, and perhaps they have heard of them too, but they "didn't take that course." Some professors who teach literature have been astonished to find students who know nothing of mythology or the Bible; allusions to Job or Icarus must be explained to those who have no intellectual furniture in their minds, no stock of literary or historical knowledge on which to draw beyond their immediate experience. In the April 11, 1980, issue of *Commonweal*, J. M. Cameron soberly observed that if Freud attended school today, he might not be able to think up the Oedipus theory because he would not have enough mythology in his head to do so. We seem now to turn to television or the movies to teach the history and literature that were neglected in school. To permit knowledge to be fragmented, as we have, by serving it up cafeteria-style, with each person choosing whether to be minimally literate or to be a specialist, contributes to the diminution and degradation of the common culture.

2

The Schools We Deserve

(1981)

"TO the casual observer, American education is a confusing and not altogether edifying spectacle. It is productive of endless fads and panaceas; it is pretentiously scientific and at the same time pathetically conventional; it is scornful of the past, yet painfully inarticulate when it speaks of the future." This strikingly contemporary observation was made by the educational philosopher Boyd Bode in the *New Republic* in 1930. Since then, American schools have lurched from crisis to crisis, and their internal confusion and aimlessness remain intact.

During the past half-century, the schools have been persistently battered by controversy and crisis, much of it growing out of efforts to redirect the purposes of the schools. In the 1930s, heated pedagogical battles between progressive educators and traditionalists were decided when the progressives secured dominance of the nation's teachers' colleges and professional educators' associations. In the postwar 1940s, the schools were handicapped by critical shortages of teachers and buildings, low teacher salaries, and the advent of the baby boom generation. In the early 1950s, the schools were attacked by a variety of critics—

45

from those who objected to the anti-intellectualism of the latest progressive fad, known as "life adjustment education," to the reactionary vigilantes who wanted to cleanse the schools of "subversive" teachers and textbooks. The orbiting of Sputnik in 1957 marked a new crisis when Americans discovered the costs of neglecting science, mathematics, and foreign languages in the secondary schools. Meanwhile, the prolonged struggle against racial inequality, both before and after the *Brown* decision, provided a recurrent source of strife. And then, in the mid-1960s, schools were again under fire, this time because of student protests and reformers who advocated such innovations as open classrooms, schools-without-walls, experiential learning, deschooling, and other arrangements whose common denominator was greater student choice and diminished adult authority.

The vast and variegated educational system that we have today, with all its virtues and flaws, is largely the product of policies shaped by responses to these events. In assessing the rising tide of criticism of the past five years, it is important to recall that the schools have tried to do, and for the most part have done successfully, what was demanded of them. Every nation gets the schools that it deserves, and we have today a system that reflects our own conflicts about the relative importance of different social and educational values.

For the past generation, no goal has been more important to educational policymakers than expanding access to educational opportunity for all youth. Whether one looks at high school graduation rates or college enrollment, it is clear that remarkable progress has been made. At mid-century, about 50 percent graduated from high school; the figure today is 75 percent. From 1968 to 1978, black enrollment grew from 6.4 percent to more than 10 percent of all college students, and the proportion of females increased from 39 percent to 48 percent. For the first time in our history, access to higher education is universal. A recent study by the College Board found that one-third of postsecondary institutions are "open door," accepting all applicants regardless of their academic credentials; more than half are "selective," accepting only those who meet their qualifications, but nonetheless accepting most or all of those who apply for admission; and just 8 percent are "competitive," accepting only a portion of qualified applicants. As college enrollments shrink in the years ahead, the number of competitive institutions will drop.

Yet having pursued the goal of increased participation so singlemindedly and successfully, educators are greeted not with laurels but with brickbats. While the schools were devising ways to retain students by meeting demands for "relevance," the pendulum began to swing, and a new critique of the schools emerged, which assumed mass education as a given but focused on the issue of quality. If there was a single event that precipitated the new public mood, it was the revelation in 1975 that scores on the Scholastic Aptitude Test for college entry had slipped steadily for a dozen years. Other pieces of what seemed to be a jigsaw puzzle began to fall into place. At opposite ends of the country, angry parents sued the local school district for granting a high school diploma to their functionally illiterate children (both lost). The National Assessment of Educational Progress released a survey that showed that 8 percent of seventeen-year-old whites were functionally illiterate, as well as a shocking 42 percent of seventeen-year-old blacks (since 70 percent of black students graduate from high schools, the diploma apparently had become merely a certificate of attendance for a substantial minority). There was a growing recognition that automatic promotion from grade to grade, regardless of attainment, had contributed to masking learning deficiencies and that the high school diploma no longer represented any particular level of proficiency. One response to the accumulation of bad news was the adoption of state-mandated minimum competency tests, which spread from one state (Arizona) in 1976 to thirty-eight states by 1980, a spontaneous national movement without a spokesman or a national organization to promote it.

An extraordinary thing has happened to achievement levels since the mid-1960s. SAT scores, which had been a consistent measure of verbal and mathematical skills, have dropped dramatically. Median verbal scores fell from a high of 478 in 1963 to a new low of 424 in 1980; in the same period, mathematical scores fell from 502 to 466. On both tests, girls' scores dropped more sharply than those of boys. The first reaction to the score drops was to attribute them to the fact that large numbers of minorities, females, and low-income students joined the college-bound pool during this time of expansion. But in fact the composition of the test takers has been fairly stable since 1970, and the score drops have been even more extensive since then. Even more alarming is that the number and proportion of high-scoring students have fallen precipitously; the number of seniors who scored over 650 fell from 53,800 (5.3 percent) in 1972 to 29,000 (2.9 percent) in 1980. The shrinkage of the top scorers has proceeded steadily since the mid-1960s and obviously is unrelated to the overall composition of the test-taking group.

When the College Board's blue-ribbon panel to investigate the causes of the score decline released its findings in 1977, it rounded up the usual suspects: the decline of the family; working mothers; television; the trauma of a decade that included Vietnam, civil disorders, and Watergate; drugs; and sex-role stereotyping. When it came to describing the responsibility of schools for the score declines, the panel noted that "there have unquestionably been changes over the past 10 to 15 years in the standards to which students at all levels of education are held. Absenteeism formerly considered intolerable is now condoned. An 'A' or 'B' means a good deal less than it used to. Promotion from one grade to another has become almost automatic. Homework has apparently been cut about in half." It pointedly concluded, too, that "less thoughtful and critical reading is now being demanded and done," and "careful writing has apparently about gone out of style." After much sociological wandering, the panel came to a simple conclusion: the retreat from thoughtful reading and careful writing may explain a good deal about declining verbal skills, and it suggests changes that are within the reach of the school.

The unusual attention paid to the SAT provoked claims that there was something peculiar about the test itself and that it was somehow out of phase with the times. Unfortunately for this thesis, the SAT declines were reflected in other standardized tests. Researchers Annegret Harnischfeger and David E. Wiley analyzed other major tests, including the American College Test (which many colleges use instead of the SAT), the Iowa testing program (used statewide in Iowa and elsewhere), and the Minnesota Scholastic Aptitude Test (administered to more than 90 percent of Minnesota high school juniors). They found strikingly consistent patterns of decline: rising achievement levels until the mid-1960s, then a steady decline that accelerates as students reach higher grades and that is particularly pronounced in verbal areas. The only exception to the overall downward trend was in the subject matter achievement tests of the SAT and the ACT science test. Rather than being contradictory, this phenomenon suggested a bifurcation between the top students and everyone else, with the best students doing exceptionally well and the others falling further behind.

Although Harnischfeger and Wiley were careful to insist

that the score declines had many causes, they nonetheless argued that substantial enrollment declines in traditional subjects "parallel closely the test score decline patterns." They reported that fewer students were taking regular English, American history, math, and science courses, although the advanced college preparatory courses did not experience a comparable dropoff in enrollment. Once again, the best students were taking the courses they needed, while everyone else was—doing what? Not enrolling in vocational or business courses, which also showed declines. Apparently the schools offered fewer instructional programs and more work-study options.

In 1980 the Gannett newspapers sent an investigative team into two dozen schools. Like Harnischfeger and Wiley, they discovered pervasive dilution of the secondary school curriculum. They described schools in which high school credit was offered for such courses as astrology, marriage simulation, cheerleading, student government, child care, and mass media. The average public school, they observed, had three hours each day of instructional time, compared to more than four hours in the average nonpublic school. In one junior high school they visited, the typical student spent two hours and twelve minutes in academic classes.

Concern about enrollment trends in science, mathematics, and foreign languages has provoked some scathing commentaries on the state of curricular requirements. The President's Commission on Foreign Language and International Studies complained in 1979 that "Americans' incompetence in foreign languages is nothing short of scandalous, and it is becoming worse." The commission pointed out that "only 15 percent of American high school students now study a foreign language—down from 24 percent in 1965. The decline continues." It also noted with alarm that only one out of twenty high school students studies a foreign language beyond the second year, while four years' study is considered necessary for competence. Equally shocking is the tiny number of Americans in high school or college who learn the languages of such major nations as Russia, China, or Japan. In fact, the number of Russian language students in American secondary schools dropped sharply, from 27,000 in 1965 to 11,000 in 1976.

In fall 1980 a report sponsored by the National Science Foundation and the Department of Education warned of "a current trend toward virtual scientific and technological illiteracy." America's scientists continue to be internationally preeminent in research and publication, but the American people are increasingly ignorant about science and technology. Again the theme of bifurcation appears: "Those who are the best seem to be learning about as much as they ever did, while the majority of students learn less and less." Will important national decisions be made by a scientific elite, or will there be a broad enough diffusion of scientific knowledge for citizens to understand vital, science-related issues?

And there have been persistent complaints about students' writing ability. Few high school students have ever had systematic writing instruction of the sort that involves thinking through a topic, preparing multiple drafts, receiving written and oral comments from the teacher, and revising papers after the teacher returns them. Recognizing that a national problem exists, many colleges have introduced remedial writing classes. People often mistakenly assume that such classes are a response to rising numbers of minority students. At one major state university in 1981, more than half the freshman class was enrolled in a remedial writing course. Bard College in New York began a different approach in the fall of 1981. All incoming Bard freshmen will have to participate in an intensive three-week "Workshop in Language and Thinking" before regular classes begin. For six days a week, eight hours a day, students will learn how to read, write, and organize ideas. They will prepare a written assignment each day, which will be returned with a critique the following day. The Bard workshop is more concentrated and individualized than most such courses and avoids taking time away from regular college studies, permitting the student to improve his or her skills before beginning first-semester courses.

Well, then, what's going on here? How is it that some students finish high school with few skills and less knowledge, that others arrive at college underprepared for college-level work, while a small minority of the same graduating class has been remarkably well educated in their special fields of interest? This diverse range of outcomes actually is consistent with the changes that have been introduced in schools, especially public schools, during the past fifteen years or so. In response to student demands for greater flexibility, colleges began to lower their entrance requirements in the mid-1960s, and high schools followed their lead by abolishing certain course requirements. (After all, goes the argument, if you don't need a foreign language to get into college, why should high schools require you to take one?) As requirements fell, the notion of a common curriculum was undermined. To maintain student interest, courses in traditional subjects were fragmented into electives and mini-courses, particularly in the "soft," humanistic areas like English and history, and requirements in the "hard" subjects like mathematics, science, and foreign language were eased or eliminated. In a time of rapidly proliferating electives, every felt need produced pressure for a new course, for values education, moral education, death education, consumer education (to name but a few), in addition to such old standbys as career education, sex education, drug education, and driver education. Inasmuch as the curriculum is a zero-sum game, with only a certain number of hours each day, every course added to a student's schedule displaces some other course. The proliferation of new courses and the easing of requirements meant that students could substitute a fun course like "mass media" for a demanding course in literature, and many evidently did.

With the authority of the common curriculum under challenge, it became difficult for educators to justify, or even to remember how to justify, any given course content. Why should students read Melville or c.e. cummings or Milton? Why did they need to know anything about the Greeks or Romans? Why learn a foreign language? If they weren't going to become scientists, why should they be compelled to study science? Wouldn't they be just as happy, happier even, if they never studied chemistry or physics or algebra or geometry? In many high schools the requirements and the common curriculum collapsed like eggshells. This meant that, after meeting minimal state-imposed requirements, students could practically design their own program. The best students, those with the highest motivation and purpose, continued to take advanced college-preparatory courses; the average and below-average students, who might have learned more if the expectations of the school had been clear and consistent, found that they could easily navigate around courses that appeared too challenging.

Uncertainty about what students should study reflected uncertainty about why they should study, and this self-doubt undermined the teachers' sense of purpose and authority. This confusion, quite understandable in a time of student unrest and societal permissiveness, made it increasingly difficult for teachers to impose demands on students, which in turn led to lower teacher expectations. Truancy began to rise, as did discipline problems, like drug use during the school day. Homework and essays, once staples of schooling, fell into disfavor. Students didn't like to do the "extra" work, and teachers were relieved of reading and grading the 100 or more papers that would be turned in by their different classes. Part of a major new study by James Coleman, comparing public and private schools, documents how little time most public high school students spend on homework. Three out of four students do one hour or less each school night, while one out of four does less than one hour each week. Not surprisingly, the students with the least homework watch the most television.

Homework may seem insignificant as an educational issue, but it does matter. Homework provides the necessary time for thoughtful writing and serious reading, time that is rarely available during school hours. Can the large majority who spend an hour or less each day on homework have time to read a novel or to write a short story? It seems not only unlikely but impossible. Homework matters, too, because of the importance of what is called "time-on-task." The phrase is educationese for the commonsense proposition that educational performance is directly related to the amount of time spent learning. Researchers have observed that a large part of the school day is consumed by changing of classes, interruptions, announcements, and disciplinary problems, and that a large part of the time even in good classrooms is not instructional time. Anything that extends the amount of time spent learning is likely to improve student performance. This does not suggest any particular method of teaching, since students can be fully engaged in individual or small group projects, but it does suggest the value of homework in stretching out the amount of learning time available to the student. It also explains why absenteeism, class cutting, and disruptive behavior in the classroom rob students of precious learning time.

The dilemma of American education has persisted since

the founding of public schools in the early nineteenth century. What kind of schooling is most appropriate for a democratic society? American educators championed a common school education, in the belief that it would promote equality, fraternity, and social progress. Common schools—the earliest public schools—usually provided what we now consider elementary education and, even today, no one doubts that the curriculum for young children should be more or less the same for all. The problem arises as children become adolescents, and their interests, talents, and abilities begin to diverge. It would be unrealistic and unsound to advocate that all young people should study the same things at the same time, in lockstep fashion, since the quick learners will find the pace too tedious and the slow learners will find it too fast. The solution to the problem of individual differences has been to establish different programs, depending on students' ability. This has taken various forms, but two especially. The first is tracking, which is determined by the students' apparent educational or occupational destinies, such as college preparatory, vocational, and general. The second approach has been ability grouping—dividing children into classes or learning groups based on ability, while having everyone learn the same subject matter. Ability grouping is used in many schools, but in a few, such as in Washington, D.C., it was banned by the courts as racially discriminatory. (The acting superintendent of the D.C. schools complained in 1981 that the black middle class pulled their children out of the District's public schools when ability grouping was discontinued.) The schools today try variants on these approaches, but find it particularly tempting to move toward lowering requirements and expanding electives. That way, the school doesn't have to have any formal policy of separating students by ability, but can rely on the students to do the sorting themselves.

But is it democratic for schools to permit students to

decide whether they should or should not learn those things that every informed citizen should know? It is not clear why educators, more than any other professional group, should become ensnared to the point of confusion by the word "democratic." Under that mantle, responsible authority has been attacked as authoritarianism, and students have been allowed to choose between an education of value and something decidedly less. Perhaps the message that schools send, when they suggest that there is no core of vital knowledge and skills, is that students can elect not only what to study but whether to come to school. If it does not matter *what* you study, why should it matter *whether* you study?

Whenever it is suggested that the schools can strive for a higher level of universal education, the refrain is quickly heard that some students don't have the brains or the inclination to study such things as history, literature, science, mathematics, foreign languages, and the arts. The challenge that has not been met is to present the same subject matter through a variety of teaching techniques and to make it immediate and valuable to all. This may be an impossible dream, but it is a dream worth pursuing. According to reports about Japan and France, universal quality education is not beyond imagination. In *Japan as Number One,* Ezra Vogel writes of a national education system that has produced a highly literate public, knowledgeable about international affairs and about the intricacies of scientific issues like nuclear power and pollution. And Paul Gagnon, a French historian at the University of Massachusetts, has written about widespread popular support in France for "the right to culture." The technological society, Gagnon notes, with its threat of alienation and boredom and its promise of extended leisure time, makes indispensable to everyone "a personal culture, a furnished mind, practiced senses, skilled hands." All French adolescents, not just the select few, receive an education by the age of fifteen or sixteen that is the equivalent of what an American student covers by the end of the sophomore year in college.

Despite our dissatisfaction, we will not soon transform our educational system. It is not that it can't be done. The problem is that we lack consensus about whether there should be a common curriculum, and whether there are knowledge and skills that everyone should have. If we believed that it was important to have a highly literate public, to have a public capable of understanding history and politics and economics, to have citizens who are knowledgeable about science and technology, to have a society in which the powers of verbal communication are developed systematically and intentionally, then we would know what we wanted of our schools. Until we do, we get the schools we deserve, which accurately reflect our own confusion about the value of education.

3

The Continuing Crisis:
Fashions in Education

(1984)

IN the spring of 1983, unsuspecting American citizens woke up one morning to discover in the morning's headlines that we were "a nation at risk"; that other countries were challenging our leadership in "commerce, industry, science, and technological innovation"; and that "a rising tide of mediocrity" was threatening "our very future as a Nation and a people." The National Commission on Excellence in Education warned, in the kind of flashy prose that commands media attention, that "if an unfriendly foreign power had attempted to impose on America the mediocre educational performance that exists today, we might well have viewed it as an act of war. . . . We have, in effect, been committing an act of unthinking, unilateral educational disarmament."

This was strong stuff, but it was only the first in a series of critical reports on the quality of American schooling. Within weeks, several other state-of-education study groups weighed in with dire pronouncements about the need for change, and the fall season opened with a new crop of critical books and studies about the schools. The daily papers and weekly newsmagazines responded to the new issue by expanding their coverage of education, but the only fact of which the media seemed certain was that the schools were in a "crisis." Customarily uninterested in long-term educational trends, the news media offered no explanation for the plethora of critiques: As first one and then another study appeared, each was duly reported, but without reference to any context to explain the tidal wave. Why did so many reports appear simultaneously? What did it mean? No one hazarded a guess.

Since the National Commission on Excellence in Education was appointed by a conservative Republican president, there was a tendency in some quarters to treat its report as a statement of Reaganism. However, this was a superficial and perhaps defensive reaction, for the commission itself did not have a partisan cast. Nor could the conclusions of the other studies and reports be dismissed out of hand as machinations of an administration intent on dismantling the federal role in education and reviving school prayer. (Indeed, one of the best of the recent studies was *High School,* written by Ernest Boyer, the last commissioner of education in the Carter administration.) Political partisanship was not a factor in any of the reports. The president had been saying that the involvement of the federal government had caused the decay of the schools, but none of the reports (including that of his own commission) supported that argument. Another federally funded commission, the National Science Board's Commission on Precollege Education in Mathematics, Science, and Technology, recommended additional federal spending of about

$1 billion a year to improve instruction in these areas, even though the president clearly opposed increased federal funding of education.

If there was a single event that precipitated the present enthusiasm for educational reform, it was probably the discovery in 1975 that scores on the Scholastic Aptitude Test had fallen steadily since 1963. This college-entry test of verbal and mathematical skills had been in use since the late 1920s, though only since the late 1950s had it been taken by large numbers of high school students. The substantial decline of the national average, especially on the verbal portion of the test, meant different things to different people. For most people, the falling SAT scores suggested that something was seriously wrong with the schools, and that the freewheeling educational experimentation of the 1960s and 1970s had undermined the teaching of basic skills. The nascent back-to-basics movement gathered momentum, and during the late 1970s nearly forty states passed minimum competency tests for high school students, to assess whether they had mastered the basics. Since minimum competency tests guaranteed only that those at the bottom had attained minimal literacy, the spread of such tests did not allay doubts about the quality of precollegiate education.

Not everyone saw the SAT score decline as a catastrophe. There were those who said that the falling scores meant nothing at all because the drop in the mean was caused by the increased numbers of poor, black, and female students taking the tests. And then there were those critics of testing who said that the test itself meant nothing at all, so it scarcely mattered whether national scores went up or down.

In search of reasons for the score decline, the College Board created a blue-ribbon panel, headed by former Secretary of Labor Willard Wirtz. The panel's report was issued in 1977 and concluded that a substantial increase in the proportion of low-scoring test takers had accounted for most of the score decline until 1970. After 1970 the demographic composition of the test takers remained relatively constant, yet test scores continued to fall (the national verbal mean went from 478 in 1963 to 460 in 1970, then dropped even faster to 429 in 1977). The perception that a real erosion of verbal skills had occurred was reinforced by the fact that the number and proportion of students scoring over 700 dropped by 50 percent between 1967 and 1974.

The Wirtz panel held that the score decline "warrants serious attention," but it was notably coy in casting stones at perpetrators. The grand villain was "pervasive change," the rise of great impersonal social forces like television, Vietnam, Watergate, and family dissolution. How these were related to falling scores other than as "distractions" was unclear. What was clear, however, was that much had changed within the school during this critical period. The panel noted, first, an expansion of electives, accompanied by a decline in enrollments in basic academic courses. For example, the number of Massachusetts schools offering courses in film making and mass media had grown, while the number offering junior-year courses in English and world history had declined. Second, standards within the schools had clearly fallen: "Absenteeism formerly considered intolerable is now condoned. An 'A' or 'B' means a good deal less than it used to. Promotion from one grade to another has become almost automatic. Homework has apparently been cut about in half." Third, one of the panel's internal studies concluded that eleventh-grade textbooks were currently written at a ninth- to tenth-grade reading level, that the portion of the typical text devoted to pictures and graphics had expanded, and that textbook assignments generally asked "only for underlining, circling and filling in of single words." Lastly, the panel concluded that "the critical factors in the relationship between curricular change and the SAT scores are (1) that less thoughtful and critical reading is now being demanded and done, and (2) that careful writing has apparently about gone out of style." The principle of Occam's razor surely should have indicated that such in-school practices were sufficient to explain declining verbal skills of the college bound, even without the social and political calamities beyond the classroom door.

As the Wirtz panel was composing its findings, citizens' groups across the country were vocally criticizing low standards, lax discipline, and social promotion. Legislatures responded to these pressures by ordering tests of students and teachers. Educators and policymakers responded by creating committees. By 1981, when President Reagan appointed the National Commission on Excellence in Education, at least two dozen committees, study groups, and task forces were already considering the condition of the schools, and most of these were specifically studying the high school. There seemed to be a general recognition that the course of study in the elementary years was essentially the same for all students, but that something was amiss in the later years (the junior high years—certainly no less important than the years that preceded or followed them—were conspicuously ignored).

As the reports began to pile up, so did the evidence of poor educational performance. The National Commission on Excellence in Education offered a broad list of particulars:

"About 13 percent of all 17-year-olds in the United States can be considered functionally illiterate"—a figure that was dwarfed by the estimate that "functional illiteracy among minority youth may run as high as 40 percent."

"Average achievement of high school students on most standardized tests is now lower than 26 years ago when Sputnik was launched."

From 1963 to 1980, SAT scores fell by more than fifty points on the verbal section and nearly forty points on the mathematics section.

"There was a steady decline in science achievement scores of U.S. 17-year-olds as measured by national assessments of science in 1969, 1973, and 1977."

"Between 1975 and 1980, remedial mathematics courses in public 4-year colleges increased by 72 percent and now constitute one-quarter of all mathematics courses taught in those institutions."

"Business and military leaders complain that they are required to spend millions of dollars on costly remedial education ... in such basic skills as reading, writing, spelling, and computation."

American high schools are usually divided into academic, vocational, and general tracks, and "the proportion of students taking a general program of study has increased from 12 percent in 1964 to 42 percent in 1979."

What did the "general track" consist of? "Twenty-five percent of the credits earned by general track high school students are in physical and health education, work experience outside the school, remedial English and mathematics, and personal service and development courses, such as training for adulthood and marriage."

Enrollments in traditional academic courses were not reassuring: "We offer intermediate algebra, but only 31 percent of our recent high school graduates complete it; we offer French I, but only 13 percent complete it. . . . Calculus is available in schools enrolling about 60 percent of all students, but only 6 percent of all students complete it."

Students were found to be doing less homework (two-thirds of high school seniors reported less than one hour per night), and "grades have risen as average student achievement has been declining."

"A 1980 State-by-State survey of high school diploma

requirements reveals that only eight States require high schools to offer foreign language instruction. Thirty-five states require only 1 year of mathematics, and 36 require only 1 year of science for a diploma."

In response to this curricular vacuity, the national commission urged that state and local graduation requirements be strengthened to include four years of English, three years of mathematics, three years of science, three years of social studies, and one-half year of computer science; in addition, it proposed that college-bound students study two years of a foreign language. The National Center for Education Statistics, the data-gathering branch of the United States Department of Education, examined transcripts for the high school graduating class of 1982 and concluded that only 2.6 percent actually met the commission's proposed graduation requirements (not including foreign language). Even among those planning to go to a four-year college, only 22.6 percent had taken as much English, mathematics, science, and social studies as the commission recommended.

In the fall of 1983, the National Science Board observed that "students in our Nation's schools are learning less mathematics, science and technology, particularly in the areas of abstract thinking and problem solving. Since the late 1960s, most students have taken fewer mathematics and science courses. Mathematics and science achievement scores of 17-year-olds have dropped steadily and dramatically during the same period." The science board's panel recommended at least sixty minutes per day of mathematics and thirty minutes per day of science in the elementary grades, and a full year of math and science in both seventh and eighth grades. In high school, it called for a requirement of at least three years of mathematics and three years of science and technology for all students.

In California, a group of business executives calling themselves the California Roundtable was several months ahead of the national commission. In 1982, the roundtable published a study on the quality of the state's schools. It pointed out that the school day and the school year had grown shorter, and that academic demands had been reduced. High school seniors received credit for work experience unrelated to their studies, and less than one-fifth of them reported completing a single homework assignment per week. As school work diminished, remedial work in the state's colleges expanded: "Over half of the students entering the state university and college systems take remedial courses in English, and about half also take remedial math courses, despite having received good grades in the required high school courses in these subjects." The roundtable's study also identified a disturbing decline in academic course enrollments, linked with a marked increase in nonacademic electives. The roundtable recommended the phasing in of higher state graduation requirements: four years of English, three years of mathematics, two years of science, one year of computer studies, three years of social studies (one year of American government, two years of history), two years of foreign language, and two years of physical education.

In the states, the national commission's report generated a flurry of activity, and new commissions were created by legislatures, state education departments, school boards, interest groups, and governors. Some of this interest predated the commission's report, since the problems that concerned the national commission were also apparent at the local level. By the fall of 1983, many states were considering educational reform, centered largely on such matters as the status and compensation of teachers and on high school graduation requirements. These two reforms are inextricably intertwined, since it will be pointless to raise curricular requirements unless there is an adequate number of skilled teachers available. A number of states have increased their graduation requirements, especially in such subjects as mathematics, science, and foreign languages, but these are areas where there have been severe teacher shortages.

Most of the national commissions and task forces have recommended a basic required curriculum for all students on the grounds that the schools must educate everyone and that a democratic society needs a citizenry in which cultural and scientific literacy is highly developed. The goal of cultural and scientific literacy need not imply a monolithic curriculum, but it does imply a minimum foundation of required studies in the centrally important academic disciplines. Common requirements, however, have long been opposed by a substantial segment of the education profession, which harbors a deeply ingrained hostility toward such words as "standards," "subject matter," and even "excellence" (which is perceived as a code word for academic elitism). Excellence, it turns out, is a threatening concept when it is defined in relation to a required curriculum.

It is instructive to note, for example, the reaction in New York State when the state board of regents proposed new graduation requirements: three years of math, science, and a foreign language, and four years of English and social studies. This proposal, though it was in line with the recommendations of the various national study groups, was soon under attack. Teachers of home economics and vocational education, and others denounced the new requirements for their narrowness (meaning that their own specialties were not among the required subjects); the chancellor of the New York City schools insisted that students in vocational programs and in art and music courses would be unduly burdened by the raising of requirements in science and mathematics; others, claiming to speak for minority youth, charged that the dropout rate would rise along with the new standards.

No one should be surprised by the degree of dissension within the education profession, for it has been virtually a canonical principle of modern pedagogy that not all children can "take" an academic curriculum, which is allegedly of value only to the college-bound student. For more than sixty years, the curriculum field has been dominated by a species of social efficiency or functionalism that judges curricular offerings by their utility and that insists on a close fit between what students study and what roles they are likely to assume as adults. Added to this orientation is a set of complementary beliefs such as: The curriculum must be constructed to meet the needs of society and of children; since children differ, the curriculum must vary according to the needs of the children; since society is constantly changing, the curriculum must constantly change to meet society's needs. In theory, any one of these precepts is defensible; children do differ, society does change, and the curriculum of the school must take into account the dynamic quality of the world around it as well as the specific abilities and needs of students. But in practice, these otherwise unassailable precepts have provided justification for educational practices that range from the unwise to the bizarre. Under their banner have marched the advocates of relevance, arguing the case for trendiness in the curriculum, and the advocates of vocational tracking, dividing children into educationally separate tracks in accordance with their presumed fitness for certain educational experiences.

Aside from the pedagogical principles that reside in many textbooks as a ready rationale for a plunge into vocationalism or politicization, Americans have a problem—or, as we would say today, a hang-up—about authority.

Education, usually, is by its nature an exercise in authority, since it implies that students are gathered to learn from teachers. The activity of teaching necessarily involves a belief in authority, since the teacher presumably seeks to impart something that the student does not know or cannot do. But many Americans have wished to find ways to avoid this inescapable relationship, and periodically the sentiment is expressed that teachers must learn from their students, that experience is corrupting, that innocence (ignorance) is bliss. Without looking abroad to Rousseau, pedagogues can cite Emerson's opposition to educational uniformity: "I suffer whenever I see that common sight of a parent or senior imposing his opinion and way of thinking and being on a young soul to which they are totally unfit. Cannot we let people be themselves, and enjoy life in their own way?" It was this same spirit of educational laissez-faire that attracted so much admiration to A. S. Neill's Summerhill, where students learned what they wanted, when they wanted, but only if they wanted. Neill's model attracted much attention during the heyday of educational romanticism, appealing to those who longed for the naturalistic style of education on demand. Summerhill went too far for public school educators, since it was not a usable model in communities that prized a semblance of order and such conventional measures of achievement as reading scores. In the late 1960s and early 1970s, though, a variety of less extreme experiments, like open education, struck a responsive chord by their claim that children learn best in the absence of authority, that their own choices were always better than anything imposed on them by coercion.

Policies were implied in the distaste for authority: the elimination or weakening of requirements for admission to and graduation from college, of requirements for graduation from high school, and of promotional standards from grade to grade. When colleges ceased requiring certain subjects for admission, many high schools could not find a good reason to maintain their requirements for graduation. Nor did it seem right to require all students to study science or mathematics, because some students didn't like those subjects. By the same token, other students didn't see why they should learn to write essays or study history. For those who planned to go to work instead of to college, there were always courses in vocational education or personal service courses, such as training for marriage and adulthood. Pushed by a philosophy of consumerism, the high school curriculum burgeoned with new electives, enrollment in mathematics and science courses diminished, homework and expository writing faded away. The guiding principle, it seemed, was to give students what they wanted; in this way, they would stay in school longer, have higher motivation to learn, and cause less trouble while there, while adults could compliment themselves for having met the needs of their students without using coercion.

It should have been a successful formula, but it was not. Once the principles of utility, relevance, and free choice became the touchstones of the curriculum, the consequences described by the Wirtz panel and the National Commission on Excellence in Education followed. When students were left on their own to decide whether to learn science, mathematics, and foreign language, it could hardly be surprising that enrollments dropped or that the supply of future teachers in these areas diminished accordingly. When student preferences determined course offerings, the explosion of electives became inevitable, particularly in history and English, where teachers were encouraged to split their courses into increasingly specialized and exotic minicourses to catch the mood of the market. Not even science was immune to the rush to electives. Paul DeHart

Hurd of Stanford University, who prepared a paper on science education for the National Commission on Excellence, reported that more than 100 new science courses were added to the junior and senior high school curriculum during the late 1960s and early 1970s, including such specialized offerings as astronomy, meteorology, oceanography, metric measurement, sex education, and human genetics.

Probably the single most significant result of these trends was the fragmentation of the curriculum—not only in content but in student enrollment in courses of vastly different quality. Responding to the new freedom from requirements, students tracked themselves into academic, vocational, and general programs. In high school, subjects like foreign language, mathematics, and science—once required of all students, regardless of their ability—became options. To liken the patterns that developed to a cafeteria—as so many critics have done—is not entirely correct; better to say that there were three different cafeterias, one for the academic track students (about 35 percent of high school students), another for the vocational track (about 25 percent), and the third for the general track (about 40 percent). The three cafeterias, where students could help themselves to the courses they wanted, differed in several ways: by the extent of academic content; by the degree of challenge; and by the intrinsic, long-range value of the offerings. Given the fairly substantial differences among the three cafeterias, it was not surprising that the wide divergence in skills and knowledge between students at the top and those at the bottom was exacerbated by the triple-track curriculum, or that high school graduates could no longer be said to share a common body of knowledge, not to mention a common culture.

The arrangement had certain virtues. For one thing, educators felt satisfied that they were meeting the needs of different children by providing them with specialized offerings; at the same time, they were meeting society's needs by keeping adolescents in school instead of on the street or in the job market, where they were not wanted. They often proclaimed as an article of faith that the diversification of the high school curriculum had lowered the dropout rate. It was true that the dropout rate had fallen steadily during the twentieth century, but, oddly, it had remained unchanged since the mid-1960s. In other words, the dilution and diffusion of the high school curriculum during the past fifteen years did not—contrary to the conventional wisdom—lower the dropout rate. Over the decades, the rise in the proportion of young people who finished high school has apparently been owing to economic and demographic factors, not to changes in the curriculum. Thus, the charge that an increase in requirements and in the assignment of essay writing and homework will cause more students to drop out is not based on evidence, but on assumptions about the educability of poor children. (It is noteworthy that the dropout rate continued to fall during the post-Sputnik years when rigor and requirements were in fashion.)

The current debate has roots that extend over the past century. In the late nineteenth century, educators worried about the seeming disorganization of the high school curriculum and wondered whether there should be differentiation between students bound for college and those bound for work. A prestigious commission was appointed, which included five college presidents (its chairman was President Charles W. Eliot of Harvard). Known as the Committee of Ten, the group, in its report of 1893, proposed that all students be liberally educated, regardless of whether they were college bound or not, and that all should study English, history, foreign language, science, and mathematics. Recognizing that only a small minority of high school graduates went on to college, the committee asserted that "the secondary schools of the United States, taken as a whole, do not exist for the purpose of preparing boys and girls for colleges." Some students might study longer than others in a given field, but the committee believed that a common liberal education was the best preparation for the duties of life, whatever the pupils' later destination.

For a time the views of the Committee of Ten were influential in the high schools, but its academic orientation was at odds with the mainstream of the new education profession. As enrollment in the high schools grew, professional educators felt constrained by the weight of academic traditionalism. John Dewey gained a substantial following for the view that the curriculum should be built around the interests of the child and should be better related to the community and to so-called real-life activities. There was a growing sense among education policymakers that the schools would never be able to play a constructive role as a social agency until they broke free of the limitations imposed by traditional academic goals. In 1918 a new group, the Commission on the Reorganization of Secondary Education, issued a statement called the "Cardinal Principles of Secondary Education." Unlike the Committee of Ten, the 1918 commission was composed largely of high school principals, professors of education, and educational bureaucrats. Its credo was that "secondary education should be determined by the needs of the society to be served, the character of the individuals to be educated, and the knowledge of educational theory and practice available." On each of these grounds, the commission argued for a fundamental shift in the means and ends of a high school education. The main objectives of education, the commission concluded, were "1. Health. 2. Command of fundamental processes. 3. Worthy home-membership. 4. Vocation. 5. Citizenship. 6. Worthy use of leisure. 7. Ethical character." The only reference to the academic function of the school was "command of fundamental processes."

The "Cardinal Principles" statement facilitated the redefinition of the high school curriculum along functional lines and conferred respectability on vocational, technical, socio-personal, and other sorts of new courses—at first in addition to, and later instead of, the academic subjects. The notion that the student should be fitted to the curriculum and vice versa legitimated what we now call tracking. The academic curriculum, no longer considered appropriate for all students, became a special program for those who intended to go to college. Others, who were heading for the workplace, were directed to more practical pursuits better fitted to their later destination. The controlling principles in this readjustment were social utility and efficiency. Every subject was judged by whether it was immediately useful and whether it met the needs of the students. By that test, students who were not going to college had no use and no need for foreign language, or for anything more than a smattering of history, science, literature, and mathematics.

In the nearly seventy years since the publication of the "Cardinal Principles," the debate has continued in a seesaw fashion. The utilitarians dominated the field in the 1940s; then the argument tilted to the champions of liberal education in the period just before and after Sputnik. During the past fifteen years, the "Cardinal Principles" have again held sway, as schools have tried to adjust the curriculum in order to reflect the changing moods of society and of students. The challenge that has never been met, whichever side was in the ascendancy, was to democratize the academic curriculum—both what was taught and who was taught—without cheapening it and without excluding large numbers of students from its reach.

What the various task forces and national commissions are now saying is that our educational systems must take on the job of making all young people literate, and their definition includes both cultural and scientific literacy. No one knows whether it can be done, because we have never tried to do it on a mass scale. If we make the attempt, it should be done with full knowledge of where we have gone astray in the past. At one extreme, the perfervid traditionalists have been content to educate those at the top without regard to the welfare of the majority of students; at the other, the perfervid progressives have cooperated in dividing and diluting the curriculum, which left the majority of students with an inadequate education. Most schools and teachers are not at the extremes, but they have little ability to blunt the lure of either progressivism or traditionalism, particularly to an indiscriminate media and hyperactive policymakers. Pedagogical practice follows educational philosophy, and it is obvious that we do not yet have a philosophical commitment to education that is sound enough and strong enough to withstand the erratic dictates of fashion.

4

Bring Literature and History Back to Elementary Schools

(1984)

DURING the national debate about education that began in April 1983 with the publication of "A Nation at Risk" by the National Commission on Excellence in Education, the elementary schools have been almost entirely ignored. This is a pity, because it is in the elementary schools that children gain (or don't gain) a firm foundation for future learning.

Perhaps the major reason so little attention has been paid to elementary schools is that there is general consensus that the significant problems of the schools begin after sixth grade. After all, unlike high schools, the elementary schools offer everyone a fairly common curriculum and they are not plagued by absenteeism or disciplinary problems. There is little doubt that the chief job of the elementary teacher is to teach a good command of basic skills and to instill good work habits. If there are problems later on, everyone seems to agree, it must be the fault of those in the junior or senior high schools.

My complacency on this score was shattered by two items that crossed my desk within a twenty-four-hour period. The first was an article that appeared in *Education Week*. The headline was "Using 'Real Books' to Teach Reading Said to Heighten Skill, Interest." The second was an exchange printed in one of the leading elementary-school journals, in which the magazine's social studies consultant was asked, "Will history ever make a comeback in the elementary-school curriculum?" His answer was, "Probably not in the near future," and he predicted that history and geography would never again be central in the social-studies curriculum because the emphasis should be on "process" skills such as "student inquiry, social problem solving, and helping kids learn to think."

These two items persuaded me that the problems of the high school are integrally related to what is happening in the elementary school. The *Education Week* story described an "experiment" in Upper Arlington, Ohio, where alternative programs are used to teach children to read by providing "real" books instead of basal readers. Lo and behold! While there was no difference in standardized test scores between those who read "real" books and those who learned with basal readers, the children who read storybooks seemed to enjoy reading more than the basal-reading children did, and their teachers in junior high said they were "superior writers" and "independent thinkers."

It shocked me to discover that educational researchers had to fall back on the customary technical jargon to demonstrate that classic children's literature is superior to basal readers. In my foolishness, I imagined that such a statement would be a self-evident proposition, needing no justification. But to my astonishment, the article on reading contains an estimate that 95 percent of elementary schools have basal readers and 65 percent use them every day. What? Is it now "experimental" and "innovative" to propose that young children should read good literature and that it might be more enjoyable than a basal reader? Is it possible that America's reading teachers think a controlled vocabulary "developed" by pedestrian writers can compete with the works of the Brothers Grimm, Hans Christian Andersen, L. Frank Baum, or the myths of many lands? Is there a single author employed by the great publishing houses whose works should be considered superior to the stories that have entertained, instructed, and challenged generations of children?

In fairness, it should be noted that many basal readers, like those produced by Lippincott and Open Court, include stories and poems of high literary quality. Even good basal readers, however, should be used as a prelude to original works of literature, whetting the child's appetite for more of "the real thing." Above all, children's literature should be presented to the reader as it was written, neither excerpted nor rewritten to cater to contemporary tastes.

How can children be motivated to read at all if what they learn isn't worth the time it takes to decipher? What child won't plead to stay up "just a little longer" if he or she is in the middle of an exciting story? I found myself wondering whether it was the publishing houses, each with its own copyrighted basal-reading series, that persuaded reading specialists that their materials were better than "real" books. Or was this incredible phenomenon a product of the reading profession's fascination with "whole-word" or "look-say" instruction, which requires a controlled vocabulary so that children don't encounter unfamiliar words?

Whether the fault lies with the publishers or the professionals, the important fact is that the basal readers somehow managed to monopolize the elementary-school "market." The basal readers may be well fitted to producing mastery of basic skills—the sort of skills that makers of standardized tests treasure. But did anyone ever love a basal reader? Did anyone ever take a flashlight to bed to read a basal reader under the covers? The dearth of literature in the elementary school may go far toward explaining some of the problems encountered by secondary-school teachers, who complain that children don't like to read, don't read well, and can't apply what they read to their own lives.

I was equally astonished to discover the contempt with which the elementary social studies consultant viewed history and geography. Like others who don't like history and never took a good history course, this educational expert associated history with "memorization and parroting of facts" rather than problem solving. As every good historian knows, history *is* problem solving. The writer of history asks: What happened? How do we know it happened? Why did it happen? Why did people respond as they did? History is about issues and controversies, about heroes and villains; it is about people struggling to improve their lives and about the ways people have devised to enslave others or to free themselves. History is the substance that students use to exercise the skills of problem solving, inquiry, and thinking.

It is certainly true that history cannot be taught in elementary school as it is taught in junior high or high school, but young children are fascinated and challenged by the incredible but true stories of human history. Biographies offer a fertile ground for involving children in the lives and stories and historical context of remarkable individuals, the men and women who overcame personal obstacles to change the world in some important way— political leaders, scientists, explorers, doctors, generals, writers, educators, civil rights leaders, and so on. History provides the framework within which the elementary teacher can use myths, legends, and fairy tales. Why shouldn't children read the fabulous Greek myths while learning about Greek history, culture, and society? Education is debased when the curriculum is stripped of its content and when skills, free of any cultural, literary, or historic context, are all that is taught.

No wonder research shows that the elementary schools are not the problem. On standardized tests of skills, the students are apparently doing fine. It is only later that their teachers report how they falter when it comes to making inferences or deductions. But it is not only higher-order skills that they lack: They are culturally illiterate. They can read the words put in front of them, but they have no "furniture" in their minds, no vocabulary of historical persons or events to draw upon, no reference to the ordinary literary images that fifth graders once imbibed in every common school in the nation.

The problem, I would suggest, lies not with the teacher, but with the experts who have told them for years that skills and process are all that matter. In this strange world of the overcredentialed but undereducated, content, knowledge, and context count for nothing. The children of this regime arrive in junior high schools and secondary schools knowing *how,* but not *why* or *what.* They have been miseducated; they have been taught to read without learning to love reading; they have been taught social studies as a package of skills rather than as a window on the varieties of human experience in other times and places. Such educationally baneful practices are part and parcel of the "rising tide of mediocrity," and it is unfortunate that they have been ignored by the national commissions.

5

American Education:
Has the Pendulum Swung
Once Too Often?

(1982)

SINCE the middle 1940s, American schools have been at the center of a tug of war between competing educational philosophies. With striking regularity, educational policy has swung from domination by "progressives" to domination by "traditionalists" in roughly ten-year periods. Since there is an extraordinary degree of diversity among the millions of teachers in the nation, both in their professional training and in their personal views, no one philosophy ever has decisive control at any moment. Yet even the teacher who closes the classroom door to the latest educational fashion cannot remain unaware of the struggles over educational policy in the political arena.

From the mid-1940s until the mid-1950s, the "good school" followed progressive practices; from the mid-1950s until the mid-1960s, the "good school" emphasized the study of science, mathematics, and foreign languages and insisted on high academic standards; from the mid-1960s until the mid-1970s, the "good school" installed open classrooms, eliminated course requirements, and experimented with minicourses and electives; since the mid-1970s, the "good school" has been eliminating frivolous courses, reinstating curricular requirements, and restoring academic standards.

Lawrence A. Cremin observed in *The Transformation of the School* that by the end of World War II, progressivism was the conventional wisdom of American education. Textbooks, teachers' organizations, local school boards, and publications of state and national agencies spoke earnestly of "meeting the needs of the whole child," "vitalizing the curriculum," and "adjusting the school to the child." Teachers-in-training learned of the historic struggle between the old-fashioned, subject-centered, rigid, authoritarian, traditional school and the modern, child-centered, flexible, democratic, progressive school. Behind the rhetoric was an acknowledgment that the extension of universal education up through the high school had created a new problem; progressives believed that the traditional academic curriculum was not appropriate for all children, and most of their innovations were devised to extend the "holding power" of the high schools so that all children would remain for twelve years of schooling.

Progressive education was difficult to define except in practice. It generally emphasized such things as active learning through experience rather than passive learning through systematic instruction; cooperative planning of classroom activities by teachers and pupils; cooperation among pupils on group projects rather than competition for grades; and the merging of traditional academic subjects into functional problem areas related to family life, community problems, or student interests. Progressive teachers rejected drill and memorization as teaching methods; the teaching of traditional subject matter unrelated to functional, "real-life" problems; traditional policies of promotion and failure; reliance on textbooks; and evaluation of the school program by tests of subject matter mastery.

Progressivism in the late 1940s was called "life adjustment education" by friend and foe alike. The United States Office of Education organized regional conferences and national commissions to encourage the spread of life adjustment education. Life adjustment education took the utilitarian, vocational thrust of progressivism to its logical extremes. It judged every subject by its everyday utility, substituting radio repair for physics, business English for the classics, and consumer arithmetic for algebra. Under the rubric of life adjustment education, schools were encouraged to merge traditional subjects like English and history with health and guidance to create "common learnings" courses, in which students could examine their personal and social problems.

Beginning in the late 1940s, critics complained that "how-to" courses and socio-personal adjustment had been substituted for history, science, mathematics, foreign languages, and literature. Life adjustment education was condemned by some because it was anti-intellectual, and by others because it aimed to teach group conformity. Authors such as Mortimer Smith, Arthur Bestor, and Robert Hutchins attacked progressivism for debasing educational standards. Scores of articles in popular journals lampooned classes where children debated whether to "pet" on the first date, what shade of nail polish was best, and how to make one's family more democratic.

After the Russians orbited Sputnik in 1957, the national press was filled with indictments of American schools for ignoring science and mathematics. The Russians' feat served as evidence for many of the critics' worst complaints about the inadequacies of American education. In reality, progressivism had already collapsed before Sputnik, a victim not only of hostile criticism but of its own intellectual ossification. While progressives prided themselves on their utilitarianism, their pedagogical blinders prevented them from seeing that the growth of mass society created a need to teach history and literature; that technological change created new needs for the teaching of science and mathematics; that global change required the teaching of foreign languages; that international tensions created the need to teach the history and literature of other societies. Instead, progressives continued to focus on the needs of youth, to the point of irrelevance.

During the late 1950s and early 1960s, educators shifted their focus from "meeting the needs of the whole child" to "excellence." Programs were developed to identify talented youth at an early age and to speed their way through rigorous courses in high school and college. While the National Education Association's *Education for All American Youth* was the prototypical educational document of the 1940s, proposing the school as a grand social service center meeting all the needs of the individual and the community, the Rockefeller Brothers Fund's *The Pursuit of Excellence* was the clarion call of the post-Sputnik era. It advocated the development of human potential as a national goal and insisted that the nation could encourage both excellence and equality without compromising either. The political climate, typified by the brief presidency of John F. Kennedy, also stimulated the popular belief that the identification of talent and the pursuit of excellence were appropriate educational goals. Part of Kennedy's image was the idea that youth, talent, intelligence, and education could right society's problems. The drive for excellence was in high gear during the early 1960s, and enrollments in advanced courses and foreign languages rose steadily, along with standardized test scores.

The sudden and remarkably quiet disappearance of the "pursuit of excellence" in the mid-1960s showed how dependent it was on the socio-political climate. A series of cataclysmic events shook national self-confidence: violence against blacks and civil rights workers in the South; Kennedy's assassination; the rediscovery of poverty; American involvement in Vietnam. By 1965, the nation's competition with the Soviets for world supremacy had lost its motivating power. As the Cold War appeared to fade, students in elite universities—the presumed beneficiaries of the post-Sputnik years—protested against technology, against the middle-class values of their parents, and against the meritocratic pressures of an achievement-oriented society.

At the elementary and secondary levels, dedication to excellence waned along with national self-esteem. Where once there had been a clear sense of purpose about educational goals, now there was uncertainty; the educational pendulum swung back towards a revival of progressivism, nudged along by an outpouring of critical books about the competitiveness and "joylessness" of American schools. Though scarcely noticed when it was first published in 1960, A. S. Neill's *Summerhill* was the bellwether of the new movement. Written by the founder of a libertarian therapeutic boarding school in England, *Summerhill* became a classic in the mid-1960s as an audience for its message of freedom and unconstrained sexuality emerged. Soon after, authors such as Paul Goodman, Edgar Z. Friedenberg, John Holt, Jonathan Kozol, George Dennison, Herbert Kohl, Ivan Illich, and James Herndon published lively books that shared a similar sensibility, attacking the oppressiveness and conformity of the traditional school and calling for teachers who encouraged spontaneity, compassion, sensitivity, and self-expression, rather than competition for grades and test scores.

Has the Pendulum Swung Once Too Often?

Times had changed. Young people had begun to absorb the manners and mores of the counterculture. Personal unkemptness and conscious inarticulateness were outward manifestations of deeply ingrained attitudes—anti-intellectualism, lack of respect for authority, and contempt for the work ethic—that created a barrier to schooling. In addition, the drug culture directly subverted educational values, since it not only dulled students' senses and their motivation to learn but established powerful peer pressures to resist education. Turmoil on the campuses, portrayed graphically each evening on the television news, provided a romantic model of rebellious youth leaders who successfully defied and humbled their elders; their example was admired and sometimes copied by high school students. As adult authority eroded, there was a sharp rise in discipline problems, truancy, and physical assaults by students against teachers and other students.

Responding to changes in the social and cultural milieu, educators sought to adapt the schools to the new conditions and to placate their numerous critics. The innovation that had the most influence in the public schools was the open education movement. In 1967, interest in open education was stirred by Joseph Featherstone's articles in the *New Republic* about informal education in British day schools; the new methods were further popularized by Charles Silberman's best-selling *Crisis in the Classroom* in 1970. In 1968, only a few dozen articles about British informal schools appeared in American educational journals, but three years later the number had soared to over 300. Several state departments of education, including those of New York and Vermont, endorsed the open education concept, and extensive teacher-training workshops in open education were conducted by schools of education.

Part of the appeal of open education was that it offered a way out of the slough of despair in which educators found themselves in the mid-1960s; there was a general consensus, based on the torrent of abuse that had flowed over the schools in a short period of time, that the attempted reforms of the 1950s and 1960s had not worked. The revisions sponsored by the National Science Foundation in the physical sciences, mathematics, and social sciences were intended to strengthen the academic side of the curriculum, a problem that did not interest the writers of the 1960s, who were concerned about social justice and personal liberation. Everything else that the government and big foundations had promoted—team teaching, ungraded classrooms, compensatory programs, and the like— was too piecemeal, too incremental, too limited to turn the school into an instrument of social reform or into a therapeutic community.

The informal approach was typified by individualized learning activities, rather than group instruction; by emphasis on play, experience, and concrete activities, rather than reading and listening; by an informal relationship between the teacher and the student; by student participation in selecting the day's activities; and by informal arrangement of classroom time, space, and materials to encourage student choice. Behind such practices was the belief that children develop and learn at different rates; that the best way to learn is through activity and experience, motivated by interest; and that children are by nature eager to learn. Some advocates went so far as to insist that the child had to be free to decide what to learn, when to learn, and how to learn, with the goal being not to "educate" the child in the traditional sense of filling him up with knowledge, but to free him from his dependence on teachers, schools, and books.

The open education philosophy answered perfectly the need for a set of educational values to fit the countercultural mood of the late 1960s; it stimulated participatory democracy; it justified the equal sharing of power between the authority figure (the teacher) and the students; it made a positive virtue of nonassertive leadership; and it implied that children should study only what they wanted. At the high school level, this philosophy led to dropping of requirements, adoption of minicourses, creation of schools-without-walls, and alternative schools.

On paper, open education was ideal. Once it was put into practice, the problems appeared. Many schools removed classroom walls, hired open educators, sent their veteran teachers to workshops to be retrained, and provisioned classrooms with the obligatory gerbils and sensory, tactile materials. Despite their training, some teachers couldn't handle the open-ended situation; children wandered about aimlessly, got into fights, demanded that the teacher tell them what to do. In some districts, parents complained bitterly that their children couldn't read, that the classroom was chaotic, and that there was no homework.

By the mid-1970s, the open education movement had gone into decline, and the journals that had hailed it in 1971 were publishing postmortems on its failure. Why did the informal methods founder in so many American schools? Certainly, open education encountered hostility from teachers and administrators who never approved of its theory or practice. Many parents objected to the lack of discipline and the absence of traditional academic work. Behind the complaints, however, was the fact that "openness" was not working in many American schools as it was said to work in British schools. Apparently, British children (in contrast to their American peers) benefited from the informal methods because they came from well-disciplined homes or because the cultural milieu instilled self-discipline. Additionally, British teachers were not merely helpful bystanders, as some American observers believed, but exercised subtle control over the direction of children's activities.

The swing away from open education was hastened by the public reaction to the news in 1975 that scores on the Scholastic Aptitude Test (SAT) had dropped steadily since 1963. Regardless of explanations blaming such factors as Vietnam, Watergate, drugs, the effect of television, and working mothers, a substantial part of the public believed that the decline of standards in the schools was primarily responsible for lower test scores. The College Board's 1977 report on the score drop confirmed that part of the drop was in fact due to lowered standards, grade inflation, absenteeism, and the widespread decline of critical reading and careful writing.

Other studies have documented a relationship between educational practices and test scores. Annegret Harnischfeger and David E. Wiley found that scores on a wide variety of standardized tests rose until the mid-1960s, then steadily declined; they noted a striking parallel between score declines and falling enrollments in traditional subjects, especially advanced courses. Enrollments in foreign language courses, the President's Commission on Foreign Languages noted in 1979, are now at their lowest point in this century.

Since the demise of the open education movement, no grand new educational campaign has emerged to enlist the energies of teachers, administrators, and educational journalists. The lack of slogans and banners may be a healthy sign. Perhaps the pendulum has swung once too often. Perhaps it may yet be possible to find a common ground on which parents, teachers, and others concerned about education may agree, a common ground that encompasses the educational ideals of the traditionalists and the compassion of the progressives. The traditionalists have a strong commitment to what should be studied; the progressives have a strong commitment to finding ways to motivate children.

Has the Pendulum Swung Once Too Often?

Suppose it were possible to agree that all children need to study history and literature and language, in order to understand themselves, their society, and the world in which they live; to study science, mathematics, and technology, in order to comprehend fully the revolutionary developments of our age; to study the arts, in their various forms, in order to awaken and develop their aesthetic sensibilities. Suppose it were further possible to agree that educators must appeal to children's interests while inspiring new ones, to teach through experiences, projects, and activities as well as books, to adapt their methods of instruction to the individual youngsters they are attempting to teach, and to kindle intellectual joy without neglecting the necessity of disciplined study. On such a common ground, adults would accept responsibility for deciding what children are expected to learn; requirements in the major disciplines would be necessary to ensure that all children are exposed to studies that they might otherwise ignore.

In recent decades, American educational policy has been pulled from extreme to extreme every ten years or so, in response to changes in the social and political climate. What protects the schools against their pendulum swings, ultimately, is the good sense of classroom teachers who are themselves well educated. Their commitment, both to knowledge and to their students, has moderated and finally blunted pedagogical fashions that were not solidly grounded in good educational practice. We should have learned by now, to save us from short-lived crusades, that panaceas are a mirage, and that the only educational improvement of lasting significance is the result of good teaching.

6

Scapegoating the Teachers

(1983)

THE most common response to the current crisis in education has been to assail public school teachers. Not only are they incompetent, goes the charge, but good people have abandoned or are shunning the teaching profession. Teacher competency tests, which have spread during the past five years to some three dozen states, have produced embarrassing results in many districts; for example, when a third of Houston's teachers took a competency test, 62 percent failed the reading section and 46 percent failed the mathematics section (and the scores of hundreds of other teachers were ruled invalid because of cheating). Those who major in education in college tend to have below-average grades in high school and lower scores on their SATs than the already depressed national average (in 1982, the national average on the SAT verbal was 426, while the average for those planning to major in education was only 394).

This state of affairs has prompted a plethora of proposals. Some call for merit pay, others for increased salaries across the board. To some reformers, the answer lies with the designation of master teachers or with the promotion of more doctorate degrees in educational practice. Still others argue that the teacher problem would be ameliorated by abolishing schools of education.

The problem of teacher competence is serious, since there is no chance that the schools will improve unless the teachers know more than the students do. Yet the rush to attack teachers for the ills of public education smacks more than a little of scapegoating. Teachers did not singlehandedly cause the debasement of educational standards, and their preparation is better today than it was twenty years ago, when test scores began to fall. Though we now look back to 1962–63 as the golden age of student achievement, these years coincided with the publication of two major critiques of teacher education, James Koerner's *The Miseducation of American Teachers* and James B. Conant's *The Education of American Teachers*. Teachers, it seems, can't win: When scores go down, they are to blame; when scores are high, they get no credit.

It is comforting to blame teachers for the low state of education, because it relieves so many others of their own responsibility for many years of educational neglect.

- Why not blame the colleges and universities for lowering entrance requirements, thus undermining high school graduation requirements? Why not blame them for accepting hordes of semiliterate students and establishing massive remedial programs, instead of complaining to the high schools that gave diplomas to the uneducated?
- Why not blame businesses and employers, who set up multi-million-dollar programs to teach basic skills to their workforce instead of telling the public, the school boards, and the legislatures that the schools were sending them uneducated people? Why didn't representatives of major employers—like the telephone company and the banks—join forces to demand improved education?

- Why not blame state legislatures, which quietly diluted or abolished high school graduation requirements? Why were they willing to pile on new requirements for nonacademic courses (drug education, family life education, consumer education, etc.) while cutting the ground away from science, math, history, and foreign languages?
- Why not blame the press, which has been indifferent to educational issues, interested only in fads, and unaware of the steady deterioration of academic standards until a national commission captured its attention?
- Why not blame the federal government, which has toyed with the curriculum and introduced programs, regulations, and practices that narrowed the teacher's professional autonomy in the classroom?
- Why not blame the courts, which have whittled away the schools' ability to maintain safety and order? (In 1983, the New Jersey Supreme Court invalidated evidence that students were selling drugs in junior high, because the drugs had been illegally seized in one student's purse and in another student's locker—the court's decision that the students' right to privacy outweighed the school's obligation to maintain order nullified the school's obligation to act *in loco parentis*.)*
- Why not blame state education departments for tolerating inferior teacher education programs, for imposing certification requirements that force students to take vapid education courses, and for burdening teachers and local school boards with a mountain of bureaucratic regulations?

With so many guilty parties still at large, it should be clear why almost everyone seems eager to pin responsibility

* The New Jersey decision was reversed by the Supreme Court in 1985.

on the teachers for the bad news about the schools. The reality is that teachers should be seen not as perpetrators of the deleterious trends in the schools, but as victims of them. As teaching conditions worsen, it is teachers who suffer the consequences. When judges rule that disruptive youths cannot be suspended, it is teachers who must lock their classroom door and worry about being assaulted.

Just as serious as the problem of teacher competence is the state of the teaching profession. Some teachers insist bitterly that teaching is no longer a profession, but has been reduced to a civil service job. Other professionals are subject to entry tests and to supervision by senior professionals, and they usually retain a large measure of control over where they work and how they perform their duties; in teaching, governmental agencies and policymakers have bureaucratized hiring practices, curriculum development, student evaluation, and other areas that once engaged the experience and participation of teachers. The effort to make schools "teacher-proof" ends by making the teachers technical functionaries, implementing remotely designed policies. With so many laws and regulations and interest groups on the scene, wise teachers look for protection to the rulebook, their union, their lawyer, or to some job with more dignity. For the person who simply wants to teach history or literature, the school has not been a receptive workplace.

In response to declining enrollments and worsening working conditions, the number of people who want to be teachers has dropped sharply over the past decade. The number of undergraduate degrees awarded in education reached a peak of 200,000 in 1973, when they were 21 percent of all bachelor's degrees awarded in the nation, but dropped to only 108,000 in 1981, fewer than 12 percent of all bachelor's degrees awarded. The tight job market has meant not only a decline in the number preparing to teach, but a decline in the ability of those who want to teach. Apparently the brighter students were smart enough to pick another field, and the flight of academically talented women to other fields has particularly depressed the quality of the pool of would-be teachers. The low starting salary for teachers is undoubtedly a factor in shrinking the pool: A college graduate with a bachelor's degree in mathematics would get a starting salary in teaching of about $13,000, while the same person would receive about $17,000 as an accountant in private industry.

The outlook for a better pool in the future is not very promising. In the fall of 1970, 19 percent of college freshmen said that they wanted to teach in elementary or secondary school. By 1982, less than 5 percent of college freshmen expressed the same ambition. Less than 2 percent wanted to teach in high school, a choice that was doubtless informed by their own recent observation of the life of high school teachers.

Would reforms in teacher education help the situation? For years, critics of education have heaped scorn on schools of education and on the required education courses that prospective teachers must take. Thirty years ago, critics like Arthur Bestor and Mortimer Smith charged that entry to the teaching profession was controlled by an "interlocking directorate" made up of schools of education, bureaucrats in state education departments, and teacher associations, and that the hurdles these groups erected (such as "Mickey Mouse" courses in educational theory and methods) excluded talented people from the public schools. Since the early 1950s was a time of baby boom and teacher shortage, nothing much came of the grumbling, and the agencies of certification and accreditation are, if anything, even more powerful today.

Students preparing to teach take most of their courses outside of the undergraduate education department. Would-be high school teachers take about 20 percent of their courses in education, and would-be elementary teachers take about 40 percent of their courses in education. Some of these courses are valuable; others are not. Some are required by state education departments without any evidence that they contribute to better teaching. On most campuses, the education department is viewed with contempt by others in the institution, and it attracts the weakest students.

Even though education majors take most of their courses outside the education department, it would be preferable if there were no education majors at the undergraduate level, if every would-be teacher majored in some subject or combination of subjects. As matters now stand, the 108,000 bachelor's degrees in education awarded in 1981 were divided up among students preparing to be elementary teachers (35 percent), physical education teachers (17 percent), special education teachers (13 percent), and teachers of such specialized areas as home economics, vocational education, prekindergarten instruction, and health education. Less than 3 percent of the education degrees went to secondary teachers, which suggests that those who want to teach in high school take their baccalaureate degree in the subjects they want to teach and get their education credits on the side or in graduate school.

Elementary teachers need a wide preparation, since they will be teaching reading, writing, mathematics, science, social studies, art, and music. But they can take the courses in how to teach these subjects to young children while majoring in a discipline or combination of disciplines. The case for requiring physical education instructors to major in a subject area is even stronger, because a large number of them teach their minor subject (usually social studies) and end up as high school principals.

Since prospective secondary teachers rarely major in education in college, they do not get counted or measured by the researchers who examine the quality of the teaching pool. In most studies and government reports, statistics are gathered only for those who major in education in college. Thus the numbers that are tossed about refer *only* to those who are academically weakest. In fact, when we are warned about the onrushing tide of incompetent teachers, we are hearing only about the coaches, the school nurses, the elementary school teachers, and the shop teachers, but not the would-be teachers of history, the sciences, English, and mathematics. We should still be concerned, particularly about the low academic ability of those who are supposed to teach young children the basic skills and impart to them their attitudes toward learning, but we should recognize that the data are biased.

Graduate schools of education have shown little interest in training teachers. Some professors and programs involve themselves with the public schools, but most of these institutions emphasize research and the training of educational administrators. Because they are parts of universities, their concept of status derives from the traditional academic model. They have low status within the university, which considers the graduate school of education little better than a vocational school.

Yet the graduate school has a useful role to play. In particular, it cares about education, which is one of the major social and economic activities in the nation. This sets it apart from the rest of the university, which tends to look down upon any interest in or involvement with the public schools. In the summer of 1983, however, the presidents of Harvard and Stanford met with leading university presidents and their education deans to discuss how to help the schools and how to overcome the traditional snobbery that has kept the "ed" schools out of the academic mainstream. Whether this resolve is translated from rhetoric into programmatic commitments remains to be seen.

Perhaps a personal note at this point will explain my own bias. In 1972, when I had been out of college for a dozen years, I decided to get a Ph.D. in history while writing a political history of the New York City public schools. I approached a young history professor at Columbia, who told me that I was a bad bet for his department: "You have three strikes against you," he said. "First, you are a woman; second, you are more than ten years away from your B.A.; and third, you are interested in education." At Teachers College, the graduate school of education at Columbia, none of those characteristics was considered a handicap, and I pursued my studies there. This lack of interest in elementary and secondary schooling and in education as a profession and as a research field is typical of major research universities.

The present crisis in education and the depressed condition of the teaching profession offer an unusual opportunity to reassess our present arrangements for preparing teachers. As Gary Sykes, until recently the National Institute of Education's specialist on the teaching profession, has observed, the profession needs both "screens and magnets," ways to keep out incompetent teachers and ways to lure in the highly talented. The traditional screen—state certification—is almost entirely ineffective, since it guarantees only that a prospective teacher has taken required courses and received a degree. Recognizing that a college degree today certifies very little, a number of states have begun to adopt teacher examinations and to reassess their requirements for entry into the profession. If school boards and state legislatures were to raise their hiring standards—to insist that new teachers have an undergraduate major other than education, for instance, and to determine whether the education courses they require are valuable—the message of the marketplace would be heeded by institutions that prepare teachers.

Developing magnets to attract good people to teaching will be far more difficult. It must involve better pay, so that a life of teaching is not equivalent to an oath of penury. It may or may not involve some form of salary differentiation for teachers who win the respect and admiration of their peers, but some salary incentives should be available to keep gifted teachers in the classroom. It should involve generous public fellowships to underwrite the education of those willing to commit themselves to the classroom for several years. It should mean a readiness by school boards to provide teachers with opportunities for continuing intellectual and professional growth. It should mean a flexibility by teachers' unions to permit the employment of graduate students in science and mathematics, college-educated housewives, and professional writers to meet critical shortages on a temporary or part-time basis. It requires a willingness by education officials to defend the teacher's professional autonomy and to preserve a climate in the schools that honors teaching and learning.

The development of teaching as a profession will also require a reconceptualization of the school as a workplace, so that excellent teachers help novices, colleagues work together as peers, and superb teachers earn as much as administrators. Until teachers have as much responsibility for their working conditions as college professors do, professionalism will remain out of reach.

As with every other educational program, the difficulty of attracting top-flight people to teaching will not yield to simple solutions. Demography contributed to the problem; smart people looked for other jobs as enrollments declined. But demography may help ease the problem, as enrollments begin to grow again, increasing the demand for new teachers. The opening of other career opportunities has shrunk the talent pool, but teaching will continue to be an attractive occupation for those who wish to combine a career with family responsibilities.

As a mass, public profession, teaching will never offer salaries that compare favorably with those of law or medicine, but it does offer satisfactions that are unique to the job. In every generation, there are people born with a love of teaching. They want to open the minds of young people to literature, history, art, science, or something else that has seized their own imagination. To recruit and hold on to such people, the nation's schools must not only reward them adequately but must provide the conditions in which good teaching can flourish. That will not come about through public incantations; it will demand realistic programs and imaginative solutions. But a nation that has led the world in popular education for more than a century owes it to itself to meet the challenge.

7

The Meaning of the New Coleman Report

(1981)

THE publication in early 1981 of James S. Coleman's study, "Public and Private Schools," unleashed national controversy that revealed more about the fears of advocates of the public school than it did about the substance of the report. Coleman, who enjoys an international reputation as a meticulous scholar, was quickly and roundly attacked as an enemy of the public schools even before his report was available. Worried that the new study would be used to promote tuition tax credits or vouchers, critics denounced Coleman's methodology and even his personal integrity in their efforts to discredit his finding that private high schools are, on the whole, better than public high schools.

If someone says that you are overweight and that this is bad for your health, do you punch that person in the mouth or do you get on the scale? The very intensity of the critical response suggested that Coleman had hit a raw nerve; those who reacted most angrily exposed their own fear that, with the availability of any form of governmental subsidy, parents would begin a stampede from public to private schools. This defensive and even hostile attitude betrayed an unbecoming lack of confidence in public education by those who are ostensibly its champions.

It would be unfortunate indeed if public school educators failed to examine the substance of the new Coleman report, for, while it contains much that will dismay them, it also contains surprisingly good news. For fifteen years, since the appearance of the original Coleman report on educational opportunity in 1966, educators have been reminded repeatedly that "schools don't make a difference" and that family background heavily determines educational achievement. The new Coleman report dramatically reverses this pessimistic conclusion and finds instead that schools *do* make a difference, regardless of the family background of students. Although there will continue to be disagreement about aspects of the new study (e.g., the way it measures the relative degree of racial integration in public and private schools), it contains important data about the relationship of various educational practices to student achievement.

"Public and Private Schools" (PPS) is part of a major longitudinal study called "High School and Beyond" (HS&B). The study was commissioned and financed by the National Center for Education Statistics, an arm of the Department of Education. In the planning stages since 1978, HS&B began with a group-administered survey in the spring of 1980 and will include follow-up surveys of the same sample in 1982 and 1984. The survey includes 58,728 high school sophomores and seniors in 1,016 schools, as well as their principals and teachers. Although researchers from various parts of the country contributed to the design of the study, the National Opinion Research Center of the University of Chicago conducted the base-year survey. PPS is the first study to use the HS&B data; others will certainly follow. When HS&B is completed, it will provide a wealth of information about schools, students, teachers, educational policies, and postsecondary outcomes. Already the data tapes of the base-year survey are available to researchers who will feast for years on the raw materials of HS&B.

Coleman's PPS (with co-writers Thomas Hoffer and Sally Kilgore) is a 233-page document that should be viewed from two distinct perspectives. One is political, the other educational. The study seeks to examine the political question of the role of private schools in U.S. education, and it also presents descriptive analyses of educational practices in public and private high schools. Spokesmen for public schools have concentrated their fire on the political debate and have paid inadequate attention to the important educational findings contained in the study.

Coleman's emphasis on the policy issues in the public versus private debate has brought the collective wrath of the public school establishment down on his head, and these issues have attracted the most attention and have sparked the greatest controversy. Coleman specifically notes that the report "is intended to provide evidence relevant" to proposals that would either increase or decrease the role of private schools, such as tuition tax credits, educational vouchers, or imposition of racial composition requirements on private schools.

In reviewing the premises underlying the policy debate, Coleman finds that:

The Meaning of the New Coleman Report

1. Private schools produce better cognitive outcomes than do public schools, even after family background factors that predict achievement are controlled. (However, Coleman is careful to point out that "despite extensive statistical controls on parental background, there may very well be other unmeasured factors in the self-selection into the private sector that are associated with higher achievement.")

2. Private schools provide a safer, more disciplined, and more orderly environment than do public schools. This factor was the single strongest difference between public and private schools.

3. Non-Catholic private schools have sharply lower student/teacher ratios than do public schools, although Catholic schools have somewhat higher ratios.

4. Private schools contribute to religious segregation, since 66 percent of all private school students are in Catholic schools, and more than 90 percent of the students in Catholic schools are Catholic. (Nonetheless, the great majority of Catholic students are in public schools.)

5. Private schools enroll a smaller proportion of blacks than do public schools, but there is less racial segregation within private schools than within public schools.

6. Private schools do not provide the educational range that public schools do, particularly in vocational and other nontraditional programs. Some of the non-Catholic private schools have limited academic offerings; for example, 44 percent of the students who attend non-Catholic private schools are not offered a third year of any foreign language.

7. Students in Catholic and public schools participate in extracurricular activities to the same extent. But students in other private schools participate more actively than do those in either Catholic or public schools.

8. Students in private schools show more self-esteem and "fate control" than do those in public schools.

Perhaps the most controversial of Coleman's conclusions are: first, that a tuition tax credit or voucher would increase the private school enrollment of blacks and Hispanics more than that of whites, and, second, that Catholic schools today "more nearly approximate the 'common school' ideal of American education than do public schools, in that the achievement levels of students from different parental educational backgrounds, of black and white students, and of Hispanic and non-Hispanic and white students are more nearly alike in Catholic schools than in public schools." It is easy to understand why both claims enrage friends of the public schools.

Whether any form of government subsidy is to be extended to nonpublic schools is above all a political question. It will not be settled by social scientists but by elected officials—perhaps ultimately by the courts. Although Coleman's research bears on the issue, its most salient findings are educational, not political. If there is a single educational message in the Coleman report of 1981, it is that schools *do* make a difference. Time and again, Coleman demonstrates that achievement follows from specific school policies, not from the particular background of the students. Since this represents such a dramatic departure from the social determinism of the past fifteen years, it is worth reviewing here the educational implications of the Coleman report of 1966 along with those of the current Coleman report.

The first Coleman report was authorized by Congress, pursuant to the Civil Rights Act of 1964, as a survey of equality of educational opportunity. Released in 1966, the report offered no policy recommendations. Its findings, however, became the source of a number of important new policies—not all of them mutually consistent. The report held that racial segregation was extensive; that the differences in resources between black schools and white schools were not great (at least not as great as had been anticipated); that levels of achievement for minority pupils were lower at every level of schooling than those of white pupils; that "schools are remarkably similar in the effect they have on the achievement of their pupils when the socioeconomic background of the students is taken into account"; that variations in the facilities and curricula of the schools "account for relatively little variation in pupil achievement"; that quality of teachers had some relationship to pupil achievement, especially for minority pupils; that "the extent to which an individual feels that he has some control over his own destiny" had a stronger relationship to pupil achievement than did all the school factors combined (and that black students in school with whites had "a greater sense of control"); that the social composition of the student body had a strong relationship to the achievement of minority pupils.

What kinds of policies flowed from these findings? The Coleman report was used repeatedly in court to argue on behalf of racial balancing. It was believed that the report had proven that integration would produce higher black achievement. It was quickly forgotten that the report's summary of "average test scores of Negro pupils" did not show the expected correspondence between black achievement and the proportion of white classmates. That is, the highest scores were registered by blacks in majority-white classes, the second highest by blacks in all-black classes, the third-highest by blacks in black-majority classes, and the lowest scores by blacks in classes that were half-and-half (and the differences from one group to the next were quite small). Coleman later complained that the courts were using his report in ways that were inappropriate. The finding of the report about the importance of "sense of control" was taken up by advocates of black community control in New York City. They argued that black children would feel a greater sense of control in a black school, where people like themselves were in positions of power. As Coleman quickly discovered, there was no way to control the way that research would be used once it was in the public domain.

Aside from the specific judicial or legislative interpretations of the report, its most pervasive effect was to encourage the conviction that schools were unable to affect student achievement very greatly. One commentator wrote in the *Harvard Educational Review*, "It is highly uncertain at this point what *school* policies, if any, can compensate for the inequalities in cognitive skills between rich and poor children that are apparent at the time they enter school." The same sentiment was expressed countless times by authors and policymakers as a demonstrated fact in the years after 1966 (Christopher Jencks's *Inequality* and the reports of the Carnegie Council on Children are prime examples). But it is impossible to assess the damage done to the self-esteem of the education profession and the consequent demoralization of the very teachers dedicated enough to inform themselves about educational research. Whether students did well or poorly in schools seemed determined for the most part by their social background, and little, if at all, by anything that teachers and schools did. Consider the consequences of this conclusion: If schools were so ineffectual in affecting the educational outcomes of their students, it becomes difficult to argue on behalf of any given curriculum, requirement, or policy. If all policies are equally ineffective, then almost any educational approach may present its claims, no matter how outlandish.

The educational side of PPS (the Coleman report of

1981) stands in striking contrast to the gloomy implications of the 1966 document. The most important finding of the new Coleman report is that, after family background is taken into account, there remains significant variation in student achievement and that this variation is related to differing educational policies. Coleman specifies the kinds of school policies that lead to higher achievement and those that contribute to lower achievement. There has been disagreement about many aspects of his study, but no one has challenged the descriptive data comparing public and private schools in terms of homework, course enrollments, discipline, and absenteeism. The relatively poorer performance of the public schools on measures such as these enables Coleman to conclude that private high schools provide better education.

Private high schools produce higher achievement than public high schools with similar students, according to Coleman, not because they are private, but because they "create higher rates of engagement in academic activities . . . school attendance is better, students do more homework, and students generally take more rigorous subjects." In addition, the disciplinary climate of the school (the effectiveness and fairness of discipline and the degree of teacher interest in students) affects student achievement. These findings, which effectively rebut the earlier claim that schools "don't make a difference," should be a source of rejoicing for educators in public and private schools alike, for they confirm the importance and efficacy of their actions. Understood rightly, the Coleman study of 1981 offers extensive documentation of the practices that make up good education.

One important difference between public and private schools that emerges from the survey is the extent of curricular tracking. Only 34 percent of public secondary students are enrolled in an academic curriculum, while 39

THE SCHOOLS WE DESERVE

percent are in a general curriculum and 27 percent are in a vocational curriculum. By contrast, 70 percent of private school students are in an academic program, 21 percent general, and 9 percent vocational. The proportion of students nationwide in an academic program has decreased by 4 percent since 1972, when comparable data were gathered. As one might expect, those in academic programs take more years of coursework in mathematics and science.

Secondary students in public schools spend less time on homework and receive higher grades than either their counterparts in private schools today or those in public schools in 1972. Only 25 percent of sophomores in public schools spend more than an hour each school night on homework, whereas 46 percent of Catholic school sophomores and 50 percent of sophomores in other private schools do so. The most homework is done by students in a special group of "high-performance" public and private high schools. In these schools 50 percent of the public school sophomores spend at least an hour each night, as do 83 percent of those in other private (non-Catholic) schools. That is, *the students who achieve the most are those who work the hardest.* The same pattern holds when students in the academic programs in public schools are compared to those in academic programs in private schools; 39 percent of the academic public students spend "at least five hours per week on homework," and 48 percent of academic private students do so; academic public students receive higher grades than their counterparts in private schools, however. The lower academic demands and expectations in the public sector cannot be accounted for by variations in students' attitudes. When students are asked if they are interested in school and if they like working hard in school, there is very little difference in the responses from students in public, Catholic, and other private schools.

Coleman concludes that, when students of similar back-

108

ground are compared, taking advanced academic courses
"brings substantially greater achievement." Here too the
contrast between public and private schools is revealing.
Students in private schools are more likely to have completed advanced academic courses, and in "high-performance" public schools these enrollments are even higher
than in Catholic or other private schools (though not as
high as those in the "high-performance" private schools).
The idea that students learn more because of taking
rigorous courses seems like a heretical notion in an age
when everyone is an armchair sociologist, armed with the
belief that only those who are already high achievers elect
to take rigorous courses. Coleman suggests a reordering of
cause and effect. He contends, with documentation, that
students do well *because* they have worked hard in demanding courses and learned from their efforts, *not* because
they come from a good family background.

The difference between private and public schools in
enrollments in advanced courses is large enough to suggest
that what is an elective in many public schools may be a
requirement in many private schools. Coleman finds, for
example, that only 6 percent of public school seniors have
taken a third-year foreign language course, whereas 14
percent of seniors in Catholic schools and 20 percent of
seniors in other kinds of private schools have done so.
These figures illuminate the alarm expressed in 1979 by
the President's Commission on Foreign Language and
International Studies, when it complained that "Americans'
incompetence in foreign languages is nothing short of
scandalous, and it is becoming worse."

Similarly, the figures compiled by Coleman on enrollments in advanced mathematics and science courses reinforce the warning of the National Science Foundation in
1980 about "a current trend toward virtual scientific and
technological illiteracy. . . ." In each subject area, fewer

public school seniors than private school seniors completed advanced academic courses: Geometry was studied by 53 percent of public school seniors, 84 percent of Catholic school seniors, and 77 percent of seniors in other private schools; second-year algebra, by 42 percent public, 70 percent Catholic, and 66 percent other private; trigonometry, by 22 percent public, 44 percent Catholic, and 42 percent other private; calculus, by 6 percent public, 11 percent Catholic, and 10 percent other private; chemistry, by 37 percent public, 53 percent Catholic, and 51 percent other private; physics, by 18 percent public, 23 percent Catholic, and 28 percent other private. Seniors in "high-performance" public and private schools have higher enrollments in advanced courses than either the public or private sector as a whole. The best private schools still have higher enrollment rates in advanced courses than the best public schools, however. In the best public schools, for example, 87 percent of the seniors have taken geometry (100 percent of the seniors in the best private schools have done so), 76 percent have taken second-year algebra (99 percent of the seniors in the best private schools have done so), and 68 percent have taken chemistry (79 percent in the best private schools have done so).

Another important difference between public and private schools is the disciplinary climate. There are enforced rules about student dress in virtually all the Catholic schools, in about two-thirds of the other private schools, and in about half of the public schools. When students are asked to rate the effectiveness and fairness of the discipline in their schools, Catholic schools receive the highest ratings and public schools the lowest. When asked to rate the teachers' interest in students, about one-third of the students in other private schools describe it as "excellent," as do one-fourth of Catholic students and only about one-tenth of the public students. The public schools in the survey had more difficulty than did the private sector with such discipline problems as absenteeism, class cutting, fighting, and threats to teachers. Such misbehavior, Coleman shows, has educational "costs." For example, Coleman demonstrates statistically that absenteeism and class cutting contribute to lower achievement levels (when family background is held constant).

What does all of this mean for the public schools? For one thing, it means that some of the sociological truisms of the past fifteen years have been demoted from fact to theory. No longer can schools be dismissed as little more than sociological cookie cutters, relegated to handing out credentials in accordance with predetermined social-class categories. The new Coleman report also gives educators, public and private, a considerable body of evidence demonstrating that school policy affects student achievement and student behavior. Most important, the report implies that school officials and education policymakers must reexamine their curricula, their programs, and their policies. It is time, once again, to consider the uses of a common curriculum and to rethink the relationship between requirements and electives. The new Coleman report reminds us that those who teach and administer schools have an important and difficult job, with the power to change the lives of their students. It is now up to the adults responsible for the schools to establish the standards, expectations, and values that create the kind of stable, purposeful environment in which all students can learn and work productively.

8

From History to
Social Studies:
Dilemmas and Problems

(1984)

WHEN I attended public school in Texas in the 1950s, I took the standard three-year social studies sequence, which included a year of world history in the ninth grade, a year of American history in the eleventh grade, and senior-year civics. I had a superb ninth-grade teacher, but the course was impossible; it covered too much material and gave students a smattering of events, dates, and cultures, picked up hastily in a forced march across thousands of years and all continents. The eleventh-grade American history course was worse: The teacher used every incident in American history to support her own cranky political bias. I realized just how poorly educated I was in history when I reached college; I felt hopelessly inadequate when I compared myself to my fellow students who had attended private schools. Many of them seemed to have a wide-ranging knowledge of ancient history, medieval history, and modern European history that was utterly beyond my grasp. What was more, their knowledge of history was enhanced by an exposure to art and literature that my school had never even attempted.

My strength, I mistakenly believed, derived from my keen interest in current events. So, in college, I majored in political science, a decision that I now believe to have been a grievous error, because I simply compounded the flaws of my high school education. The issues that seemed so urgent in the late 1950s are today of merely antiquarian interest. Why should anyone care about Quemoy and Matsu anymore, those offshore islands that John F. Kennedy and Richard Nixon argued about during the 1960 Presidential campaign, except as a footnote to contemporary Asian history? Does Sputnik really matter now except as a milestone in the history of technology? Why should anyone recall the confrontation between Governor Faubus of Arkansas and President Eisenhower in 1958 except as an incident in the history of racial relations in America? Almost everything that once seemed important has now faded, to be remembered only by those who are interested in history.

I eventually turned to the full-time study of history when I realized that I could not understand the present without studying the past. My continued interest in contemporary issues made me a historian; there was simply no other intelligent way to understand the origins of our present institutions, problems, and ideas. As a latecomer to the study of history, I am—like all converts—a zealous advocate; I believe in the importance and value of the study of history, and I would like to see it strengthened in the schools. It is from this perspective that I began to inquire into the condition of history in the schools and how it got that way. As of mid-1984, however, it was nearly impossible to determine the current state of history in the secondary schools. Educational data collection is today so inadequate that no one can accurately say how history is taught, how well it is taught, what is taught, or what is learned. Most states have tabulated course enrollments, and some national surveys have totaled up the percentage of children who are enrolled in courses that are titled "history," but these figures are highly suspect. Because of the enormous variety of practice extant, there is not necessarily any identity of content among courses bearing the same label.

Furthermore, we have no reliable measures of achievement or mastery for the field of history; the makers of standardized tests long ago abandoned the attempt to assess historical or literary knowledge and instead devote their entire attention to abstract verbal and mathematical skills. We cannot say with certainty whether high school graduates today know more or less than their counterparts of ten, twenty, or thirty years ago; we have no good measures of historical knowledge at present, nor did we have any in the past. The possibility of agreeing on such a measure today seems remote. Because we live in a time of cultural fragmentation, the idea of testing large numbers of students for their knowledge of history seems outrageous. It was not surprising, for example, that the many national reports of 1983 cited test scores in mathematics, science, and verbal skills, but their bill of particulars omitted any mention of the humanities. We have no objective data to tell us how we are doing, because we lack consensus on the minimum knowledge that we expect of all students. We do not agree on what literature is important, nor do we agree on what history should be taught to all American youngsters.

We know that many states require high school students to study at least one year of U.S. history, but we do not know what lurks behind the course label. National data tell us that 65 percent of high school graduates in 1982 took at least three years of social studies, but—in view of the minimal history requirement—it is almost certain that few of these credits were taken in history.[1] A survey published by the Organization of American Historians (OAH) in 1975 revealed that in at least five states—New York, Indiana, Iowa, Oklahoma, and Oregon—virtually no training in history was required for high school history teachers.[2] In New York City, the history teacher's license was abolished in 1946, and at present no formal study of history is required for a license as a high school social studies teacher.[3]

If one were to judge by the accumulation of anecdotal reports—a notoriously unreliable source of evidence— many college professors think that freshmen know little about American history, European history, or any other history. One frequently hears complaints about students who know next to nothing about events that occurred before the twentieth century; or who are ignorant of the Bible, Shakespeare, the Greek myths, or other material that was once common knowledge. Or, as one Berkeley professor put it to me a few years ago, "They have no furniture in their minds. You can assume nothing in the way of prior knowledge. Skills, yes; but not knowledge."

While it is not possible to know definitively how history is faring in the schools today, there is increasing reason to fear that history is losing its integrity and identity as a field of study within the umbrella called the social studies. The field of social studies, in the view of a number of its leaders, is in deep trouble. Bob L. Taylor and John D. Haas claimed in 1973 that "secondary school social studies curricula are in a state of 'curriculum anarchy'; which is to say that local curriculum patterns are more varied than at any other time in this century. No longer is it possible to describe a typical state, regional, or national pattern of social studies curriculum. Furthermore, it appears [that] each junior or senior high school in a given school district is 'doing its own thing.' "[4] A 1977 study by Richard E. Gross of Stanford University found that the field was characterized by increased fragmentation and dilution of programs; by a growth of electives and minicourses; by a rapid proliferation of social science courses; by a drop in required courses; and by a tendency toward curricular anarchy. In keeping with these trends, other reviews of the field noted a singular absence of agreement about the content and definition of the field.[5]

While the field of the social studies was having an identity crisis, history as a subject was struggling for survival. The 1975 study by the OAH reported a significant dilution and fragmentation in the teaching of secondary school history. In New Mexico, the trend was toward ethnocultural courses; in Hawaii, the trend was toward integrating history into a social science framework focused on problem solving, decision making, and social action; in Minnesota, teachers were encouraged to shift away from historical study toward an emphasis on concepts that transcend "any given historical situation"; the OAH representative in California predicted that history would lose time to such "relevant" topics as multicultural studies, ethnic studies, consumer affairs, and ecology. Similar reports about the deteriorating position of history within the social studies curriculum came from Vermont, Rhode Island, Connecticut, New York, Maryland, Wisconsin, Missouri, Nebraska, North Carolina, Oklahoma, West Virginia, Illinois, and Iowa. The OAH report confirmed what many had long feared: that the study of history in public high schools has been seriously eroded, absorbed within the increasingly vague and amorphous field of the social studies.[6]

The OAH survey, like the Gross survey, was conducted

in the mid-1970s and reflected the curricular fragmentation of that time. A survey conducted a decade later would doubtless show that many states, cities, and school districts substantially raised their graduation requirements. Yet even a cursory review of the actions taken in the early 1980s demonstrates that history continues to be left out in the cold, and that social studies requirements have been increased without reference to history. Even the tough-minded National Commission on Excellence in Education failed to mention history as a necessary subject of study for all American students. In view of the currently unfocused nature of the social studies, students may meet the higher requirements by taking courses in current events, drug education, sex education, environmental education, citizenship education, values education, law studies, economics, psychology, or other nonhistorical studies.

How did history fall to this sorry state? A review of the "history of history teaching" suggests that certain ideological and political trends caused history to lose its rightful place in the public high school curriculum. History as a regular subject of study entered the public school curriculum before the Civil War but did not become well established until the end of the nineteenth century, as secondary school enrollments grew. History, English, modern foreign languages, and science entered the curriculum as modern subjects, in contrast to the classical curriculum of mathematics and ancient languages.[7] Most public schools offered one or more history courses, such as ancient history, medieval history, English history, modern European history, and U.S. history. The schools of the nineteenth century also offered courses that were predecessors of the social sciences: courses, for example, in civil government, political economy, and moral philosophy. By 1895, 70 percent of the nation's universities and colleges required a course in U.S. history for admission, and more than a quarter required the study of Greek and/or Roman history.[8]

In order to understand the fate of history over the years, it is necessary to follow the rationale for its inclusion in the curriculum. Why study history? It was argued, first, that history offers valuable lessons in morals by demonstrating the kind of personal and national behavior that should be admired or abhorred; second, that history enhances personal culture by revealing the great achievements and ideas of the past; third, that history inspires patriotism; fourth, that history trains good citizens by defining civic virtue; fifth, that history reinforces religious ideals; and sixth, that history strengthens and disciplines the mind.

Some of these rationales were profoundly damaging to the integrity of the subject. Using history as an instrument for the teaching of morals, religion, and patriotism undermined respect for history by turning it into propaganda. It distorted the most essential value in history, which is the search for truth. The subject of history was even more severely injured by the proponents of mental discipline, who believed that rote memorization of the textbook strengthened the mind; this method must have destroyed student interest in the content of history, and it certainly reared up legions of people who hated historical study rather than the tyrannical method by which it was taught.

Between the years 1893 and 1918, three major reports were issued on the public school curriculum that bore directly on the teaching of history; these reports were important not only because they influenced practice, in some cases quite substantially, but also because they vividly portrayed the ideas that were dominant or gaining ascendancy among leaders of the educational profession. Everyone interested in history as a secondary school subject should read them, because by reading between the lines, it is possible to discover the answer to the question: What happened to history?

The first major report on the curriculum appeared in 1893, the product of a group called the Committee of Ten. During the late nineteenth century, it appeared to many educators that the high school curriculum was growing in an uncontrolled fashion, without rational plan. In response to this sentiment, the Committee of Ten was created by the National Education Association (NEA) as the first national commission on the high school curriculum. (See pp. 71–72, 137–143.) Its chairman, Harvard's President Charles W. Eliot, was widely known as a proponent of the elective system and the modern subjects. The committee established nine subject-matter groups to make recommendations on content and methodology. One of the most important issues that the Committee of Ten was asked to address was whether there should be different curricula for children who were going to college and those who were not. The committee, and all of its subject matter consultants, agreed that all children should receive a broad, liberal education, regardless of their future occupation or when their education was likely to end.[9]

The report of the history conference was remarkable. This group, which included both academic scholars (one was a young Princeton professor named Woodrow Wilson) and school officials, attacked the rote memorization method of teaching history. Memorizing facts, they said, was "the most difficult and the least important outcome of historical study." The history group commented that "when the facts are chosen with as little discrimination as in many school textbooks, when they are mere lists of lifeless dates, details of military movements, or unexplained genealogies, they are repellant." To know such facts, they held, was like "a curious character in Ohio" who was said to remember what he had eaten for dinner every day for the past thirty years. The committee insisted that they would rather see history eliminated than to see it taught "the old fashioned way," through painful and pointless rote memorization.[10]

The committee argued that when history and its allied branches were taught in a manner that teaches judgment and thinking, and when they were taught in conjunction with other studies, such as literature, geography, art, and languages, they "serve to broaden and cultivate the mind . . . they counteract a narrow and provincial spirit . . . they prepare the pupil in an eminent degree for enlightened and intellectual enjoyment in after years . . . and they assist him to exercise a salutary influence upon the affairs of his country." The "newer methods" endorsed by the committee included inquiry, comparative studies, informal presentations by students, individualized work, field trips, debates, and audiovisual aids; in addition, the committee advocated better textbooks, better trained teachers, and better-equipped libraries.[11]

The committee recommended an eight-year course in history, beginning in the fifth and sixth grades with biography and mythology. American history and government would be taught in the seventh grade; Greek and Roman history, in the eighth grade; French history (as an illustration of European history in general), in the ninth grade; English history (because of its contribution to American institutions), in the tenth grade; American history, in the eleventh grade; and intensive study of a special historical topic, in the twelfth grade.

The history committee insisted that their recommendations were not intended for the college bound. On the contrary, they said, "We believe that the colleges can take care of themselves; our interest is in the school children who have no expectation of going to college, the larger number of whom will not enter even a high school." They argued that there should not be separate courses for the college bound and others. Under this system, they said, those who will get the most education later on are the only ones to get any training in history in the schools. Such a distinction, "especially in schools provided by public taxation, is bad for all classes of pupils. It is the duty of the schools to furnish a well grounded and complete education for the child," regardless of his later destination.[12]

The specific influence of this report is hard to estimate, but it did encourage good relations between professional historians and the school establishment, and it helped to undermine the legitimacy of rote memory methods. A few years later, the National Education Association invited the American Historical Association to create yet another committee, this time devoted entirely to the subject of the history curriculum and college entrance requirements. This group, called the Committee of Seven, wrote a document that affected the teaching of history for many years. Like the Committee of Ten's history conference, the Committee of Seven was deeply critical of the rote system of teaching. Its report endorsed the use of varied methods to stimulate the interest and participation of pupils in the learning process. It criticized the typical textbook as "mental pabulum" and urged the introduction of supplementary materials. It recommended the inclusion of biographies, primary source materials, and innovative techniques. It conceived of history not only in terms of political institutions and states but also as the study of the social and economic fabric of human activity. It recommended a four-year course in history for the secondary school: first year, ancient history to A.D. 800; second year, medieval and modern European history; third year, English history; fourth year, American history and civil government. The committee made these recommendations not because this sequence would prepare students for college, but because the members believed that historical study was the very best sort of general education for all children. The curriculum, they insisted, "must be prepared with the purpose of developing boys and girls into young men and women, not with the purpose of fitting them to meet entrance examinations. . . ." They believed that history was "peculiarly appropriate in a secondary course, which is fashioned with the thought of preparing boys and girls for the duties of daily life and intelligent citizenship. . . ."[13]

The committee complained that there were too many people teaching history who lacked appropriate training. "In one good school, for example, history a short time ago was turned over to the professor of athletics, not because he knew history, but apparently in order to fill up his time. In another school a teacher was seen at work who evidently did not have the first qualifications for the task; when the examiner inquired why this teacher was asked to teach history when she knew no history, the answer was that she did not know anything else."[14] The committee expressed the belief that history teachers should have a firm knowledge of their subject, should have command of professional skills and methods, should be fired with the enthusiasm to inspire students to the struggles and conflicts of the past, and should themselves be not only teachers but lifelong students of history.

The Committee of Seven believed that the best way to understand the problems of the present was through study of the past; that students would best understand their duties as citizens by studying the origins and evolution of political institutions, not only in their own society but in other societies and in other times; that the ability to change society for the better depends on knowledge of our institutions and our ideals in their historical setting. Further, they believed that historical study teaches students to think, cultivates their judgment, and encourages accuracy of thought.

In viewing this curricular history, one must bear in mind

the rationale that is offered for the study of history. The Committee of Seven's rationale was that history honestly taught yields valuable benefits. Study of the past, they believed, would create intelligent, thinking, responsible citizens, men and women who had "acquaintance with political and social environment, some appreciation of the nature of the state and society, some sense of the duties and responsibilities of citizenship, some capacity in dealing with political and governmental questions, something of the broad and tolerant spirit which is bred by the study of past times and conditions."[15] They were convinced that the study of history was valuable both intrinsically and extrinsically. They believed that history was a synthesizing subject that belonged at the center of the curriculum because it gave meaning and coherence to everything else that was studied.

The report of the Committee of Seven in 1899 set a national pattern for the history curriculum. By 1915, the overwhelming majority of high schools offered courses in ancient history, medieval and modern European history, English history, and American history. Furthermore, in most high schools, American and ancient history became required subjects. An historical survey of history teaching in 1935 held that the history departments of the nation's high schools "attempted to swallow the report of the Committee of Seven 'hook, line, and sinker.'" The so-called "four-block" plan was widely adopted, and there was an increase in both history courses offered and history courses required of all students. Further strengthening the influence of the Committee of Seven report, textbook publishers used the report as a model for their history series.[16] This situation, following the Committee's report, was a far cry from 1893, when history was still struggling to gain legitimacy as a proper subject of study in the high school.

If the story of the history curriculum ended in 1915,

there would now be good news about the status of history. The overwhelming majority of high schools, we would discover, would offer at least three years of history, including ancient history, European history, and American history, and nearly half would offer English history.[7] It would be necessary to recall the reports of several other numerically named committees—the Committee of Eight, the Committee of Fifteen, and the Committee of Five, among others, and to note the emphasis on biography, mythology, legends, and hero tales in the elementary grades. The same approach, brought up to date in the 1980s, would certainly include histories of non-Western societies. But 1915, alas, was the high-water mark for traditional, narrative, chronological history in the schools.

Nascent social and political trends made their mark on the public school curriculum, deeply affecting the teaching of history. In the 1890s, history was considered a modern subject, but only a few years later, during the first decade of the twentieth century, educational progressives began to treat it as part of the "traditional" curriculum. The traditional curriculum became a target for progressives, who sought to modernize the schools and to make them responsive to the needs and problems of contemporary life. In the opening decades of the twentieth century, progressivism emerged as a dynamic movement in American life, committed to social progress, social betterment, and social reform. Many of the ills of the nation were associated with the vast hordes of poor immigrants who crowded into the cities. The schools were given the primary responsibility for Americanizing immigrant children. Not only were they to function as academic institutions, teaching English to their charges, but to assume a custodial role, preparing the newcomers to be good citizens, training them for the job market, and introducing them to the ordinary necessities of daily life, like nutrition and hygiene.

To meet some of these needs, new courses entered the high school curriculum, such as training for specific trades, sewing, cooking, and commercial studies. As high schools added practical courses, curricular differentiation became common. In many schools, there was a manual training course of study, a vocational course, a commercial course—and, for the academic elite, a college preparatory course. A "course of study" was a carefully sequenced series of individual courses, lasting two, three, or four years; in schools where curricular differentiation was fully developed, in keeping with the latest pedagogical thinking, the students' selection of a course of study was often tantamount to the choice of a vocation. The admonitions of the Committee of Ten and the Committee of Seven on behalf of liberal education for all children were scorned by progressives as an attempt to force everyone into a narrow academic curriculum. The reformers insisted that an academic curriculum was inappropriate for children who intended to go to work, and that there must be different programs for the small minority who were college bound and for the vast majority who were work bound.

Progressive educators became accustomed to thinking of the schools in terms of their social function and to asserting that the work of the schools must meet the test of social efficiency. In education, social efficiency meant that every subject, every program, every study must be judged by whether it was socially useful. Did it meet the needs of society? No doubt, to the new profession of curriculum makers and policymakers, the prospect of shaping society was far more exciting than merely teaching literature or history or science. In contrast, the traditional subject-matter based curriculum seemed anachronistic. What point was there in teaching history, science, literature, mathematics, and foreign language to children who would never go to college? How was society served by wasting their time in such manifestly "useless" and impractical studies? Although not all school officials or teachers agreed (and many strongly disagreed), educational leaders in national organizations and in major schools of education repeatedly asserted that the traditional curriculum was intended only for the children of the elite and was inappropriate for the schools in a democracy. Teaching children to think and imparting to them knowledge about science and culture clearly did not make the grade to those who made social utility their touchstone.

By the time of World War I, social efficiency was widely accepted as the chief goal of education, and this consensus emerged full-blown in the third major report on the secondary curriculum, prepared by the National Education Association's Commission on the Reorganization of Secondary Education. Published in 1918, the report of this group was known as the "Cardinal Principles of Secondary Education," and it is generally considered the single most important document in the history of American education.[18] It proclaimed a utilitarian credo that deeply influenced the nation's schools for decades to come. (See pp. 72–73, 146–149.) In contrast to the Committee of Ten and the Committee of Seven, the "Cardinal Principles" strongly endorsed differentiated curricula, based on future vocational interests, such as agricultural, business, clerical, industrial, fine arts, and household arts. The report gave a powerful boost to proponents of vocational education, curricular tracking, and useful subjects; it disappointed those who wanted all children to have a liberal education and reinforced the belief that academic studies were only for the college-bound elite.

Like the earlier Committee of Ten, the commission established subject matter committees, which wrote individual reports. There was no committee on history. Instead, there was a Committee on Social Studies, whose report appeared in 1916. The committee defined the social studies as "those whose subject matter relates directly to the organization and development of human society, and to man as a member of social groups." The major purpose of modern education, said the committee, is "social efficiency." By their very nature, the social studies "afford peculiar opportunities for the training of the individual as a member of society. Whatever their value from the point of view of personal culture, unless they contribute directly to the cultivation of social efficiency on the part of the pupil they fail in their most important function."[19] By this standard of utility and relevance, there was scant justification for the study of ancient civilizations or premodern societies. From the outset, the social studies as a field was associated with social action, social history, contemporary issues, and social efficiency.

The "constant and conscious purpose" of social studies, said the committee, was "the cultivation of good citizenship." Unlike history, which had no obvious social utility, the social studies promised to address issues of immediate concern. "Facts, conditions, theories, and activities that do not contribute rather directly to the appreciation of methods of human betterment have no claim," said the committee on social studies. This principle of selection cut the ground away from ancient and medieval history and attached greater value to current events than to history. But history was not to be jettisoned altogether. The principle espoused by the committee for deciding what history to teach was this: "The selection of a topic in history and the amount of attention given to it should depend ... chiefly upon the degree to which such topic can be related to the present life interests of the pupil, or can be used by him in his present processes of growth." The committee was blunt in stating that the widely adopted four-year history sequence set out by the Committee of Seven less than twenty years earlier was "more or less discredited," based as it was on "the traditions of the historian and the requirements of the college."[20] Appeal to pupils' interests, not transmission of knowledge, was to determine the content of history courses.

The "Cardinal Principles" and the report of the Committee on the Social Studies accurately enunciated the new canon of professional educators. These two statements projected the concept that the public schools were society's instrument for guiding the rising generation into socially useful roles. Those who objected that the primary responsibility of the schools was to democratize and distribute knowledge, and that they accomplished this by expanding children's intellectual power, by transmitting the accumulated wisdom of the past, and by enabling young people to make their own decisions about how to be socially useful, were likely to be dismissed as reactionaries, out of touch with the times and with the findings of modern pedagogical science.

The acceptance of social efficiency as the touchstone of the high school curriculum proved disastrous to the study of history. What claim could be advanced for the utility of history? Knowing history didn't make anyone a better worker; it didn't improve anyone's health; it was not nearly so useful for citizenship training as a course in civics. When judged by the stern measure of direct utility, history had no measurable claim except its utility for meeting college entrance requirements; without these, there was scant defense for history's study. Professional historians might have argued that the study of history teaches children how to think, how to reach judgments, how to see their own lives and contemporary issues in context, but they seemed content to abandon curricular decisions to the pedagogues, who scorned these claims. Nor could history meet the immediate needs of young people, in the sense that it did not tell adolescents how to behave on a date, how to be popular with the crowd, or how to get a job. In the new era of social efficiency and pupil interests, the year-long course in ancient history began to disappear from American schools, and before long the four-year history sequence was telescoped to three, then two, and in many places, only a single year of American history.

In the decades that followed the 1916 report of the Committee on the Social Studies, the emphasis in the social studies curriculum shifted decisively towards current events, relevant issues, and pupil-centered programs. The introduction of such courses was not, in itself, a bad thing. A modern, dynamic society needs schools in which students study the vital problems of the day and learn how to participate in the democratic process. But the time for the new subjects was taken away from history. Except for American history, which was thought to be useful as preparation for citizenship, the place of historical studies shrunk in the schools. Even in the elementary schools, where earlier generations had studied biography and mythology as basic historical materials, the emphasis shifted to study of the neighborhood, the community, and pre-literate peoples, a trend encouraged by the report's recommendation of courses in "community civics."

Of course, it was not the report of the Committee on Social Studies in 1916 that was responsible for the erosion of the position of history; the report itself merely reflected the ideas, values, and attitudes of the newly emerging education profession. These ideas, values, and attitudes were not—unfortunately—congenial to the study of history for its own sake, nor even to the study of history as a means to improve the intelligence of the younger generation. The ideology expressed in the 1916 report was hostile to a study that had no demonstrable claim, no practical value, that offered so little promise of immediate social betterment.

Subsequent efforts to reexamine the social studies curriculum did little to resuscitate the position of history, because the ideology of social efficiency maintained its dominance. When the American Historical Association created a commission to analyze the social studies in the midst of the Great Depression, the commission declared that the most important purpose of the social studies was to produce "rich and many-sided personalities."[21] Whatever the other courses in the social studies may have been capable of doing to promote personal development, it is difficult to imagine anyone claiming that the study of history produces "rich and many-sided personalities."

Even the innovative curricula produced after Sputnik, known collectively as "the new social studies," failed to restore history in the secondary schools. This was not because the case for history was weak, but because the case that should have been made was never made at all. The approach of the "new history" of the 1960s proceeded on the assumption that children should be taught to think like historians and to learn the historical method, just as students of science were learning to think like scientists and learning the scientific method. The problems with this approach were many: First, few children then or now actually know enough history, enough context, to make it worthwhile or possible for them to conduct a genuine historical investigation; second, historians themselves do not agree on the definition of a single "historical method"; third, learning the process of how to write history is appropriate to graduate students but not to students in school, and it is certainly less interesting than learning the actual stuff of history.

If history is ever to regain its rightful place in the schools, this will occur only if educators accord value to the study of history both for its own sake and for its value as a generator of individual and social intelligence. History has a right to exist as an independent study; it should be taught by people who have studied history, just as science and mathematics must be taught by those who have studied those subjects. The other social studies also have their unique contributions to make, but their contribution should not be made by stealing time from history or by burying the study of history in non-historical approaches.

In 1932, Henry Johnson of Teachers College, Columbia University, wrote a delightful review of the teaching of history throughout the ages, somewhat misleadingly titled *An Introduction to the History of the Social Sciences.* Johnson quoted a sixteenth-century Spanish scholar, Juan Luis Vives, to explain why it is valuable to study history. "Where there is history," wrote Vives, "children have transferred to them the advantages of old men; where history is absent, old men are as children." Without history, according to Vives, "no one would know anything about his father or ancestors; no one could know his own rights or those of another or how to maintain them; no one would know how his ancestors came to the country he inhabits." Vives pointed out that everything "has changed and is changing every day," except "the essential nature of human beings." Johnson referred to seventeenth-century French oratorians, who believed that the study of history cultivated judgment and stimulated right conduct. He cited their view that "history is a grand mirror in which we see ourselves. . . . The secret of knowing and judging ourselves rightly is to see ourselves in others, and history can make us the contemporaries of all centuries in all countries."[22]

History will never be restored as a subject of value unless it is detached from the vulgar utilitarianism that originally swamped it. History should not be expected to teach patriotism, morals, values clarification, or decision making. Properly taught, history teaches the pursuit of truth and understanding; properly taught, history establishes a context of human life in a particular time and place, relating art, literature, philosophy, law, architecture, language, government, economics, and social life; properly taught, it portrays the great achievements and the terrible disasters of the human race; properly taught, it awakens youngsters to the universality of the human experience as well as to the magnificence and the brutality of which humans are capable; properly taught, history encourages the development of intelligence, civility, and a sense of perspective. Unique among subjects taught in school, history is necessarily interdisciplinary, encompassing all other fields of thought and endeavor. It endows its students with a broad knowledge of other times, other cultures, other places. It leaves its students with cultural resources on which they may draw for the rest of their lives. These are values and virtues that are gained through the study of history. Beyond these, history needs no further justification.

9

Curriculum in Crisis: Connections Between Past and Present

(1985)

WITH the publication of the report of the National Commission on Excellence in Education in the spring of 1983, and with the near-simultaneous appearance of several other critical studies of the condition of American education, school reform suddenly rose to the top of the domestic policy agenda. Governors, state legislators, professional educators, presidential candidates, and citizen groups debated a wide variety of proposals for improving the schools. Among the proposed reforms, two issues dominated: first, the quality of the teaching staff and, second, the quality of the curriculum. As problems, these issues were closely interrelated, since there would be no point in requiring students to take more science, for example, if the schools were unable to hire sufficient numbers of science teachers. The remedies under discussion necessarily differed, with the teacher issue focused on increased incentives for talented individuals and the curriculum issue focused on increased high school graduation requirements. Insofar as it is translated into programs for study, retraining, and compensation, the teacher issue may be characterized as a question of public-sector resource allocation (whether such responses are adequate to provide well-educated teachers in the public's classrooms is by no means clear). The curriculum issue, however, is a question less of how much money is spent than of resolving conflicts among deeply held attitudes about education and building consensus about what studies, if any, are to be required of all students.

The common theme of most of the education reports of the early 1980s was the importance of providing a common educational experience for all students. Both the report of the National Commission on Excellence in Education and the report by former Commissioner of Education Ernest Boyer stressed the value of a common core of learning. Other studies, such as the report by the National Science Board Commission on Precollege Education in Mathematics, Science and Technology, urged the adoption of increased requirements in particular areas. "Simply put," said the science panel, "students in our Nation's schools are learning less mathematics, science and technology, particularly in the areas of abstract thinking and problem solving. Since the late 1960s, most students have taken fewer mathematics and science courses. Mathematics and science achievement scores of 17-year-olds have dropped steadily and dramatically during the same period." The need for a common core of studies was demonstrated by studies in the late 1970s that showed a sharp drop in enrollments in the basic academic disciplines at the same time that enrollments were rising in nonacademic courses like driver education, home economics, and general shop.[1]

By late 1983, a national survey found that forty-six states

had either raised their graduation requirements recently or were debating proposals to do so. Yet the apparent stampede to require students to study the traditional academic subjects was not unimpeded. A national shortage of teachers of science and mathematics made the imposition of new requirements problematic. There was no similar rush to set requirements for foreign language instruction, in part because of doubt about its value but also because of the shortage of certified teachers in any non-English language. Other doubts were expressed: How would the states pay for strengthening the curriculum? Would the dropout rate soar if graduation standards were toughened? Would disproportionate numbers of black and Hispanic students fail to meet the higher standards? Would vocational programs be undermined by the new emphasis on academic courses? Would the new requirements stifle the artistically oriented students who dislike mathematics and science, as well as the scientifically gifted students who dislike history and literature? Not far from the surface of the public debate hovered the suspicion that there was something elitist and mean-spirited about the new reforms, that they represented little more than an effort to fit a diversity of children into a Procrustean bed meant only for the college bound.[2]

The struggle over the "right" curriculum for the high school has been nearly continuous ever since there was a significant number of public high schools. The earliest high schools were academies, pay schools that offered a wide variety of courses. To satisfy student demand, academies usually offered both college preparatory courses (consisting primarily of Latin, Greek, and mathematics) and such courses as English grammar, rhetoric, logic, composition, geography, surveying, bookkeeping, navigation, moral philosophy, and astronomy. At their peak, in 1850, there were some 6,000 academies which enrolled some 260,000 students. Although a number of states subsidized them, the academies in the 1870s and the 1880s were overtaken by the public high schools, which were controlled by public authorities and paid for by public funds. The curriculum of the public high schools tended to follow a two-track pattern: the "classical" curriculum of Greek, Latin, and mathematics for the few who were preparing for college; and the "English" curriculum, which usually included the diverse modern academic and practical courses found in the academy. Some of the larger public high schools offered a third or fourth curriculum, such as "Latin-Scientific," which was the classical curriculum with Latin but not Greek, and the Modern Language curriculum, in which German or French was taught instead of a classical language.[3]

In the late nineteenth century, the lines separating colleges and high schools were blurred. Admission to college was based on examinations, not on the credits presented, and many colleges contained departments where students prepared for the examinations. By 1890, there were about 200,000 students in public high schools (and almost 100,000 in private high schools); like academy students, all attended voluntarily, and about 10 percent remained to graduate. As the public high school expanded, educators' interest in practical courses grew, as did criticism of Greek and Latin. At professional conferences, there were repeated calls for courses that were better suited to preparing students for the real world than the languages of the ancient world were. The classicists responded to their critics by claiming that their time-honored subjects were superior for disciplining the mind and the will. The boy or girl who mastered Greek, Latin, and higher mathematics, it was said, could do anything else well.

There were four troublesome issues for high schools in the early 1890s. First was the antagonism between the classical curriculum and the modern academic subjects like science, English literature, and modern foreign languages; since only a tiny minority was actually preparing for college, many teachers and principals resented the "tyranny" (and elevated social status) associated with Greek and Latin. (According to Edward A. Krug, even though a reading knowledge of Greek was required by some colleges for admission, in 1889–90 only 3 percent of public high school pupils studied it, and only 7 percent of those in private high schools.) Second was the problem of preparing students to meet college entrance requirements. Each college had its own requirements even for the same subjects: In Greek, one insisted on Homer, another on Xenophon; in English literature (a "modern" subject), one demanded Chaucer and Burke, while another insisted on Milton and Shakespeare; still other colleges had no specific readings at all. The third issue derived from the increasing pressure by forward-looking educators to include practical courses like manual training, in order to prepare students for the real world. The fourth issue, intimately related to the other three, was whether the high school should have different curricula for those who were college bound and those who were not.[4]

Uncertainty about these issues led the National Education Association, the organizational voice of administrators, to create what must have been the first national blue-ribbon panel to examine the high school curriculum in 1892 (See pp. 71–72, 119–120). Chaired by Harvard's President Charles W. Eliot, the Committee of Ten on Secondary School Studies organized nine "conferences" of teachers and scholars to consider the school subjects and make recommendations as to how they should be taught and whether it was appropriate to differentiate between the college bound and others. The Committee of Ten surveyed forty high schools and discovered that thirty-six different subjects were offered, a number that must have suggested the "disorder" and miscellaneousness of the high school curriculum. The thirty-six subjects included five languages (Greek, Latin, French, German, and Spanish); six mathematics courses; four science courses; four history and government courses; English courses; and such miscellany as stenography, penmanship, and music. How astonished Eliot and his colleagues would have been by a survey of 741 Illinois high schools in 1977, which found 2,100 separate courses, most of them in nonacademic fields![5]

The 1893 report of the Committee of Ten was surprisingly bereft of the rhetorical flights of fancy that for the next ninety years came to be standard in statements on the role of education in American society. In a spare and understated tone, the Ten made several recommendations. First, it came down firmly against differentiation; indeed, all nine subject-matter conferences agreed "that every subject which is taught at all in a secondary school should be taught in the same way and to the same extent to every pupil so long as he pursues it, no matter what the probable destination of the pupil may be, or at what point his education is to cease." Since so small a number of high school graduates went to college, the Ten insisted that "the secondary schools of the United States, taken as a whole, do not exist for the purpose of preparing boys and girls for colleges." Their chief function was to prepare students for "the duties of life." The case against differentiation was best stated by the history conference, which complained that in some institutions "those who are to get most training hereafter [i.e., the college bound] are the only ones who have any training in history in the schools." The history teachers held "that such a distinction, especially in schools provided for the children by public taxation, is bad for all classes of pupils. It is the duty of the schools to furnish a well grounded and complete education. . . ."[6]

The second major recommendation by the Committee of Ten was that the modern academic subjects should be made equal in status to the classical curriculum and should be equally acceptable for the purposes of college admission. To this end, it proposed four model curricula, all of which should be acceptable to colleges: classical (containing three foreign languages, including Greek and Latin); Latin-Scientific (containing two foreign languages, one modern); modern languages (containing two modern foreign languages); and English (containing only one foreign language, either ancient or modern). The model curricula offered by the committee implied that neither Latin nor Greek was absolutely necessary for college preparation, and that students should be able to choose from among different programs (even within the different curricula, there was a modest degree of choice among sciences or languages). But all four of the model curricula included courses in English, mathematics, history, science, and foreign language: All were variations of what would today be called a liberal education curriculum.

The report was widely discussed and debated for years after its publication, and it ultimately suffered a curious fate. The progressive educator Francis Parker saluted its stand against "class education," saying, "There is no reason why one child should study Latin and another be limited to the 3R's." But G. Stanley Hall, the leader of the child study movement, castigated the Ten as elitists who put too much emphasis on preparation for college, instead of for life, and who ignored what he called "the great army of incapables, shading down to those who should be in schools for dullards or subnormal children." Hall complained that the report of the Ten was responsible for rising enrollments in Latin, which he thought decadent. In response to Hall's critique, Eliot said that early division of pupils into "future peasants, mechanics, trades-people, merchants, and professional people" was common in Europe but unsuited to a democratic society. He insisted that there was no conflict between preparing for life and preparing for college, since all good education is good preparation for life. Eliot insisted that there were only a small number of "incapables" in school and "that any school superintendent or principal who should construct his program with the incapables chiefly in mind would be a person professionally demented."[7]

The strange fate of the report of the Committee of Ten was that the critics successfully branded it a reactionary document that ignored individual differences, written by college presidents who wanted to force all children to take a college preparatory curriculum. Edward A. Krug, the historian of the high school, called this reversal a paradox: "The idea of giving early and separate treatment to those who could identify themselves as college-bound pupils became known as a 'liberal' point of view; while the opposite notion, that of providing the broadest possible entry for all pupils to college, became known as 'conservative.' "[8]

The problem with the report of the Ten was that it was out of joint with the times. The influx of millions of immigrants to the nation's cities put new strains on the schools. The fact that most of them came from eastern and southern Europe caused popular and scholarly commentators to bemoan the future of Anglo-Saxon America, deluged as it was by a genetically inferior and culturally backward mass. The gravest social problem, in the eyes of most contemporary observers, was how to assimilate these illiterate hordes. The schools were, of course, expected to play a leading role in the mission of Americanizing the immigrants through their children. This meant not only teaching them English but also assuming a custodial role, which forced the schools to take responsibility for training them as good citizens and to tell them how to prepare for jobs, how to keep clean, and what was expected of them in everyday life. To meet some of these needs, new courses joined the high school curriculum, such as training for specific trades, sewing, cooking, and commercial studies. In response to what were perceived to be the needs of immigrant children, some educators avidly campaigned for vocational education, industrial education, and trade schools. Because these educators based their advocacy on the needs of a changing society and economy as well as on a recognition of the diversity of children, they were clothed in the garb of reformers; those who resisted the onslaught and contended that all children should be liberally educated were pigeonholed as conservatives, tied to the academic status quo, indifferent to new educational theories fitting the curriculum to the child, and insensitive to the changing conditions about them.

The Committee of Ten's proposal to permit students to choose from among four different curricula ran afoul of more than the new economic conditions. Within the profession, there was a strong sentiment for flexibility and student choice. In 1899, the NEA appointed a committee, called the Committee on College-Entrance Requirements, which offered a new solution to the problems of the high school curriculum. Instead of parallel courses of study, the new committee recommended the concept of "constants," studies to be taken by all pupils, leaving the rest of their program for free electives. The committee recommended that all students take four years of foreign language, two of mathematics, two of English, one of history, and one of science. This simple suggestion seemed a brilliant stroke, suddening freeing the high schools of the legacy of discrete courses of study ("classical," "English," and so on).[9]

Yet even the turn to "constants" was for some a transitory expedient: The chairman of the Committee on

College-Entrance Requirements declared less than a year after presenting his report that he personally did not believe there should be any "constants" and that the high school diploma should go to any students who had persisted for four years, regardless of whether they had studied any foreign language, science, mathematics, or history. "It is not what our young people study," he said, "but how they study and how they are taught, that give them power." High schools in five large cities experimented with the free-elective system at the turn of the century, and the principal of a Boston high school explained that the ideal high school was one with a pleasant room for study, a good library, and helpful teachers. The high school, he said, was the people's college, and the school "must not prescribe to the people what the people shall study."[10]

However, the interest in an elective system organized around certain "constants" or even a totally free elective system was not nearly as persistent as the practice of directing students into separate courses. As more and more practical subjects entered the high school curriculum, new courses of study appeared: a manual training course, a vocational course, a commercial course, and—of course— a college preparatory course. With the arrival of the new practical subjects, the distinction between the classical curriculum and the modern academic subjects disappeared. Progressive reformers lumped the two together as the college preparatory curriculum. And what had once been a contest between the classical curriculum and the modern subjects became converted in a short space of years into a rivalry between a traditional curriculum and a practical curriculum. School leaders insisted that it was inappropriate to force students to take college preparatory courses if they intended to go directly to work, that what they needed were the skills to prepare for life. The development of separate curricula was inevitably based on presumptions about students' future occupations, as Charles Eliot had feared. It was odd that less than fifteen years after the Committee of Ten had inveighed against differentiating on grounds of students' occupational destination, the practice was not only widespread but was also considered progressive and liberal.

In the decade before World War I, industrial education was the wave of the future. The growth of American industry, the worldwide competition for markets, the need to train immigrants to be good workers—all presented compelling arguments for making the work of the schools more practical. Critics complained that the schools' stubborn adherence to abstract and academic studies was failing to meet either the needs of modern society or the needs of children. What was required was more job training, more preparation for specific occupations. Poor people, said the social reformers, didn't need to learn history and mathematics and literature; they needed the skills to be farmers and homemakers. Caught up in the new enthusiasm for industrial education, President Theodore Roosevelt declared in 1907 that "our school system is gravely defective in so far as it puts a premium upon mere literacy training and tends therefore to train the boy away from the farm and the workshop. Nothing is more needed than the best type of industrial school, the school for mechanical industries in the city, the school for practically teaching agriculture in the country.""

Industrial education had a certain appeal to educators, especially those who felt besieged by the children of immigrants. Many of them were illiterate and overage; the spectacle of twelve-year-old boys sitting in first-grade classes did not please principals. Among the children of poverty, there were inevitably large numbers who had difficulty learning, which was hardly surprising since so many urban classes had more than fifty pupils. It must

143

have been easy to conclude that the children of poor immigrants needed an education to fit them quickly for the job market; not much more rationalization was needed to reach the view that an academic preparation should be reserved for the few who planned to go to college. Schools around the country introduced different curricula based on their pupils' probable occupations, and in 1915 the NEA's Department of Superintendence passed a resolution approving "the increasing tendency to establish, beginning with the seventh grade, differentiated courses of study aimed more effectively to prepare the child for his probable future activities."[12]

There was another element in the emerging pattern, stemming from the progressive spirit of social uplift. Social and political reformers ousted corrupt machine politicians, provided medical and social services for the poor, built playgrounds, improved working conditions, established settlement houses in the slums, and battled slum landlords. Naturally, the schools attracted the interest of progressive reformers, who saw them as laboratories of social experimentation. The sociologist Albion W. Small told a general meeting of the NEA in 1896, "Sociology demands of educators, finally, that they shall not rate themselves as leaders of children, but as makers of society." In an era when social reform was ascendant, educators too had a vital role as agents of social improvement, as soon as they recognized that the real purpose of the schools in a democracy was not simply to empower individuals but also to meet the needs of society. As one school superintendent put it in 1913, "In a political and social democracy such as ours, children must be taught to live and to work together co-operatively; to submit their individual wills to the will of the majority; and to conform to social requirements whether they approve of them or not."[13]

The concept of social efficiency, which was popular

among progressive reformers, put education into a new context. It informed educators that they had a critical role to play in shaping society, a far more exciting prospect than merely teaching children about literature or history or science. The possibility of not just serving society but of actually directing its destiny was irresistible, or at least more interesting. The traditional curriculum was inefficient; under its sway, children were taught history, literature, mathematics, and foreign language even though they were not going to college; it was not only wasteful of the children's time but also served no useful social purpose. It became conventional in educational meetings to assert that the traditional curriculum, everything associated with a liberal education, was designed for an aristocratic class and was therefore unsuited to schools in a democracy. When a group of high school English teachers defined the purposes of their subject as the development of the ability to write and speak, the knowledge of the best literature, the cultivation of a sense of style, and the inculcation of love for literature, a professional journal complained that they were too intellectual: "Where does trigonometry apply in a good woman's life? Will it contribute anything toward peace, happiness and contentment in the home? Will it bake any bread, sew on any buttons or rock any cradles?" Then there was the educational writer who read a story about Lady Jane Grey, who had preferred to read Plato rather than to go hunting with her friends in the park. The writer said, "If such a child were found to-day, I dare say she would be hurried off to a physician or a brain specialist."[4]

By the time of World War I, a strong consensus had formed around social efficiency as the goal of education, and this consensus undergirded the report of the NEA's Commission on the Reorganization of Secondary Education. The commission organized subject matter groups, as the earlier Committee of Ten had. The committee on ancient languages lamely tried to make a case for the utility of Latin; the committee on modern languages talked of stimulating interest in other nations. The committee on mathematics proposed dividing mathematics courses on the basis of the subject's probable utility to students in their future occupations. The committee on social studies held that the aim of their subject was good citizenship. "Facts, conditions, theories, and activities that do not contribute rather directly to the appreciation of methods of human betterment have no claim," it held, thus effectively disposing of ancient and medieval history and putting current events on a higher plane than history. The science committee tried to show the relevance of biology and chemistry to everyday living, but it was difficult to make a case for physics. As Krug observed, the effect of the emphasis on social utility was to put each subject into the docket to prove its value. The burden of proof was on those who believed in the liberating qualities of the academic studies; those who challenged them had to prove nothing.[15]

The Commission on the Reorganization of Secondary Education issued its report in 1918, which went down in educational history as the "Cardinal Principles of Secondary Education." The main objectives of high school education, said the commission, were "1. Health. 2. Command of fundamental processes. 3. Worthy home-membership. 4. Vocation. 5. Citizenship. 6. Worthy use of leisure. 7. Ethical character." According to Krug, the single reference to intellectual development, called "command of fundamental processes," did not appear in the early drafts of the report. Not surprisingly, the report endorsed differentiated curricula, based on future vocational interests, such as agricultural, business, clerical, industrial, fine arts, and household arts. Almost as an aside, the report added, "Provision should be made also for those having distinctively academic interests and needs."[16]

The committee did not intend to limit access to higher education; on the contrary, it believed that those who took a vocational curriculum should also be eligible for college admission. The vocational and antiacademic bent of the "Cardinal Principles" was not lost on high school officials. An NEA survey in 1928 of some 1,200 high school principals revealed that more than half had reorganized their curriculum as a result of the 1918 report. The subjects most often added were commercial studies, home economics, sciences, industrial arts, and social studies; the subjects most often dropped were Latin, French, ancient history, and advanced mathematics.[17]

The "Cardinal Principles" crystallized the new canon of professional educators. It was by no means innovative; it brought together a variety of complementary strands of the progressive era that merged into an ideology in which the schools were society's instrument for guiding the rising generation into socially useful roles. Anyone who protested that the schools were supposed to give children intellectual power, to transmit the accumulated wisdom of the past, and to empower young people to make their own decisions about how to be socially useful was apt to be dismissed as a conservative, imbued with reactionary and individualistic ideas. In order for schools to take their place as agencies of social change, educators had to shed antiquated views about the transmission of knowledge. To be a good teacher was well and good, but it could scarcely compare to the power that flowed to those who took responsibility for shaping and sorting the youth of the nation. No more would educators be "only" teachers, the somewhat impractical and underpaid Ichabod Cranes and schoolmasters to an ungrateful and uncultured people. With the "Cardinal Principles" as their banner, they had the satisfaction of seeing themselves as engineers of social change, marching in the forefront of reform.[18]

The education profession was not uniquely responsible

for this new view of its historic mission: It was pushed, pulled, and prodded by reformers, economists, sociologists, even university presidents who believed that it was wasteful to give an academic education to those who were not planning to go to college. It was accepted as incontrovertible truth that an academic curriculum was appropriate only for those who needed it to get into college, but that it was both inappropriate and distasteful for the overwhelming majority who would not go to college. What possible reason would a future farmer or machinist have for learning history or science or literature? Educators believed as a matter of faith that the failure to introduce vocational courses would cause students to drop out in droves, especially students from poor and minority backgrounds. The odd thing was that they continued to voice this fear even as enrollments spiraled upward. In 1890, there were about 200,000 students in public high schools; in 1900, there were 519,000; high school enrollment passed the 1 million mark in 1912 and reached 2.2 million in 1920. As it happened, this growth occurred without the assistance of compulsory education laws. But it was not enough, for there continued to be millions who were not in high school. High school leaders kept rediscovering the dropout problem, even though high school graduation rates remained the same from 1890 to 1910, and they continued to deplore their failure to draw all in. Despite the rapid growth of high school enrollments, educational thinkers insisted that the curriculum was keeping potential students away and driving out others.

Curiously, educators seemed more certain of the irrelevance of the academic studies than did students or parents. Not more than 12 to 13 percent of the high school students graduated from high school in 1910, but fully 49 percent studied Latin, to the despair and disapproval of enlightened schoolmen. By 1915, Latin still enrolled 37 percent of high school students, even though most educational leaders believed that it was inappropriate for any but the college bound. Indeed, many educators doubted that even the college bound should study Latin or any other foreign language. In 1910, 84 percent of all high school students studied some foreign language, a figure that dropped to 73.2 percent in 1915. The "Cardinal Principles," which contained no encouragement for the study of any foreign language, supported the trend away from language study, and the world war decimated enrollments in the German language, which fell from 24.4 percent of all students before the war to 1 percent in 1922.[19]

Much of the rhetoric on behalf of the introduction of vocational curricula centered on the supposed needs of the children of immigrants. It was they, said the educators, who needed to be gathered in, and it was they who needed vocational skills, courses that were immediately practical, studies that had direct utility in the job market; the academic curriculum would never do for children with their special needs. But the parents of these children were never surveyed about what they wanted, for the judgment was based on the educators' understanding of society's needs, not on the parents' or students' idea of their own needs. An interesting illustration of these different perceptions occurred in 1917, when progressive reformers in New York City tried to install the "Gary plan," in which students alternated between academic and prevocational activities during the school day. The Gary plan, also called "the platoon system," had won national acclaim from Randolph Bourne, John Dewey, and others, but its intended beneficiaries were not impressed. Immigrant parents and students demonstrated noisily for three weeks to protest the plan, which they believed would close the doors of opportunity to their children. A Tammany candidate for mayor was elected, having pledged to prevent the introduction of the Gary plan into the public schools.[20]

The aim of this investigation is to identify the origins of present-day debates about the curriculum. In the early 1980s, some educators and national commissions argued that all students should be enrolled in an academic curriculum; that certain subjects (like English, science, mathematics, and history) should be "constants" in everyone's high school program; and that requirements were necessary to ensure that all students take the necessary courses. Those who offered these recommendations were criticized for ignoring the differences among children; for ignoring the special needs of minority children, who needed job training; for placing too much emphasis on academic subjects; for risking an increase in the number of dropouts by raising academic requirements; for neglecting the need for courses that are immediately practical in the job market.

There is some irony in the fact that the case for the academic subjects was made in the early 1980s on grounds of social utility: It was said, for example, that students should learn foreign languages because of job opportunities in international trade or because of the importance of understanding other nations and cultures, and that students should study mathematics and science because of the nation's need for engineers and scientists. Advocates of literature and history struggled with little success to find the appropriate justification that might commend their studies to the near-instinctive demand for social utility.

The argument that students should be well educated because education is a good in itself was rarely heard, least of all from educators. Perhaps they feared that no one would believe them. Or perhaps their own unexamined intellectual heritage inclined them not to believe it themselves.

10

Is Education Really a Federal Issue?

(1983)

FOR the first time since Sputnik was orbited in 1957, education is a major political issue. The warning by the National Commission on Excellence in Education that the schools—and our society—are threatened by "a rising tide of mediocrity," and similar appraisals by other national study panels have made the public aware that the condition of the schools cannot be taken for granted. The question now is, can the momentum for school improvement be sustained?

All the recent reports have complained that national indicators of academic achievement and of literacy have fallen over the past twenty years, despite the vast expansion of our educational system. Educators disagree about why this is so and even whether the measures of achievement are valid, but there is no doubt that the trend has been down. Not only did average college entrance examination scores drop steadily from 1964 until 1982, but the number of high-scoring students has shrunk dramatically. Since the mid-1960s, the same downward pattern has also been recorded on standardized tests given in junior high school and senior high school.

Test scores, of course, are but a symptom of the larger problem. During the past decade, researchers have pointed to disturbing practices: lower requirements for high school graduation and college admission, which led to smaller enrollments in foreign languages and in advanced courses in mathematics and science; dissolution of the history and English curriculum, which promoted the proliferation of specialized or nonacademic electives; less time spent reading, writing, or doing homework, which undermined verbal skills. Student behavior in school has also changed for the worse; reports of absenteeism, vandalism, and fighting by students have been widespread. During the same period, grade inflation and social promotion reflected the low value placed on academic achievement.

Although there has been a tendency to place much of the blame for these developments on the teaching profession, it seems clear that the larger trends were not caused by teachers. For the person who loves to teach poetry or history or science, the schools have not been a happy workplace. Because of the poor conditions of teaching, it is little wonder that the schools have had an increasingly difficult time attracting or holding on to talented teachers.

The dire descriptions of our educational problems are no cause for negativism. In a democracy, the first step necessary for dealing with a problem is to recognize it, and this is the service performed by the national reports. At the time of Sputnik, heightened public concern about the schools led to effective action at all levels—federal, state, and local. Real changes occurred as a result, such as increased enrollments in foreign languages, science, and mathematics and the development of new curricula.

Thus, the bad news about our educational needs may actually be good news because it means that we now have the political consensus to do something about improving the schools. The seriousness of our long academic slide provides fair warning that no quick fixes will do. The recent commission reports contain many sensible suggestions, and they make clear that the job of improving the schools will require thoughtful and consistent efforts by teachers, administrators, parents, state legislators, and federal officials.

Yes, there is a federal role in education, and it has nothing to do with prayer or private school subsidies. The federal government must continue to be concerned about both the quality and equality of educational opportunity. The value of a strong national voice is exemplified by the admirable report of the National Commission on Excellence in Education, which has already raised the level of discourse about education across the country.

Federal policies must be designed to address local needs. Federal action can help to alleviate the shortage of teachers in subject areas like foreign languages, mathematics, and science by offering fellowships and loans to prospective teachers and by creating a mechanism to recognize and reward outstanding teachers. The National Science Foundation can play a constructive role by furthering contacts between high school students, teachers, and the larger world of science and technology.

The recent efforts by the National Endowment for the Humanities to improve the teaching of history, literature, and foreign languages in high school should be encouraged. On Chairman William Bennett's initiative, the endowment is offering summer seminars for high school teachers to increase their knowledge of history and literature and has sponsored collaborative activities for teachers of the humanities in high schools and colleges. In addition, the endowment's interest in the high schools has prompted many state humanities councils to involve teachers and students in their programs.

Instead of cutting the bilingual education budget, Congress should turn the program into a national literacy campaign with an even larger budget. The federal government should state clearly, as the Twentieth Century Fund task force on federal policy recently recommended, that "the most important objective of elementary and secondary education in the United States is the development of literacy in the English language." The task force (on which I served) proposed that the federal government establish the goal—literacy in the English language for every child—and that each district be free to decide which methods (including bilingual education) are most appropriate.

A wise federal policy would include expanded funding of educational research and information in order to keep policymakers, educators, and citizens well informed. The National Center for Education Statistics, already an invaluable barometer of education trends, should have the capacity to keep tabs on the performance of students, teachers, and schools across the nation. With better information, we are less likely to be surprised by educational crises in the future.

The federal government should also grant financial assistance to school districts that are overwhelmed by an influx of immigrant children. The well-funded "impact aid" program, intended originally to subsidize districts with large numbers of military personnel, could be redirected for this purpose.

Properly conceived, the federal role is to inspire, prod, and assist localities to improve the quality of education available to all children. But even under ideal circumstances, the federal role can be only subsidiary to local and state efforts. Educational change that is more than cosmetic will require the cooperation of many different actors. Public education continues to be primarily a state responsibility, and the day-to-day functioning of schools depends on the attitudes and actions of teachers, administrators, school board members, parents, and students.

To improve student achievement, teachers will have to assign more homework, expect students to do more reading and writing, and spend more time correcting essays. Parents will have to see that their children spend more time on homework and less time on entertainment. Colleges should raise their admissions requirements, which would immediately affect high school curricula. Schools should strengthen the basic curriculum for all students so that everyone studies history, literature, science, mathematics, the arts, and foreign language. Those who are not going to college may not have another opportunity to learn what is taught in school.

For everyone involved, the critical factor that must change is the attitude toward the importance of good education. Technological changes demand higher standards of literacy for the entire population. Schools are not simply custodial institutions designed to keep young people off the streets and out of the labor market. They are vital in developing the abilities and intelligence of young people. Our future well-being as a society depends in large measure on the capacity of our schools to nurture productive, thoughtful, and adaptive young men and women.

The impetus for school improvement that followed Sputnik lasted only seven or eight years before other social crises captured the attention of the public and the education profession. It fell victim, too, because its stress on the needs of the gifted conflicted with a rising tide of egalitarianism. School reformers today plead not for the needs of the few but for the right of all American children to a better education. If it is true that public education has the chance only once in a generation to gain enough national attention to produce substantial change, then the time is now.

11

60s Education, 70s Benefits

(1978)

SINCE the late 1960s, American schools have been the object of intense criticism by those who claim that they have failed to promote equality of opportunity. One of the linchpins in this attack is the charge that the educational reforms of the Great Society era failed and that this failure demonstrates the bankruptcy of American social policy.

The legislative programs of the late 1960s did not eliminate educational inequality. Yet to ignore the substantial changes brought about during this period is to misunderstand recent history.

The major thrust of the Great Society educational reforms was the expansion of educational opportunity. This did not represent a break with the past, but rather a speeding up of long-term democratizing trends in education. If one uses participation as a measure, it is clear that there has been rapid growth in the enrollment of those not compelled to attend school. The proportion of three- and four-year-olds in nursery school has jumped from 10 percent to 32 percent. The number enrolled in college has doubled since 1965, from 6 million to 12 million.

Even more significant than the growth in numbers has been the profound change in the way people use educational institutions. People of all ages are moving in and out of postsecondary programs, changing careers, finishing interrupted degrees, learning new skills, exploring dormant interests. The concept of lifelong education has taken hold among a large segment of the population. Indeed, almost one-third of all college students attend part-time, and some 36 percent are over twenty-five years old.

The broadening of college opportunities for minority youth has been striking: Between 1965 and 1977, the number of black college students quadrupled, from 274,000 to 1.1 million; black students now are 10.8 percent of all college students. Five years ago, only 8 percent of blacks between twenty-five and twenty-nine years old had completed college, compared to 21 percent of whites; in 1977, 12 percent of blacks in that age group had finished college, compared to 25 percent of whites. While the black–white differential remains large, the absolute number of black college graduates has risen sharply: In 1974, there were 700,000 black college graduates in the entire country; by 1977, that number had grown to 984,000.

Below the college level, the Great Society reforms have not yet redeemed their promise, in part because they were prematurely declared failures. The belief that schools could make a difference was the major rationale for programs like Head Start, which provides preschool education for the poor, and Title I of the Elementary and Secondary Education Act of 1965, which distributes federal funds to improve the education of poor children.

Early evaluations of these programs yielded disappointing results about their effect on student achievement, which led some people to conclude (wrongly) that educational performance is wholly predetermined by genetics or family background. As a result, the Head Start program was sharply curtailed. However, a recent major review of the long-term effects of Head Start found that Head Start children ultimately performed better in school than poor children who were not in the program.

The Title I program remained intact because it became politically popular: In the decade after 1966, some $20 billion was allotted to 90 percent of the nation's school districts. One reason that national evaluations of Title I revealed minimal impact on student achievement was that the quality of local programs ranged from excellent to ineffectual. When the good and the bad were averaged together, the results were unimpressive.

In the best Title I classrooms, student achievement is clearly related to the content and intensity of instruction, suggesting that good teachers and effective schools do make a difference. Yet no education authority—national, state, or local—has been willing to compel change in unsuccessful programs. Unfortunately, those who administer Title I are more concerned to see that federal dollars are well distributed rather than well used. What is needed are responsible public officials to restore Title I to its unfulfilled educational goals.

Assessing the effects of the Great Society educational reforms is somewhat like debating whether a glass is half empty or half full. Those who see a half-empty glass focus on the number of minority students who never finish high school, the high attrition rate of minority college students, and the small proportions of minority students in graduate schools. And they are right to do so. This sort of self-criticism, which continually raises aspirations, is part of the very nature of American society.

Yet it is important to see the hypothetical glass in relation to its contents in 1965—that is, to recognize both how much has been accomplished and how much remains to be done. Those who argue, against the evidence, that all efforts at educational reform have failed are actually insisting on the futility of any reform. Such a perspective leads to apathy and despair, not to a realistic assessment of the past nor to a renewed sense of purpose and efficacy.

12

The Case of
Tuition Tax Credits

(1984)

ON the surface, the issue of tuition tax credits is not complicated. On one side are defenders of the public schools, who fear that the egalitarian mission of public education will be jeopardized if states or the federal government permit tax deductions for private school tuition. On the other are champions of nonpublic education, who contend that public policy should provide tax incentives to encourage choice, pluralism, and diversity in schooling. Tax credits will foster competition and excellence, say the nonpublic school advocates. Tax credits will destroy the public schools, reply the public school partisans. The lines are drawn, and the battleground is the common school, that distinctively American institution.

Of course, political controversies are rarely as simple as they seem, and this issue is no exception. Each side clings to its own mythology. The public school forces pledge to defend to the end a high and impregnable wall between church and state, but that wall has historically been of uneven height and has frequently been breached over the years. The nonpublic school forces propose tax credits on grounds of equity, but such credits would undoubtedly be inequitably distributed.

Few issues have been as tortuous for our political system as trying to define the appropriate relation between the state and nonpublic schools, especially sectarian schools. There were private schools long before there were public schools, and the line between public and private was not always so clear as it seems today. In the nineteenth century, many states allocated public land and funds to private academies, including those with denominational sponsors. Church schools in New York City in the first quarter of the nineteenth century shared proportionately in state funds for schooling, in recognition of their public function.

Nineteenth-century public schools were decidedly Protestant in their orientation. Many common school leaders were militant Protestants or ministers *manque*. The public schools had daily readings of the Protestant Bible, their students sang Protestant hymns, and their textbooks reflected the Protestant view of European history. In the 1840s, Catholics in New York argued that the state should support Catholic public schools, since it already funded Protestant public schools. In an era when major eastern cities experienced anti-Catholic rioting, the political climate was unsurprisingly hostile to such a proposal. After the Catholic plea was denied, American Catholics set about building a school system of their own.

During the balance of the nineteenth century, the religious issue provoked numerous disputes, including an unsuccessful campaign in the 1870s to pass a constitutional amendment barring public support for religious schools.

In the 1920s, war-inspired xenophobia prompted legal attacks on religious schools, which turned to the courts for protection. In 1923, the Supreme Court's ruling in *Meyer* v. *Nebraska* voided laws in several midwestern states that prohibited foreign language instruction (the defendants were parochial school teachers of German); in the *Pierce* v. *Society of Sisters* decision of 1925, the Supreme Court invalidated an Oregon law requiring all children to attend public schools.

The *Pierce* decision has often been called the Magna Carta of private education in the United States. The Court declared that the state had unreasonably interfered "with the liberty of parents and guardians to direct the upbringing and education of children under their control. . . . The fundamental theory of liberty upon which all governments in this Union repose excludes any general power of the State to standardize its children by forcing them to accept instruction from public teachers only. The child is not the mere creature of the State. . . ." Less often noted is the fact that the decision affirmed the state's right to regulate nonpublic schools, "to inspect, supervise and examine them, their teachers and pupils; to require that all children of proper age attend some school, that teachers shall be of good moral character and patriotic disposition, that certain studies plainly essential to good citizenship must be taught, and that nothing be taught which is manifestly inimical to the public welfare.'"

If the message of the *Pierce* case was straightforward—private schools have a right to exist, and the state has a right to impose reasonable regulations—the line of Supreme Court decisions since the 1940s about the relation between the state and religious schooling has been anything but clear. The Court approved the use of public funds for transportation of children to parochial schools, disapproved released time for religious instruction (in public school buildings) in Illinois, approved released time for religious instruction (out of public school buildings) in New York, disapproved prayer in the public schools, approved the provision of secular textbooks to nonpublic schools, and disapproved reimbursements for teachers' salaries and materials. The wall of separation, it should be obvious, has numerous chinks and crannies. The treatment of tuition tax credits by the high court has been similarly inconsistent. In 1973, the Supreme Court overturned a New York law which provided tax benefits to nonpublic school parents, but in 1983 endorsed (by five to four) a Minnesota statute which provides tax deductions for educational expenses of all state taxpayers (the $500–700 deduction obviously is worth more to the 10 percent who pay private school tuition than to the 90 percent whose only expenses are for gym suits and school supplies).

This last decision by the Court reinvigorated discussion of a federal program of tuition tax credits. Since 1978, its major proponents in Congress have been Senators Bob Packwood (R.-Ore.) and Daniel Patrick Moynihan (D.-N.Y.). Initially, their legislation passed the House but failed in the Senate; on another occasion, it passed both houses, but in forms so different that no legislation resulted. While President Jimmy Carter opposed tuition tax credits, the Reagan administration championed the cause as its own.

Yet even with a sympathetic president, a potentially sympathetic Supreme Court, and strong proponents in the Congress, the prospect for tuition tax credits remained doubtful. Even after four years of enthusiastic support by the Reagan administration, such legislation gained no more than warm rhetoric and a long waltz through the legislative process.

Having been in dispute for more than a century, the question of whether and how the public should support nonpublic schools is not likely to be easily resolved or to go away. This being the case, it is unfortunate that the nature of the public debate about this difficult and complex issue has been so unsatisfactory. The alarmist rhetoric of public school advocates would lead one to believe that private schools were steadily encroaching on the public schools. Yet the proportion of American children enrolled in private schools has declined from 13 percent in 1960 to little more than 10 percent in the early 1980s. Similarly, one might expect that Catholic schools were the primary beneficiaries of any tax credit plan, but Catholic school enrollment dropped from more than 5 million in 1960 to only 3 million in 1982. Some 35 percent of the children in private schools are non-Catholics, and the fastest-growing private schools are non-Catholic, Christian day schools.

In response to persistent demands for public support for the private sector, the arguments made on behalf of the common school are disappointingly tendentious. Friends of the public schools say that tuition tax credits must be rejected because they would subvert the public school; that the public school must be defended because it promotes political socialization, social solidarity, egalitarianism, and civic virtue; that educational choice is reprehensible because it is synonymous with inequality; that equal opportunity requires a similar curriculum for all children, which is available only in the public schools; and that erosion of the public school would advance inequality of opportunity and of resources.

If these assertions were true, they would amount to a powerful argument for the public school; but they are assertions from ideology, not from evidence. There is no evidence, for example, that students in nonpublic schools are less committed to democratic ideals or less likely to be good citizens than students in public schools. There is no reason to claim that private school graduates are socialized to unworthy political or social values. No one has looked at military enlistment rates or voter registration or any other evidence of civic engagement to compare the consequences of public and private schooling. Nor can anyone fairly deny the substantial inequalities among public schools; the schools of wealthy suburbs are more akin to private nonsectarian schools than they are to the public schools in the central city. To pretend that all public schools have equal resources or that they offer the same curriculum—neither of which is true—does not advance the cause of the public school.

Equally obscure is the issue of educational choice. Opponents of tuition tax credits denigrate choice as an undemocratic value, as a value inconsistent with equality. But most Americans do not see a necessary conflict between those values. Most people think that their right to choose among candidates, their right to choose where to live, their right to choose a field of work, their right to choose between public and nonpublic schools—that these rights are as important as the national commitment to equal opportunity. Furthermore, insisting that the public school stands for equality while the private school stands for choice neatly ignores the millions of people who have already chosen to leave the cities and to place their children in public schools in well-to-do suburbs.

Some critics believe that demands for tuition tax credits were stimulated by such relatively recent events as school desegregation, the banning of school prayer, and the spread of school finance reform, and that these changes launched the pressure for schools that reflect particular religious, social, or political values; although these events probably contributed to middle-class flight from urban schools and to the rise of Christian day schools, it should not be imagined that political claims on behalf of private education began with the *Brown* decision in 1954, the school prayer decision in 1962, or the school finance reform activities of the 1970s. Opponents of tuition tax credits insist that the public is being asked to subsidize inequality or a religious environment or schools that can reject troublesome children, which in many instances is true. Recognizing that choice has a measure of legitimacy, many public schools have tried to introduce forms of diversity within a public setting—like magnet schools, schools with parental involvement, mini-schools within large schools, or open enrollment within a school district. But none of these options goes far enough to satisfy the parent who wants a religious school or a distinctive value orientation.

Supporters of some form of public support for private schools argue that it is in the public interest to permit parents to choose their children's schools. In a comparison of public and private schools, James Coleman held that private schools were characterized by better discipline, higher student achievement, better student behavior, and more demanding student coursework than were public schools; he proposed that public subsidies would facilitate choice (and therefore better educational opportunities) for those who could not now afford private schools. In his view, support for choice would enhance equity, not undermine it. Nathan Glazer claims that "some degree of homogeneity is necessary for effective education to take place," and he does not mean either racial or economic homogeneity but "some degree of agreement on values among students themselves and among students, parents, and teachers." Without this agreement, too much time is wasted on discipline problems instead of spent effectively on education.[2]

A strong case against tuition tax credits has been made by economist David W. Breneman. Based on his analysis of the potential effects of the credits, he doubts that they would generate many shifts from public to private schools;

the amount of saving would be too little to affect low-income families and not enough to affect most other families. Instead of spurring choice, he contends that the credits will be "pure windfall gains to those with children already enrolled in private schools, a high price to pay for the relatively few families whose decisions might be affected."[3]

One intriguing idea that has not to date received serious consideration is the possibility of modeling school aid on the need-based grant programs in higher education. The federal government and many states make grants and loans to low-income students for higher education, regardless of whether they attend public or private institutions; it is difficult to see why this approach is appropriate for college, but not for schooling. In the late 1970s, Senator Moynihan proposed "baby BEOGs," that is, vouchers for low-income school children, following the example of the popular Basic Educational Opportunity Grants for needy college students; the idea fell flat because it didn't satisfy those clamoring for tax credits for all parents, and it didn't placate those who opposed any form of aid to private schools.

It may be that in the years ahead some program to provide public aid to parents of private school students will succeed. Those on opposite sides of the issue agree that tax credits would not substantially change public school enrollment, since only those who are at the margins would shift their children from public to private schools. Of course, there would be other consequences, and these are worth considering. Leaving aside the question of cost to the public treasury, the most significant effect is likely to be on the private schools themselves. If they should become recipients of major government funding, the level of government regulation seems likely to increase. This raises troublesome problems for the private schools. Once they are subject to the same regulations as public schools, will they lose the qualities that make them special?

A study by Dennis J. Encarnation of the Harvard Business School concludes that government aid to nonpublic schools and government regulation are extensive. Nonpublic schools benefit by their tax-exempt status, eliminating their liability for local property taxes, and they receive tax-deductible contributions. In addition, they receive direct benefits from federal, state, and local programs, which directly subsidize such services as pupil transportation, special education for the handicapped, secular textbooks, and health and welfare programs. Encarnation contends that 26 percent of the revenues of nonpublic schools comes from direct and indirect government aid.[4]

No private school is entirely beyond government regulation, Encarnation finds. All fifty states require private elementary schools to register with the state and to supply regular reports. Five states require nonpublic schools to meet state accreditation standards; thirteen states require all teachers to have state certification; forty-six states require nonpublic schools to offer a curriculum "equivalent" to the public school curriculum. Encarnation predicts that the adoption of tuition tax credits would undoubtedly increase the scope of direct government regulation of private schools.

This, I believe, is the real specter of tuition tax credits: not the destruction of the public schools, but the absorption of private schools into the public sector. Tax credits seem likely to stimulate much greater government regulation of student admissions, teacher certification, curriculum standards, and disciplinary practices. If this occurs, then the very practices and policies that make private schools distinctive will be eliminated.

Regulation of student admissions might force private schools towards a common school approach, away from the distinctiveness that many private schools now treasure. Regulation of teacher hiring might force private schools to hire only teachers with state-mandated credentials, instead of hiring artists to teach art, actors to teach acting, and historians to teach history. Imposition of curriculum standards might impair both the Summerhills and the starchy traditionalists who choose to march to a different drummer. Application of the judicially circumscribed disciplinary practices of public schools to the private sector would deprive them of the power to expel disruptive students (which is most effective simply because it exists, not because it is used).

Advocates of tuition tax credits disparage this prospect by pointing out that nonpublic schools, colleges, and universities already receive extensive governmental subsidy without being unduly burdened by government regulation. The analogy between precollegiate schooling and higher education may not be appropriate, however, since governmental agencies have traditionally monitored elementary and secondary schooling in all its aspects while eschewing direct involvement in student admissions, faculty hiring, or curriculum standards in higher education.

Tuition tax credits have gained support in recent years because of the expectation that they will not unleash higher levels of government regulation, since the financial benefits would go to parents rather than to institutions. But the validity of this argument may have been undermined by the Supreme Court's Grove City College decision in early 1984. In a little noted but significant section of the decision, the Court ruled unanimously that federal loans to the college's students represented aid to the college itself, even though the college scrupulously refused any direct loans, grants, or contracts from the federal government. Based on this precedent, federal and state courts might eventually decide that tuition tax credits—no less than student loans—benefit the institutions and make them recipients of public assistance. If this occurs, there might even come a time when the courts determine that the schools receiving these public benefits must banish religion from their curriculum, which would be a bitter irony for those religious schools hoping to be rescued from rising costs by tuition tax credits for parents. This prediction could be wrong, but the risk remains.

During the past century, public schools replaced private schools as the dominant educational institution. Private schools survived as an alternative for those who wanted something better (in their own eyes) or something different from the public schools. Whether they are religious or secular, they are freely chosen by parents, often at great cost to themselves. They are usually communities of the like-minded, who share values, either religious, academic, social, or political. Some are freewheeling in their progressivism; some are bastions of academic traditionalism; some look remarkably like the local public school, except for their religious practices. To the extent that they are genuinely different from the public schools, they represent a source of diversity and pluralism in American education. It would be a shame to see these distinctive qualities sacrificed for the financial relief promised by tuition tax credits.

13

The Uses and Misuses

of Tests

(1984)

THE debate about standardized testing has been one of
the most rancorous educational issues of the past decade.
Since the case against standardized testing has received a
great deal of attention in the popular and scholarly media,
the nature of the indictment is by now familiar. Articulate
critics have charged that such tests measure only a narrow
spectrum of abilities; that the tests by their very nature
discourage creative and imaginative thinking; that the
results of the tests have far too significant an effect on the
life chances of young people; that the emphasis in a
multiple-choice test is wrongly on "the right answer" and
on simplicity instead of thoughtful judgments; that the
tests favor the advantaged over the disadvantaged while
claiming to be neutral; and that the tests are inherently
biased against those who are unfamiliar with the language

and concepts of the majority culture. In short, say the critics, the tests corrupt education, subjugate millions of students to their mechanistic requirements, and limit access to educational opportunity.

In examining the uses and misuses of testing, it is necessary to reflect on this upsurge of hostility to the testing process and to ask why it has occurred now.

My own view is that the tests have become increasingly controversial because they have become increasingly indispensable. Objections to standardized testing have accompanied the period in which the tests have become a fixture not only in educational decision making but in entry to the labor market. One of the sources of this increased criticism of the tests is egalitarianism, for the egalitarian complaint is that the tests discriminate among test takers and favor those with the best education and the most verbal ability. But the force that makes standardized testing an omnipresent feature of our society is also egalitarianism, because testing continues to be the most objective mechanism available to allocate benefits. In education, tests have grown more important to the extent that other measures have been discarded or discredited. Although it is easy to forget the past, we should recall that the tests helped to replace an era in which many institutions of higher education made their selections with due regard to the student's race, religion, class, and family connections. For many years, the objectivity of the tests was believed to be the best guarantee that selections would be made on the basis of ability, rather than status.

The tests have assumed an exceptional importance in college admissions, because other measures have been rendered useless. Personal recommendations today carry far less weight than they once did, because letter writers can no longer rely on the confidentiality of their statements. High school grades are a questionable standard, not only because of the variability from one school to another but because of the prevalence of grade inflation. If almost everyone applying for admission to a select college presents an A record, then the grade point average becomes meaningless in the admissions process. In the current situation, the students who selected demanding courses and the schools that resisted grade inflation are handicapped when colleges attach importance to the grade point average. Personal interviews are helpful, but they are limited in value by the interviewer's prejudices and the student's ability to present himself. When all of these factors are considered, the tests—despite all of their flaws—are left as the fairest measure of a student's academic ability.

Thus the contemporary paradox. The more egalitarian our society becomes, the more important are standardized tests. Yet the more important the tests are, the more they are subject to egalitarian criticism for assuming too much power in determining future life chances. So long as there are educational institutions where there are more applicants than places, there must be an objective way to decide who gets in. This being so, the egalitarian critique of testing founders precisely because no other objective means has been discovered to take the place of ability testing.

Unless some more objective means is devised, testing will continue to be pervasive, perhaps even more than it is now. This is not necessarily a development to be welcomed, since it goes hand-in-hand with the growing bureaucratization of American education. However, it is important to note that the influence of standardized testing in college admissions is limited by demographic factors. Although critics frequently complain about the unconstrained power of the testers, a recent survey by the College Board showed that fewer than 10 percent of all institutions of higher education are highly selective. Most colleges and universities accept all prospective students who apply or require only that they meet minimal standards. For the overwhelming majority of students, the tests are used for placement, not for exclusion from educational opportunity.

While they are certainly not perfect instruments of assessment or prediction, tests have appropriate uses for students, teachers, and educational institutions. Students who take the Preliminary Scholastic Aptitude Test (PSAT) or the SAT, for example, get a measure of their strengths and weaknesses relative to other students. Correctly read, not as a life sentence but as a one-shot assessment of verbal and mathematical abilities, the test score can direct the student toward appropriate study to improve areas of academic weakness. For teachers and schools, the tests are useful as rough indicators of how well students are learning the specific skills that are tested. The test scores can help the school in diagnosing educational problems and in prescribing appropriate remedies.

The chief virtue of the standardized test is that it may serve as an early warning system. If a student scores a 350 on the SAT, counselors and teachers should be alerted to find out why and to do something about it. If a school administrator sees a steady downward trend in the scores for a school or a district, it should also be considered a warning of possible problems in the teaching of academic skills.

The best example of how the tests function as an early warning system occurred during the past several years. In 1975, the College Board acknowledged that SAT scores had steadily and sharply declined since 1963–4. More than any other single factor, the phenomenon of falling test scores stimulated a national debate about education policies. As a result, the public and policymakers became concerned about the decline of academic standards and of literacy.

Initially, some in the educational field tried to explain away the score decline, either by questioning the validity of the SAT or by pointing to the increased numbers of minority students in the pool of test takers. These attempts to allay public concern were soon rebutted, however, as additional research provided evidence that other standardized tests of verbal skills showed the same pattern of falling scores over the same period. In particular, Annegret Harnischfeger and David E. Wiley's article, "Achievement Test Score Decline: Do We Need to Worry?" documented a parallel drop in scores in a wide variety of tests, beginning in about the fifth grade.[1]

The second claim—that the score decline was caused by the inclusion of large numbers of poor and minority students in the test cohort—was effectively dismissed by the blue-ribbon panel appointed by the College Board and chaired by Willard Wirtz. The Wirtz panel found that the new students had contributed to the decline until about 1970; after that date, the composition of the test-taking population had stabilized, yet the SAT averages continued to fall and to fall even faster than before 1970.

The report of the Wirtz panel identified a number of in-school practices that probably contributed to the score decline. It observed that absenteeism, grade inflation, and social promotion had become widespread, while the assignment of homework had shrunk. One of its internal studies, prepared by Harvard reading expert Jeanne Chall, found that the verbal content of widely used high school textbooks had been reduced by as much as two grade levels. Although the panel was careful not to pin the blame for the score decline on any particular factor, it did note that there was "almost certainly some causal relationship between the shift in the high schools from courses in the traditional disciplines to newer electives." It further pointed out that its "firmest conclusion is that the critical factors in the relationship between curricular change and the SAT scores are (1) that less thoughtful and critical reading is now being demanded and done and (2) that careful writing has apparently about gone out of style."[2]

The SAT score decline sounded a national warning bell that something might be terribly wrong in the schools. The reaction was not long in coming, and it was not always wisely considered. In almost every discipline, teachers reported the pressures of a "back-to-basics" movement that demanded greater attention to basic skills and disparaged innovative practices. Within five years after the news of the score decline broke, nearly forty state legislatures had adopted minimum competency tests in an effort to restore value to the high school diploma; such tests of minimal skills did little to raise overall educational quality. In response to these developments, more than two dozen commissions, task forces, and study panels were established to examine the problems of American education, with special focus on the high schools.

The spring of 1983 saw the release of reports from four of these groups, and several more followed in the fall of the same year. For the first time in a generation, the public became deeply concerned about the problems of American education. Hardly a day went by without an article in the news about merit pay, teacher education, curricular change, tightened standards for high school graduation or college admission, or some other educational subject that a year earlier would have not made it into the papers, let alone onto the agenda of the state legislature.

This time of ferment and reform was directly stimulated by the impact of the SAT score decline. No other single indicator had the power to alert the public to a national erosion of educational quality, nor the power to elicit research focusing on problems of educational quality. Though one would wish it were possible to generate interest in educational reform without developing so drastic a symptom, nonetheless the SAT score drop dramatically

177

raised the level of public attention to education.

These then are the uses of well-made standardized tests: as an assessment tool to help individual students identify their strengths and weaknesses, as a diagnostic and prescriptive technique to improve individualized learning programs, as a yardstick to help competitive colleges select their students, as a barometer to gauge the learning of academic skills, and as an early warning system to measure national trends in learning these skills.

But the tests are not an unmixed blessing. Many of the criticisms that have been made of them are on the mark. The tests can easily be misused and become an end in themselves, rather than a means. It is true that standardized tests measure only a narrow spectrum of abilities and that they cannot measure many valuable ways of thinking. The tests have validity only because the narrow spectrum of abilities that they do measure tends to be central to the learning process in college. The odds favor the future academic success of the student who scores 700 over the student who scores 400, yet the odds are not always right. We all know students who don't test well, who freeze up in the test situation, or who have gifts that the tests don't measure. Sensible admissions officers know this and are on the lookout for youngsters who have the imagination, creativity, or drive that doesn't register on the SAT.

The critics also have a point when they speak of the simplistic thinking that multiple-choice questions promote. While it is true that many questions asked on the SAT and on achievement tests have only one correct answer among those presented, the very emphasis on the right answer may itself be educationally counterproductive. As an historian, I am aware that the more I know, the less I am sure of. I am troubled when one of my children is asked to give the three reasons for the outbreak of some war or the four causes of some movement. When the event or movement in question is still being debated by historians, as most everything is, then I am especially annoyed by the idea that test makers and teachers should treat them as settled issues. As a parent, I want my children to see history, politics, literature, and art in relation to one another, and not as compartmentalized events that can be defined in short answers or in multiple-choice questions. Furthermore, I want them to learn that most questions cannot be answered with a "yes" or a "no," that most judgments must be hedged by qualifications, and that questions about literature and history usually require complicated answers that must be explained, justified, and defined. In a better world, educational testers would value the slow, thoughtful response over the fast, reflexive answer.

Overreliance on standardized testing may be dangerous to the health of education. It is certainly dangerous to the integrity of the high school curriculum. The introduction of the SAT, which (in its verbal component) is curriculum free, left many high schools without a good argument for requiring students to take history, literature, science, or anything not specifically demanded by the college of their choice. The old College Boards were based on a very specific curriculum and on specific works of literature and periods of history; the elite secondary schools agreed on what was important to teach, and their students were well prepared for the examinations, which relied heavily on essay answers. It was a move toward democratic admissions when the SAT was adopted, because the SAT tested scholastic aptitude and made no assumptions about what curriculum the student had studied. As a result, public school students all over the country were able to compete fairly for places in the prestigious colleges. Unlike the authors of the College Entrance Examinations, the makers of the SAT do not care whether the student has ever read

Jane Austen or Charles Dickens or any particular work.

Now, it is not the fault of the Educational Testing Service that students may arrive at college with high test scores and appallingly little substantive knowledge of history or literature. But the curriculum-free SAT has presented no impediment to high schools that thoughtlessly decimated their own curricular requirements. Because the SAT is curriculum free, students who are good test takers are justified in thinking that they can do very well in the admissions process even if their preparation for college has been haphazard. Again, I want to stress that the SAT did not cause the curricular chaos that has come to be the bane of American high schools. But any admissions officer who relies on SAT scores without scrutinizing the content of the student's high school coursework is gravely misusing the test.

Standardized tests are misused when teachers, textbook publishers, curriculum planners, and administrators permit ordinary classroom practice to be dominated by the fill-in-the-blanks mentality, to the virtual exclusion of writing. Researchers have reported a sharp increase in the time spent in elementary schools and even in high schools on workbooks and busywork. The study of textbooks by Jeanne Chall for the Wirtz panel documented a marked increase in emphasis on "objective answers." Chall found that "generally, the assignments in the Reading, History and Literature textbooks [ask] only for underlining, circling and filling in of single words." When these busywork activities are substituted for student writing, they are anti-intellectual and subversive of good learning. Filling in the blanks is not equivalent educationally to the intellectual tasks involved in writing an essay, in which the student must think through what he wants to say, must organize his thoughts, must choose his words with care, and must present his ideas with precision.[3]

The harm in minimizing the practice of writing in the

classroom is not merely to the student; teachers are also injured. Workbook activity requires minimal skill and thought by teachers; they become technicians, checking for the correct answer, a rather low-grade form of labor. When they teach writing, their own intelligence and judgment and skill are brought into play. In order to teach writing, they must make decisions; they must provide guidance; they must set standards of accomplishment. In short, they must wear the mantle of professionalism. The shift in the classroom from teacher control to materials control no doubt contributes to what some observers have called the "deskilling" or the "technicization" of teaching, a process that converts teachers from professionals to civil servants.

In sum, there can be no doubt that the tests have their uses as well as their misuses. The standardized test should be seen as a measuring device, an assessment tool, never as an end in itself. The skills that it measures are important, but it does not measure every important skill. The information that it gives us about the state of a student's learning is never definitive, but tentative and subject to future change. Above all, we should not permit the standardized test to become the be-all and end-all of educational endeavor; we send our children to school not in order to do well on tests but in order to become educated people, knowledgeable about the past and the present, and prepared to continue learning in the future. Tests help us check up on how well children are learning, and this is their major value. Their uses are clear and limited. The mastery of tests should not be permitted to fill in the blank of what should be our educational philosophy.

Those who believe in the value of tests have a particular responsibility to guard against their misuse in the classroom, the press, admissions offices, and the workplace.

14

On the History of Minority Group Education in the United States

(1976)

BECAUSE of the heterogeneous character of the American population, the education of minority groups is a controversial subject—one which is frequently politicized by those who study it. Educational historians have tended to interpret this issue in accordance with their own political and social orientation. The dominant perspective, until the past decade, was that the American public schools were the highest realization of the democratic ideal, that they provided equal opportunity to all and rapid mobility to the deserving. This view, even at its most popular, never received universal assent; such distinguished scholars as George Counts and Merle Curti criticized it vigorously. Since the late 1960s, this idealistic and optimistic vision has been dethroned by a barrage of criticism, and a new construct has been raised up in its place. The new interpretation holds that public schooling has been a capitalist tool of indoctrination, that it has been purposefully used to stamp out cultural diversity, and that it has been slyly (or brutally) imposed on unwilling masses by arrogant reformers.

Whereas the old concept was oversimplified in its optimism, the new concept—which permeates the work of contemporary New Left historians of education—is oversimplified in its cynicism. The former too easily proclaimed the inevitable triumph of democracy, equality, and opportunity; the latter too glibly perceives oppression, indoctrination, and conspiratorial behavior.[1]

Both interpretations are highly ideological, the one intent on proving the success of American education, the other intent on proving its failure. And it is not surprising that researchers with ideological blinders tend to find what they seek, to confirm what they previously believed. Today there are few adherents to the success theory. For a variety of reasons—the despair that followed the political assassinations of the Kennedy brothers and Martin Luther King, the anger that flowed from urban riots and the Vietnam War, and the cynicism that followed the Watergate disclosures—the failure theory of the radical revisionists is strongly in the ascendancy.

None of us is entirely free from a value orientation, but I submit that a dispassionate effort to see the broad spectrum of minority group education in American history leads to the conclusion that neither of these interpretations is adequate, that both are cliches that mislead rather than enlighten. As general interpretations, they are both distortions of history.

It is not that the truth lies in the middle, somewhere between optimism and cynicism, but that it is too complicated to be explained by simplistic slogans. Not every minority group is or was similar; some did not want to be assimilated, but others did. Each group must be studied separately, within the context of its own interests and with due respect for the historical situation.

Consideration of the various minorities in American history suggests the broad diversity of problems and responses that has characterized educational efforts. There have been (and are) racial minorities, religious minorities, linguistic minorities, and national minorities. Each has had its own educational needs, which have been met or not been met in different ways; it is historically unjustified to assert that all have been crushed by their education into a homogeneous, deracinated mass.

When each group is looked at on its own terms, several important points emerge. First, most groups are not monolithic; it is fallacious to speak of the views of all Catholics or Poles or blacks or any other group. Second, the way a particular group was treated differed, sometimes dramatically, from one time period to another. Third, even within the same time period, a particular group often encountered inconsistent policies in different locales. Fourth, not all education of minorities took place in public schools; further, the decision to respect the right of minority groups to maintain private schools was itself public policy. Fifth, the current emphasis on oppression of minority groups is usually lacking crossnational perspective; Americanization through schooling, even at its most assimilationist, was more benign than the physical elimination of those who are different (which has occurred in some countries with minority populations).[2]

How Should a Nation School Its People?

For most of the United States' existence, there has been no national policy of education. Communities and states devised their own arrangements for schooling, free of any pressure from the federal government. While there were many variations, there were two basic approaches: One was the common school, open to all children in the community (though "all children" was often defined as "all white children") and supported at least in part by public funds; the other approach was state subsidy of private schools. Various communities experimented with the latter approach (sometimes in combination with common schools). Some states sponsored private academies; some cities granted public funds to private philanthropic societies to educate poor children. New York City, during the first quarter of the nineteenth century, directly funded nearly a dozen church schools.[3]

The New England common school, originally set up by the Protestant leadership for its own educational purposes in the seventeenth century, was secularized during the eighteenth century, and by 1826 was hailed as the quintessential American common school by Massachusetts school reformer James G. Carter. The common school was not merely a good and useful way of providing the elements of knowledge; in Carter's view, it was America's example "to the civilized world," a school supported by all members of the community for the instruction of "all classes of the community—the high, the low, the rich, and the poor."[4] And this common school, as Carter described it, was more than just a school. It was a form of egalitarian social action because it promised to eliminate factitious distinctions and to guard against the formation of an aristocratic class by democratizing knowledge. The idea that the common school was an agency of social and political reform was widely popularized in the late 1830s and 1840s by Horace Mann.

However, the common school itself was not the invention of zealous reformers like James Carter, Horace Mann, and Henry Barnard. Most communities outside the South moved spontaneously toward some variant of common schooling, not for ideological reasons but because it seemed to be the most practical and economical way of setting up schools. Horace Mann and his generation of reformers may have been the articulators, rather than the initiators, of a trend that was already well grounded. Interest in public schooling can be found in many cities and states in the first quarter of the nineteenth century; Albert Fishlow has documented a high level of school enrollment which predated the flowering of the common school movement. In Wisconsin, still a frontier region in the early nineteenth century, community-sponsored schools were organized which became the forerunners of a state system of common schools. As early as 1818, the Virginia state legislature, by a single vote, failed to establish a state school system. Even without the New Englanders' ideology, state-supported common schools were under consideration or in rudimentary form in many states.[5]

During the second half of the nineteenth century, public schools were firmly established throughout the country; the New England ideology, which asserted that the survival of the American republic was dependent on the common schools, became widespread. The ideology seems to have been more a selling point for public support than an article of faith, however. If Americans really believed that their nation's institutions and freedom depended on the strength of the common schools, they would have prohibited nonpublic education. But Americans apparently respected freedom of choice more than the common school ideology, for private schools abounded. Many minorities took full advantage of the freedom to maintain their own schools, and there were Catholic schools, Jewish schools, German schools, French schools, Polish schools, and numerous other schools run by benevolent agencies and small sects.

While there were bitter struggles over subsidizing Catholic schools, the right of nonpublic institutions to exist was never seriously in jeopardy until the 1920s. An initiative measure was narrowly adopted by the voters of Oregon in 1922 that would require all parents to send their children to public schools. The bill, the sponsors of which included the Ku Klux Klan, was a product of the superpatriotism of the postwar period. The purpose of the measure, aimed especially at immigrants and Catholics, was to forcibly Americanize all children by putting them into the same public classrooms. David Tyack has described how the Klan publicists employed a twisted version of the common school ideal to argue "that the public school should mix children of all the people—all ethnic groups, all economic classes—in order to produce social solidarity. . . ." Klan spokesmen did not recognize the irony of their advocacy of social, racial, and economic integration. The attorney for Oregon used traditional egalitarian rhetoric to maintain that "the great danger overshadowing all others which confront the American people is the danger of class hatred. History will demonstrate the fact that it is the rock upon which many a republic has been broken and I don't know any better way to fortify the next generation against that insidious poison than to require that the poor and the rich, the people of all classes and distinction, and of all different religious beliefs, shall meet in the common schools, which are the great American melting pot. . . ."[6]

Fortunately for the nation's nonpublic schools, the United

States Supreme Court in 1925 declared Oregon's law unconstitutional and held it to be an unreasonable interference with the liberty of parents to direct their children's education. The state does not have the power, wrote the court in *Pierce* v. *Society of Sisters*, "to standardize its children by forcing them to accept instruction from public teachers only."[7]

After World War I

The period during and after World War I was characterized by heightened patriotism, xenophobia, and fear of subversion by un-American elements. After years of partial restrictions, immigration was finally reduced to a trickle, and educators turned their attention to Americanizing the nation's large immigrant population. In many public schools, Americanization took the form of citizenship instruction and literacy classes for all ages; it invariably meant a strong emphasis on patriotic exercises and the teaching of idealized American history and hero tales.

There is little evidence that immigrants were spiritually destroyed by these kinds of Americanization efforts. Those historians who infer that they were apparently see the immigrants as easily intimidated. To be sure, Americanization efforts were frequently crude and chauvinistic, and many an immigrant child was made to feel ashamed of his family's speech and customs. But to understand this process solely as a one-way relationship between victim and oppressor is to miss an interesting aspect of American history. Many immigrants had a strong sense of the value of their own heritage. Jane Addams recalled lecturing Greek immigrants on the glories of America's past; when she was done, one of her audience remarked, quietly but assuredly, that his own Greek ancestors were better than her Anglo-Saxon forebears.[8] While imbibing the public and private Americanization programs, the immigrants participated in a vigorous cultural life which flourished among those groups that wished to preserve ties to their heritage and to their compatriots from the old country. Germans, Irish, Italians, Slavs, Jews, Finns, Hungarians, Greeks, Poles, and others had ethnic associations, their own press, and a broad range of communal activities.

A remarkable fact, which is rarely noted by historians bent on proving the cultural rapacity of Americanization programs, is that immigrant groups themselves were frequently sponsors of Americanization efforts. Timothy L. Smith has documented an immigrant thirst for education that is sharply at variance with the radical historians' image of coerced and brutalized immigrants. Smith points out that the night school movement was started by immigrant associations, then adopted by public school agencies. Early parochial schools "stressed the learning of English quite as much as the preservation of Old World culture." Far from fighting to withdraw to ethnic enclaves, immigrants "realized that to learn to speak and read English was to make their investment of time, expense, and emotion gilt-edged. The earliest volumes of virtually any Slavic newspaper published by religious or secular organizations in America carried lessons in English, announced the publication of simple dictionaries or grammars, and exhorted readers to learn the new tongue as a means of getting and holding a better job." But their self-Americanization was not necessarily at the expense of their cultural values; Slovaks, Greeks, Hungarians, Serbs, Roumanians, and Russians sent their children to public schools, but also "insisted upon frequent and sometimes daily attendance at the church for catechetical instruction, precisely as Orthodox Jewish parents sent their youngsters from public schools to the synagogue in the late afternoon or on Sunday."[9]

Similarly, Mordecai Soltes' study of the Yiddish press describes it as "an Americanizing agency." At the time of World War I, there were five Yiddish-language newspapers with a circulation of half a million readers. These newspapers consistently supported the public schools as well as supplementary religious instruction. The Yiddish press, wrote Soltes, "actively cooperates with the civic and patriotic purposes of the school." To assume today that immigrants who accepted and furthered Americanization had been indoctrinated is to credit the immigrants with little intelligence or self-interest. It is more likely that they took from Americanization programs what they wanted and ignored what they did not want.[10]

The ugly side of the postwar Americanization crusade stemmed from intense anti-German feelings, which caused most states to adopt laws restricting foreign language instruction in both public and private schools. Many states required English as the basic language of instruction (there were foreign language schools where English was rarely spoken). Some states, like Nebraska, went further; in 1919, it prohibited the teaching of any modern language in the first eight grades of all public and nonpublic schools. When a parochial school teacher in Nebraska was convicted of teaching German, he carried his appeal to the Supreme Court. In *Meyer* v. *Nebraska* (1923), without questioning the state's power to require English instruction, the Supreme Court overturned Nebraska's law and reaffirmed the teacher's right to teach and the parent's right to engage a teacher without state interference. Similarly, when Americanizers passed a law in Hawaii to force the use of English as the exclusive language of instruction in Japanese private schools, the Japanese went to court and won.[11]

What tends to be overlooked in focusing on the efforts to suppress diversity is the remarkable diversity that did exist in many public and private schools. Private foreign language schools were established by Germans, Poles, French Canadians, Czechs, Norwegians, Dutch, Lithuanians, Jews, Japanese, Koreans, and Chinese, among others. Bilingual programs could be found in many nineteenth-century public schools, particularly in the Midwest, where there were large islands of Germans, and in the Far West, where both California and New Mexico had Spanish bilingual schools. Baltimore and Indianapolis had German bilingual school systems during the nineteenth century, and Cincinnati had a strong German bilingual program from 1840 until 1917.[12]

Heinz Kloss, a German scholar of national minority laws, has found American policy towards its non-English-speaking minorities to be remarkably tolerant. Americans have the right to use their mother tongue at home and in public; the right to establish private cultural, economic, and social institutions in which their mother tongue is spoken; the right to cultivate their mother tongue in private schools—which are not only tolerated but granted a state charter of tax-exempt status. Kloss does not agree with those radical historians who argue that the homogeneity of the American people is the result of persistently coercive educational efforts to strip minorities of their differences. He holds that

. . . the non-English ethnic groups in the United States of America were Anglicized not because of nationality laws which were unfavorable towards their languages but in spite of nationality laws favorable to them. Not by legal provisions and measures of authorities, not by the state did the nationalities become assimilated, but by the absorbing power of the unusually highly developed American society. The nationalities could be given as many opportunities as possible to retain their identity, yet the achievements of the Anglo-American society and the possibilities for individual achievements and advancements which this society offered were so attractive that the descendants of the "aliens" sooner or later voluntarily integrated themselves into this society.[13]

In much the same vein, Joshua Fishman attributes the rapid absorption of non-English-speaking minorities to the openness of American society, not to educational coercion. Noting that American nationalism has always been "non-ethnic" in character, Fishman writes that "there was no apparent logical opposition between the ethnicity of incoming immigrants and the ideology of America. Individually and collectively immigrants could accept the latter without consciously denying the former. However, once they accepted the goals and values of Americans, the immigrants were already on the road to accepting their life-styles, their customs, and their language."[14]

Assimilation was facilitated, if Kloss and Fishman are correct, by *lack* of oppression. Specific instances of discrimination against foreign children have usually been traced to the attitudes of teachers, an Anglocentric curriculum, and a generalized American disparagement of old world cultures. More often than not, this discrimination was sporadic rather than systematic. Had it been more substantive and more threatening, it would probably have impeded assimilation by raising immigrant self-consciousness and resistance.

The Case of the American Indian

Where educational oppression of a minority was blatant and purposeful, as in the case of the American Indian, the policy was a disaster that neither educated nor assimilated. Through most of American history, missionaries and government officials took it as their duty to civilize and

Christianize the Indians; usually this meant that Indian culture and language and folkways had to be eliminated. While some were "weaned away from the blanket," as the saying went, most simply developed a strong internal resistance to the new behavior. Forced efforts at assimilation tended to produce precisely the opposite of what was intended.[15]

Christian missionaries tried to bring white civilization to the Indians throughout the colonial period. In the mission schools, Indian children were given English names, haircuts, and baths; they learned to sit at benches and to use knives and forks. Missionaries strove to teach them the work ethic; they wanted the Indians to take up farming and to appreciate the value of private property. Though there were some successes for the missionaries, they were time and again frustrated by the Indians' cultural stubbornness. To the chagrin of the missionaries, many Indians never ceased to doubt the superiority or at least equality of their own values.[16]

From 1778 until 1871, the federal government signed treaties with Indian tribes in which the Indians ceded land and the government pledged various public services, such as education and medical care. In 1802 and 1819, Congress appropriated funds to promote "civilization among the aborigines." This money, commonly called the "civilization fund," was apportioned among missionary organizations that cooperated with government agents. Government policy during the nineteenth century was to push the Indians farther and farther west, forcibly when necessary, to satisfy the expanding American nation's hunger for land. Education policy was an adjunct of the government's land policy: By civilizing the Indians and turning them from hunters to farmers, it was hoped that their need for land would diminish.

Most missionary schools favored bilingual instruction

using Indian languages, but after the Civil War the federal government began to insist on faster assimilation. A government report in 1868 urged the establishment of Indian schools with compulsory attendance where "their barbarous dialects would be blotted out and the English language substituted." After the treaty period ended in 1871, the government began to displace the bilingual mission schools with government schools where only English was spoken. The establishment of these schools also caused the elimination of many Indian-initiated schools. The Cherokees, in particular, had created their own school system, which sent graduates to eastern colleges; further, they published a bilingual newspaper using a Cherokee alphabet devised by a member of the tribe in 1821. Schools were also run by Choctaws, Creeks, and Seminoles.[17]

In the 1870s, with several Indian tribes making their last stand in ferocious battles, the federal government launched a new educational program designed to extirpate Indian culture. The model for the new system was the Carlisle Indian School in Pennsylvania, a boarding school founded in 1879:

The school was run in a rigid military fashion, with heavy emphasis on rustic vocational education. The goal was to provide a maximum of rapid coercive assimilation into white society. It was designed to separate a child from his reservation and family, strip him of his tribal lore and mores, force the complete abandonment of his native language, and prepare him in such a way that he would never return to his people. . . . The children were usually kept in boarding school for 8 years during which time they were not permitted to see their parents or relatives.[18]

The founder of Carlisle, General R.H. Pratt, had a slogan: "Get the Indian away from the reservation into civilization, and when you get him there, keep him." By 1886, no federal funds went to any school where Indian children were instructed in any language other than English."[19]

The federal government, relying on the Carlisle philosophy, provided both day schools and boarding schools, emphasizing the latter. It should be noted, however, that many Indian children were not in federal schools but in state-run public schools and in mission schools. In the early 1920s, before there had been any serious criticism of the Carlisle approach, there were as many Indian children in public schools as in federal schools.

Not until 1926 did government officials begin to question the effectiveness of their Indian education policies. For one thing, the 1920 census revealed that Indian illiteracy was a shocking 36 percent, as compared to 6 percent for the population as a whole. The secretary of the interior commissioned a study of the government's Indian policies by the Institute for Governmental Research (later called the Brookings Institution). This study, called the Meriam report for its director, Lewis Meriam, had a dramatic effect on the assumptions that undergirded government policy.

Published in 1928, the Meriam report was a sharp repudiation of the policies of the previous half century. It urged the government to renounce coercive assimilation and, in its stead, to "respect the rights of the Indian . . . as a human being living in a free country," to recognize "the good in the economic and social life of the Indians in their religion and ethics," and to seek "to develop it and build on it rather than to crush out all that is Indian." The report criticized the emphasis on boarding schools, where nearly 40 percent of Indian children were enrolled. Many of these schools were overcrowded, poorly maintained, and "grossly inadequate." But the worst indictment was that they separated the Indian child from his family and community, "where he belongs."[20]

The Meriam report embodied pluralistic ideas whose time had come; its recommendations became guideposts during the New Deal era under the leadership of John Collier, Commissioner of Indian Affairs from 1933 until 1945. Congress passed an act in 1934 to strengthen tribal self-government, and Collier launched a program of cultural freedom for the Indians. For the first time, the Bureau of Indian Affairs repudiated coercive assimilationism and emphasized bilingualism, native teachers, adult education, and preservation of the Indians' cultural heritage. In 1933, the federal schools were still overwhelmingly boarding schools; by 1943, most federal schools had become day schools.

During most of Collier's tenure, his innovative approaches were under attack by Congress, which grew increasingly suspicious of Collier's emphasis on Indian culture and de-emphasis of assimilation. With a resurgence of superpatriotism in the 1950s, congressional pressure finally forced a reversal of federal policy and a return to the boarding school approach. The Commissioner of Indian Affairs appointed in 1950 to revive this policy was Dillon S. Myer, who had supervised the relocation of thousands of Japanese-Americans during World War II.

Coercive assimilation was again repudiated in the 1960s, at first tentatively during the Kennedy years, then decisively during the Johnson administration. Both the Economic Opportunity Act of 1964 and the Elementary and Secondary Education Act of 1965 gave impetus to policies based on respect for the rights of Indian parents and Indian communities; furthermore, they set into motion political forces within the Indian communities that would make any future reversion extremely improbable. The implicit trends received official recognition by President Johnson in 1968, when he urged that the highest priority be given to improving Indian education and transferring the control of Indian schools to Indians.[21]

The story of Indian education in the United States illustrates the variability of the historical experience—even when it is that of a clearly oppressed group. It is a history that most nearly fits the radical concept of education as a tool of coercion and imposition. Yet to read it only from that perspective would be to miss a number of intriguing divergences. The very substantial shift to pluralistic policies in the late 1920s and then again in the 1960s underlines the struggle between opposing philosophies and the differentness of time periods. The existence of a Cherokee school system in the nineteenth century suggests that Indians themselves were not necessarily hostile to schooling—as the radical analysis would have it—but to cultural suppression. It further suggests that a policy of cultural respect, in this as in other instances, might have stimulated Indian educational efforts and, ultimately, Indian assimilation on terms set by Indians.

Black Education

The case of black educational history, like that of other minority groups, also defies the simplistic labels of ideologists, but for different reasons. Whereas government policy attempted to force the assimilation and de-ethnicization of the Indians, it explicitly sought to prevent the assimilation of blacks. Whereas the cultural aspirations of European immigrant groups were at least tolerated and frequently encouraged, those of blacks were ignored, or worse, mocked. The racist doctrine of white supremacy was used to justify social and economic repression of blacks in both the North and the South.

Here, too, broad generalizations tend to oversimplify and distort a complicated picture. Those radical historians who speak assuredly of education as a tool of oppression fail to explain the slaveholders' deadly fear of education.

"Believing that slaves could not be enlightened without developing in them a longing for liberty," the slave states one after another adopted laws prohibiting the education of slaves. Some states, viewing ignorance as the best social control, expelled free Negroes because they might have access to abolitionist literature and spread the contagion of insurrection to illiterate blacks. To salve their Christian consciences, some planters encouraged verbal religious instruction for their slaves.[22]

To portray blacks solely as victims locked into illiteracy is to overlook the tenacious struggle of countless individual blacks to obtain an education even within the slave system. Some slaves developed personal relationships with their masters and, as house servants, acquired literacy; some plantations, for their own internal purposes, trained slaves as artisans, carpenters, blacksmiths, weavers, and tailors. Both Woodson and Bullock have found numerous accounts of slaves whose zeal for learning could not be denied, no matter how many laws were passed.[23]

Another source of education in the antebellum South was mission schools. They were available to only a few blacks, principally those who were favored household servants and those who were free. (The number of free blacks in the South was not insignificant: Bullock holds that it grew from 32,523 in 1790 to 258,346 in 1860.) Despite the state laws, courageous blacks and whites maintained clandestine schools for blacks.[24]

These educational opportunities, limited though they were, provided what Bullock has called "a hidden passage" within the institution of slavery—one which permitted the development of a potential middle class. Far from having schooling imposed on them by arrogant reformers, blacks resorted to extraordinary means to obtain an education that state law denied them. Indeed, some former slaves who had by stealth and iron-willed persistence acquired literacy while in bondage became highly effective spokesmen for the abolitionist movement in the North.

Blacks in the antebellum North, usually a small minority, were generally either confined to segregated schools or excluded from public schools altogether. Many colored schools had been opened by philanthropists at a time when the only free schools were pauper schools. Consequently, when common schools were introduced, the practice of racial segregation was already commonplace in many cities. New Jersey was unusual in that it never practiced legal segregation. Most northern and western states, for varying periods and in various communities, maintained racially segregated schools. In at least two instances (Boston and Hartford), separate schools were instituted at the request of the black population,[25] largely because of the desire to protect black children from white hostility.

After the Civil War, the Freedmen's Bureau was responsible for providing southern blacks with education. A network of schools run by benevolent societies, missionaries, and the Freedmen's Bureau sprang into existence, staffed mostly by northern teachers, many of them trained in New England colleges and fired with Christian zeal. The curricula in the mission schools, which reflected the New England bias of their teachers, stressed liberal arts rather than practical education. Many of them taught classical languages, which southern whites thought absurd. Senator John C. Calhoun of South Carolina had once said that he would be willing to believe in the possibility of black equality if ever he met a black who could parse a Latin verb or write the Greek alphabet. According to Horace Mann Bond, this oft-quoted remark was frequently cited in the autobiographical accounts of college-educated blacks of the first free generation. In Bond's view, the New Englanders' faith in liberal education was eventually justified: "Based on the academic successes of first, second, and even third generation descendants of the students of the early mission schools, available evidence suggests that these institutions provided for Southern Negroes some of the most effective educational institutions the world has ever known."[26]

Southerners complained that the Yankee schoolteachers imposed their ideals and aspirations on their Negro students, but there is abundant evidence that the newly freed blacks eagerly sought the formal schooling so long denied them. Furthermore, those blacks who were delegates to state constitutional conventions in the South took a positive attitude towards the spread of public schooling. Echoing the sentiments of common school reformers of an earlier generation, black representatives argued for compulsory schooling and for schools that would be open to all, without regard to race. Despite enormous political and financial obstacles, public school systems began to operate during Reconstruction and Negroes responded enthusiastically.[27]

The end of Reconstruction and the abandonment of southern blacks by the federal government coincided with the onset of a series of civil rights reversals in the Supreme Court, the effect of which was to erode the Negro's constitutional protection and to sanction the system of segregation that the South fashioned to supplant slavery. The political enfeeblement of the black population, achieved by intimidation after Reconstruction, was written into law across the South in the two decades after 1890; loss of the ballot through such devices as poll taxes and literacy tests assured the Negro's political impotence. A disenfranchised people could have no influence in the shaping of educational policy, no voice when school funds were unfairly apportioned. It was a classically vicious circle: Illiteracy was the justification given for excluding blacks from the polls (though equally illiterate whites could vote by grace of grandfather clauses); their exclusion left them powerless to contest for educational facilities with which to remedy their illiteracy.

Just as General Pratt's Carlisle Indian School became the model for Indian education, General S.C. Armstrong's Hampton Normal and Agricultural Institute became the southern model for Negro education (Pratt was following the Hampton example when he established Carlisle). Founded in 1868, Hampton embodied Armstrong's views about the special educational needs of the Negro race; Armstrong championed industrial education, not only to make the black an efficient worker but to improve his moral character. His most influential disciple was Booker T. Washington, who opened Tuskegee Institute in 1881; as an educator, Washington came to symbolize the idea that blacks required a special education, one that equipped them to adjust to their place in a caste system. The Hampton-Tuskegee idea was applauded by the white South as an appropriate education for blacks; it quickly found favor with influential white philanthropists, who seized on the chance to aid black education without offending white southern sensibilities. Critics of this emphasis on industrial education included not only W.E.B. Dubois but also W.T. Harris, the United States Commissioner of Education, who argued forcefully (but unsuccessfully) on behalf of liberal education for blacks.[28]

What guaranteed the predominance of the Hampton-Tuskegee model was the political impotence of blacks. As late as 1889, according to Bullock, there was little difference between white and black schools in the apportionment of funds, the length of the school term, or teachers' salaries; but with the legal disenfranchisement of blacks in the 1890s, discrimination grew. The industrial education idea provided a convenient rationale for spending less on black schools and teachers, since industrial education was supposedly simpler and cheaper than the traditional schooling given to whites. But historians today do not know with any certainty to what extent black schools in the South adopted, rejected, or combined industrial and academic education. What is needed is a painstaking investigation of individual schools, which is unlikely to occur so long as historians consider the question of black educational history to be a settled one.

It is rare to discover an exploration of black successes such as Horace Mann Bond's *Black American Scholars,* a study of the family background and schooling of black recipients of the doctoral degree in the period 1957–62.[29] Bond identifies certain remarkable black families whose educational aspirations and achievements have been repeated across several generations. He locates black high schools that produced unusual numbers of scholars. Foremost among these was the M. Street School (later called the Paul Laurence Dunbar High School) in Washington, D.C. Founded in 1870, the school consistently symbolized academic excellence. Its teachers were graduates of the nation's best colleges, its curriculum was college preparatory, its standards were high, and its graduates went to top colleges. Dunbar graduates received more doctorates than those of any other black high school in the period studied by Bond. Bond singled out other urban schools from which doctoral recipients had graduated, like the Frederick Douglass High School in Baltimore and the McDonough 25 High School in New Orleans. Certain black schools in small towns produced unusual numbers of doctorates in relation to their size. Some of these schools were former mission schools with high academic standards; others were located in towns where there were one or more black families with strong educational backgrounds or where there was even a single black educator who inspired young people to go to college. There was no evident explanation for the Wayne County

Training School in Jessup, Georgia, which had the highest ratio of doctorates to graduates of any black school in the country. Three of its graduates received doctorates between 1957 and 1962, though its typical graduating class was only fourteen. The point about these black schools in the South is not that they were good, but that we know so little about them; and the more we are tied to the familiar ideological labels applied to black educational history, the less we are inclined to try to reconstruct what was actually happening in individual schools.

The number of black doctorate holders was small, and the barriers blocking their academic paths were high. Their success is a tribute to them, not to the racist system that they overcame. Yet, it is noteworthy that the system made their success extremely difficult but not impossible. Blacks were more often oppressed by the education that they did not receive than by the education that they did receive.

Another fresh approach to black educational history is embodied in Vincent P. Franklin's *The Education of Black Philadelphia: The Social and Educational History of a Minority Community, 1900–1950.* Franklin critically examines the education of blacks in Philadelphia within a broad social, economic, and political context. A lesser historian would have been content merely to document white racism in school policies. Franklin, however, analyzes the energetic response of black Philadelphians to the school system, and in particular, their struggle to change repugnant policies. His illustration of indigenous community education programs, both formal and informal, evokes a sense of a community that was determined to maintain its dignity and its cultural heritage.

Black Education Since 1954

In the years since state-enforced school segregation was ruled unconstitutional, the education of blacks has been as varied from one school to the next and from one city to the next as it is for other groups. Most whites and blacks are uncertain about the best education for blacks, surely as uncertain as they are about the best education for whites. At different times and in different communities, some have advocated the pursuit of excellence in black education, which others have attacked as elitism; some have advocated egalitarian educational policies, which others have attacked as catering to the lowest common denominator; some have advocated racial integration as a first principle, which others have attacked as mindless assimilationism; some have advocated black control of black schools, which others have attacked as naive separatism. A large part of the uncertainty about the right direction for the education of blacks is the confusion of educational and social issues. It is not clear today whether the major problem is how to raise the educational level of the black population or how to bring about full racial integration. At the time of the *Brown* decision, racial integration appeared to be synonymous with quality education—that to achieve one was to achieve the other. There is mounting evidence that this is not necessarily so, but there remain many who believe that racial integration is an end in itself, not a means.

To the extent that a governmental policy has developed towards black education in the years since 1954, it embodies the view of the integration movement that all-black schools are inherently inferior. This derives from the statement in *Brown* that "separate educational facilities are inherently unequal." At first it seemed that separate educational facilities were unequal because the state had set them aside for blacks and compelled blacks to attend them; it now seems that such facilities are unequal because only blacks attend them.

The shift in meaning is subtle but significant, for it suggests that stigma is attached not just to the illegal act of segregation but to the concentration of blacks themselves. "Real" integration is taken to mean that no school has a black majority. To effect this, the courts have been asked and have ordered the dispersion of black pupils throughout school districts, or in some instances across traditional district lines. If such a policy emanated from the government, it might appear to be a policy of coerced homogenization since one of its purposes is to break up black concentrations.

This trend toward dispersion of blacks as an educational and social strategy is a development of the last decade, and it is unique in the history of minority group education. Other groups have asked to be let alone, either in public or in private schools; or to have governmental support for the promotion of their own cultures; or to be given the same treatment as other groups and access to the same facilities. At times, blacks have asked for some or all of these approaches. Only in the past decade have black organizations asked, as a matter of right, that the children of their racial group be dispersed among the majority population.

Some Conclusions

This brief attempt at synthesizing the experiences of a broad variety of minority groups has necessarily condensed the lives and experiences of millions of diverse people into a short essay. To try to do so in a sense violates the point

I have been stressing about the complexity of each group's experience. What I have hoped to do is to rescue the topic from an ideological bog and to argue for investigations that go beyond the radical homilies of the late 1960s. Some of the conclusions I draw are as follows: In a free society with a free press, education liberates more often than it oppresses; in such a society, ignorance and illiteracy are the most dangerous instruments of social control; advocates of schooling had mixed motives, which were more good than bad; every individual and every group should have the freedom to decide whether to assimilate into the general population; political powerlessness is a precondition to educational discrimination; different members of different groups have different educational goals at different times and in different places. In historiographical terms, this essay is a plea for less assertion and more documentation, less ideological posturing and more mining of source materials.

Until late in the nineteenth century, this nation was considered by its majority to be a white Protestant country; at some time near the turn of the century, it became a white Christian country; after World War II, it was a white man's country. During the past several years it has become a multiethnic, multiracial country intensely aware of differences of every kind, a country in which almost everyone thinks of himself or herself as a member of a minority group. Having once been a society in which differences were shunned, accents studiously unlearned, and foreignness somewhat suspect, the United States has become a nation where people are seeking out their long-forgotten roots, learning ancestral languages, celebrating the traditions that their fathers (and mothers) rejected.

This very celebration of our differences may signal the relative unimportance of those differences. Joshua Fishman, referring to language groups, wrote that ethnic group schools teach about ethnicity, whereas authentic ethnicity consists of living ethnically: "In the school, ethnicity became self-conscious. It was something to be 'studied,' 'valued,' 'appreciated,' and 'believed in.' It became a 'cause.' As it was raised to the level of ideology, belief system, national symbolism, or selective sentimentality it also ceased being ethnic in the original and authentic sense." Thus, Italians and Poles and Irishmen and Jews can march in each others' parades; their daughters and sons can and do intermarry without causing any family rupture. Relations between blacks and whites have not reached that point, though interracial contacts at all levels have increased steadily over the past generation.[30]

But what do we want? Do we want cultures that differ significantly from each other, or do we want cultures that differ in name and history only? Do we want schooling that accentuates awareness of cultural differences, or do we want schooling that minimizes them? Do we want ethnicity to persist, or do we want it to slip away unobtrusively? It is this very ambivalence about the value of ethnicity and pluralism that prevents our educational patterns from having a single guiding principle.

To study the history of the education of minority groups is to become aware of the inappropriateness of applying sweeping ideological labels to the diverse experiences of all minorities. What is needed from historians is more nuance and more discernment, not less. The task for historians of education today is to set aside tendentious generalizations and to search for a sense of once-living people with once-vital aspirations, for the culture within which they lived, and for the processes by which they were educated.

15

Integration, Segregation, Pluralism

(1976)

IN 1954, when the Supreme Court banned state-imposed school segregation, almost two dozen states had laws that regulated citizens on the basis of their race. There were laws to prevent interracial marriage, laws requiring racially separate schools, and laws to limit access to public facilities. In most southern states, wherever interracial contact might occur, there was a law to prevent or regulate it. This legal superstructure was purposeful, not haphazard. It reinforced a caste system with a code of behavior based on white supremacy. The code's primary intent was to contain and control black people. Deviant whites could sample black life at no risk other than ostracism by their own kind; blacks who stepped outside the bounds ran afoul of the law, the police, and the courts.

The unwritten rules of caste required black deference.

Law or no law, a black entered a white person's home through the back door. Law or no law, black people in the deep South stepped off the sidewalk onto the street when passing a white person. In department stores, blacks could sweep the floor but not sell merchandise; in beauty shops, they could shampoo white women's hair, but not set it in curlers. If a black murdered another black in a Saturday night brawl, the police might look the other way; a black who murdered or assaulted a white sometimes did not survive the back room of the police station.

The *Brown* v. *Board of Education* decision, more than any other single event, destroyed the foundation of this racial caste system. Not only did it inspire the civil rights movement, which educated blacks about their rights and political power, but it began the process of dismantling institutional segregation. After *Brown,* the Constitution, the law, and the courts could no longer be used to prop up the caste system. However haltingly and grudgingly this elementary principle was accepted in formerly segregated states, there is no longer any doubt that the power of the state may not be employed to discriminate against people on the basis of their color.

While it is fashionable in some quarters to scoff at the *Brown* decision and to say that it changed very little, anyone who knew the South before 1954 realizes that *Brown* launched a social revolution. At that time, few blacks voted and those who did were offered a choice among white racist candidates. Today, blacks vote and wield political power; this fact has transformed the nature of southern politics and permitted the victory of moderate and liberal candidates. It is no longer remarkable in the South to see blacks and whites patronizing the same restaurants, the same cinemas, the same shops. Deference is dead, and little is left of the caste system other than the nostalgia of unreconstructed white racists.

Still, there is concern today that a resegregation phenomenon is under way, not only in the South, but in
almost every major American metropolitan area; that we
are moving inexorably toward de facto apartheid, as the
nation's central cities become blacker and the white suburbs
grow larger. Since the 1950s, vast numbers of southern
blacks have moved to the cities and whites have moved
out. All of America's largest cities have substantial black
minorities. Some, like Atlanta, Washington, D.C., Newark,
Gary, and Detroit, have black majorities. Others, like
Baltimore, St. Louis, Cleveland, New Orleans, Memphis,
and Birmingham, are close to 50 percent black. The
suburbs that ring these cities are generally more than 90
percent white. As a result of these population trends,
sixteen of our twenty largest cities in 1976 had a minority
of whites in their public schools.

Why are whites leaving the cities? Some have suggested
that nothing more is involved than white racism, fear of
living in close proximity to blacks. Yet while racism may
be one reason for white flight, it is not the only reason.
Suburbanization started long before blacks arrived in the
cities in great numbers and occurs in cities where there are
relatively few blacks. Some whites move to the suburbs
because it represents a step up in personal status; some
prefer clean air, safe streets, and small-town life. These
same motives no doubt account for the suburban exodus
of middle-class blacks as well.

Alongside the familiar black city–white suburb dichot-
omy, other facts must also be considered. For one thing, 4
million blacks (17 percent of the black population) now
live in the suburbs, an increase of 19.5 percent in the past
five years alone. The suburbs *are* permeable. Second, the
black migration from the South to the urban North has
not only stopped, but has reversed itself; according to the
Census Bureau, blacks have been leaving the North and
moving into the West and South.

These are the demographic facts, but how they are interpreted depends on the perspective of the interpreter. The integrationist sees the black concentration in the cities as the onset of a new and insidious form of racial segregation. The cultural pluralist sees the great black urban migration in the same light as previous migrations, and recalls the dire predictions that accompanied the arrival of the Irish, the Jews, and the Italians.

Integration and pluralism are both versions of assimilation, and it is worth noting that in a scant quarter-century the central issue of race has shifted from whether to segregate to whether and how to assimilate. In the early 1950s, the combined power of law and tradition limited black assimilation to those few light-skinned Negroes who "passed" surreptitiously into the white majority. This notion of passing was rather like escaping from blackness, and it fitted in appropriately with the racist belief that blackness was a curse, not a culture.

Intimations of this disparagement of black culture come through in considering both pluralism and integration. Cultural pluralism has been discussed for most of this century, but usually in relation to white ethnic and religious groups that had a distinct cultural heritage and wanted to preserve it; the unwritten assumption seemed to be either that blacks did not have a culture worth preserving or that blacks themselves wanted to flee their racial identity. Similarly, the rhetoric of integration seemed to assume that blacks wanted to merge into the white majority and lose their racial identity. It has been said, for example, that the racial problems of America will lessen as racial intermarriages increase, which is an unsubtle way of suggesting that blacks should lose their blackness and be absorbed by the white majority.

In this country of diverse groups, problems of assimilation underlie many social and political controversies. How should society balance the needs of the common culture against the needs of particular groups? What does American nationality require of Americans? Should the requirements of nationality cancel out other loyalties in pursuit of a homogeneous citizenry? Should government encourage cultural diversity? Should government have a hands-off policy where cultural preferences are involved? Is it good or bad to have neighborhoods and schools that are distinctly Italian or Jewish or black or Oriental? Is it possible to have an American community that is both integrated and pluralistic?

These questions have been agitated for the entire 200 years of our nationhood, but only in recent years have they fully pertained to the position of blacks. Racial segregation was, in fact, the ultimate form of state-mandated nonassimilation. Segregation set blacks apart and made them easier to exploit. Every black who grew up under legalized segregation retains vivid memories of unfair treatment, of neighborhoods with unpaved streets, of schools with broken windows and leaky roofs, of calculated and systematic disadvantage.

Since state-imposed segregation is unconstitutional, the issue today is how and on whose terms blacks should be assimilated into American society. Some Americans believe that any black concentration in schools or neighborhoods suggests segregation and must be eliminated. The heritage of segregation has implanted the assumption that every all-black school is inferior and every black neighborhood is a slum. There are black nationalists who see any kind of assimilation as a threat to black cultural aspirations, but their numbers are few. And there are cultural pluralists who sense that their perspective has been lost in the polarized verbal duels between integrationists and separatists.

These tensions have historically been played out in educational policy. This has happened for two reasons:

first, because of the formative impact that is generally attributed to schooling as it pertains to one's attitudes, values, skills, and opportunities; and second, because public schools are nearly universal in their reach. The great breach of state segregation came through the public schools, and, just as characteristically, the Supreme Court's desegregation decisions have provided virtually the only public forum for consideration of assimilation policy.

It was the Supreme Court that made segregation illegal, and it is the Court that now mediates among the competing demands of integration and pluralism. Proceeding a step at a time, each decision following logically on the previous one, the Court has moved toward an increasingly detailed definition of how blacks are to be assimilated through the public schools. At the time of *Brown,* the Court evidently believed that striking down segregation laws would suffice to bring about desegregation. For a dozen years, lower courts in the South understood the *Brown* decision to mean that the Constitution did not require integration, but merely forbade discrimination.

However, in the decade after 1954, the southern states were so obstinate and devious in their refusal to dismantle dual school systems that the Supreme Court was forced to take a more activist role in bringing about actual desegregation. Freedom-of-choice plans that did not produce measurable desegregation were struck down by the Court in 1968 in the landmark *Green* v. *County School Board* case. New Kent County, Virginia, had two schools, one white and one black, and no residential segregation. Under its freedom-of-choice plan, 15 percent of the blacks attended the formerly white school, but no whites chose to go to the black school. The Supreme Court required the local school board to develop a plan that "promises realistically to work now," one that would produce "a system without a 'white' school and a 'Negro' school, but just schools."

213

It was relatively simple in rural New Kent County to decree the elimination of racially identifiable schools. The issue became more complex in Charlotte-Mecklenburg, North Carolina, another formerly de jure segregated system. Charlotte-Mecklenburg did have residential segregation, and a neighborhood school policy produced racially identifiable schools. But, following the principle in *Green* that the schools had to produce a remedy that "works now," in 1971 the Court went further in *Swann* v. *Charlotte-Mecklenburg,* directing district judges and school authorities to "make every effort to achieve the greatest possible degree of actual desegregation." This was measured in terms of how many blacks and whites were in the same schools. The requirement had changed from desegregation, which might leave many one-race schools intact, to a conscious policy of integration, which aims to eliminate one-race schools altogether. Accordingly, "racially neutral" assignments by neighborhood were unacceptable if they left many one-race schools. So the Court told local officials to do whatever was necessary—including the use of racial quotas, the gerrymandering of districts, and the creation of noncontiguous attendance zones—in order to redistribute white and black pupil populations into the same schools.

Swann was the first decision in which the Supreme Court declared that the Constitution required racial dispersion in order to achieve "the greatest possible degree of actual desegregation." This formulation was derived from the philosophy of the melting pot—of public schools that bring every element of the community together and reconcile their differences into a harmonious whole. This shift grew out of the original ambivalence in the *Brown* decision. On the one hand, *Brown* made it unconstitutional for the state to use racial classifications, except for remedial purposes. But on the other, *Brown* held that separate schools are inherently unequal. One approach implied a colorblind principle in the assignment of children to school, while the other implied that children must be assigned by race in order to achieve integration. In the *Swann* decision, the Supreme Court seemed to accept the idea that a racially identifiable school is unconstitutional because the function of the public schools requires that all groups are taught together. This interpretation, which interweaves a theory of society and a theory of education, came to fruition in the *Swann* decision.

After *Swann*, it would be increasingly difficult to make a valid distinction between de jure and de facto segregation. Though the Court held that not every school in every community would be expected to reflect the racial composition of the school system as a whole, it made it plain that school authorities would have the burden of justifying the existence of any one-race schools.

There was no reason why the logic of *Swann* should be limited to formerly de jure segregated school systems, and the *Keyes* v. *Denver School District No. 1* decision in 1973 proved that it would not be. In that decision the Supreme Court took the principles that had accumulated with reference to southern schools and applied them in Denver, which had never operated legally segregated schools. The Denver school board was found to have pursued certain policies, such as zoning, site selection, staff assignment, and neighborhood schools, that had segregated 38 percent of the black school population in identifiably black schools. Having determined that segregation existed "in a substantial portion of the district," the Court declared that Denver was unconstitutionally operating a dual system of de jure segregated schools. Neither a neighborhood school policy nor the plea that the illegal actions had occurred before 1954 was an adequate defense to the charges.

After *Keyes*, civil rights lawyers understood that diligent research was likely to produce the evidence to prove that a seemingly de facto segregated school system was actually an unconstitutional de jure segregated system. A permissive transfer policy was one such piece of evidence, for it was often used by white students to transfer out of schools that were growing blacker. Assignment of minority teachers to minority schools was another indication of a de jure policy, as was a conscious decision to build a school in a minority neighborhood. In one northern city after another, civil rights lawyers have found such evidence. In Pontiac, Michigan, school officials and real estate agents worked together to maintain racially homogeneous neighborhoods and schools; in Detroit, school attendance zones were manipulated to keep black and white students in different schools; in Boston, predominantly white schools were overcrowded while predominantly black schools had seats available.

But when such evidence has been found, it is not always certain that the policymakers intended to bring about racial segregation. In some instances, educationally valid assumptions had led to policies that were segregatory. Judges have condemned school authorities for building small schools; the district judge in Detroit held that a school for 300 to 400 pupils "negates opportunities to integrate, 'contains' the black population and perpetuates and compounds school segregation." But educators for at least the past decade have been saying that small schools are educationally preferable to large and impersonal schools. Another reason for small, neighborhood-based schools is to maximize parent and community involvement in the schools, a goal that most educators today believe is an essential part of the educational process. Citywide integration must be planned, administered, and enforced centrally, not locally. Parental involvement, moreover, becomes more difficult when children attend school in distant neighborhoods.

Many black educators believe that it is educationally

desirable to assign black teachers to predominantly black schools. But when judges and officials at the Department of Health, Education and Welfare's Office of Civil Rights look at faculty assignments for evidence of segregation, they expect that a properly integrated system will have distributed black teachers and administrators evenly throughout the schools. A western city recruited black teachers who had been specially trained to teach in inner-city schools and promised them inner-city assignments; yet HEW officials insisted that the black teachers had to be assigned evenly throughout the system in the interests of better staff integration. Similarly, a Boston judge, Arthur Garrity, rejected the argument that black teachers and black parents had requested assignment of minority staff to minority schools; the practice was unconstitutional, "whatever may be the desires of black teachers or parents."

What has become incredibly vague in the past several years is the precise meaning of "segregation," "desegregation," and "integration." In 1954, a segregated school system was one in which the state required or permitted separation of pupils on the basis of race. Black children were bused past white schools to attend distant black schools, and whites were similarly bused to white schools. Desegregation in 1954 appeared to mean that schools had to be color-blind and to accept whoever lived nearby or wanted to attend, regardless of their race or color.

But since the *Swann* decision, the Supreme Court has specifically rejected a color-blind policy or any other policy that is apparently racially neutral, if such policies leave large numbers of racially identifiable schools intact. Given this standard, district courts have understood a segregated school to be one that is not racially balanced in relation to the entire district.

Thus, in Boston, Judge Garrity held that any school that deviated by more than 10 percent from the citywide white–black pupil ratio of 61–32 percent was a segregated school. He found: "At least 80 percent of Boston's schools are segregated in the sense that their racial compositions are sharply out of line with the racial composition of the Boston public school system as a whole." A segregated school, under this definition, included a school that was 60 percent black and 40 percent white; technically, it would include even a school that was 50–50.

The logic of the racial balance definition reached the heights of absurdity in Detroit. Its schools in 1976 were 71 percent black. After the Supreme Court overruled a district court's merger of Detroit with nearby suburban school systems (*Milliken* v. *Bradley*), the problem of desegregating Detroit by itself was returned to a lower court. The NAACP proposed that every school have approximately 71 percent black children, and that any school varying by more than 15 percent would be considered segregated. The district judge turned down this plan as "rigid and inflexible . . . treating [pupils] as pigmented pawns to be shuffled about and counted solely to achieve an abstraction called 'racial mix.' " Under the plaintiffs' plan, he pointed out, a school that was 55 percent black would be considered a "racially identifiable white" school, while a school that was 85 percent black would be desegregated.

The states of Massachusetts and New York have defined a school that is composed of more than 50 percent minority pupils as a "racially imbalanced" school. State officials have taken the position that a racially imbalanced school is incapable of providing equal educational opportunity. In policy terms, this means that any school that is more than 50 percent black and/or Hispanic is an inferior school. From this perspective, real integration requires both racial balance and a white majority. Courts can order racial balance, but few major cities still have a white pupil majority.

As the black pupil population has grown in the cities, civil rights groups have urged that a segregated school is one where the racial balance varies sharply from the racial composition of the metropolitan area as a whole. When the Supreme Court refused to merge Detroit with its surrounding suburbs, it was because there had been no evidence that the suburban districts had practiced racially exclusionary policies. Civil rights lawyers believe they will be able to document segregatory practices on both sides of the city–suburban lines and will sooner or later win metropolitanwide integration orders in northern cities. This would involve cross-district exchanges of black and white pupils and would make it possible to eliminate predominantly black schools.

The policy that the civil rights lawyers seek, and one that the reasoning of recent Supreme Court decisions appears to support, is a policy of governmentally mandated racial dispersion. During the past several years, and especially since the *Swann* decision, the Supreme Court appears to have declared that the law of the land supports the ideals of the melting pot.

The melting pot has been a strong and recurrent ideal in American history. It sets forth the hope that America would take the people of all nations and races and blend them together into a new and harmonious race. This new race of people would shed their ancient allegiances, rivalries, languages, and customs. "The melting and intermixture" of diverse nations, tribes, and races, in Ralph Waldo Emerson's words, would produce "a new race, a new religion, a new state, a new literature." According to Frederick Jackson Turner, it offered "the possibility of a newer and richer civilization . . . a new product, which held the promise of world brotherhood."

The melting-pot theory has always had its critics. In recent years, they have been divided between those who contend that it never worked and those who fear that it worked all too well. The former maintain that social planners should acknowledge the persistence and vitality of ethnicity in American life; the latter hold that the homogenization of American society has bred rootlessness, culturelessness, and anomie. Nearly all the critics agree that public policy should encourage cultural diversity.

The principle of cultural pluralism is as thoroughly American as the melting-pot idea. What pluralism means in practice is that diverse groups have the right to be left alone, so long as their members fulfill the basic obligations of citizenship. The state, in other words, cannot compel people to "melt," either culturally or racially. John Dewey described the American concept of pluralism as "a complete separation of nationality from citizenship. Not only have we separated language, cultural traditions, all that is called a race, from the state—that is, from problems of political organization and power. To us language, literature, creed, group ways, national culture, are social rather than political, human rather than national, interests."

How do these basic principles—the melting pot and cultural pluralism—apply to the issue of school integration? They are at the heart of the issue, but they mean different things to different people.

To those who support a policy of racial dispersion, the alternatives available are either integration or segregation; anything in between is construed as a rationale for continuing the caste system. "The newly excited self-consciousness of 'white ethnics' is nothing more than a fresh awareness of what the institutions and customs of American society, including the segregated schools, have taught them from childhood, namely, that the United States of America is a white man's country," wrote a white NAACP official recently. "Desegregation is not the answer. It merely brings the races together; it does not supply the cement for a single society." The goal is "a pluralistic unitary society." From this perspective, the ideal school system would be one in which blacks and whites were evenly dispersed throughout a large metropolitan area so that no school could be stigmatized as a one-race school. This was the Supreme Court's assumption in the *Swann* decision, and it is the principle that the NAACP hopes to establish eventually in northern cities as well. The underlying social ideal is the melting-pot theory, the belief that in a truly free and nondiscriminatory society people would tend to settle in racially and ethnically mixed neighborhoods. Wherever they have not, runs the argument, it is only because of the workings of overt or covert patterns of discrimination, which government must remedy.

The pluralist response is that people must be permitted to cluster in whatever way they choose, even if it results in some one-race schools. So long as distinct neighborhoods and racially identifiable schools are not the consequence of any state action, argues the pluralist, then neither the schools nor the neighborhoods should be considered segregated in a legal sense. It is government's role to assure equal access to housing and schools and to remedy particular instances of discrimination, but it is not government's role to require specific percentages of racial mixing in neighborhoods or schools.

Each side believes the other to be racist, and both are at least partly right. The pluralist argument could be exploited by those who just do not want blacks to live in their neighborhood or go to their children's schools. The dispersionist argument is popularly understood to mean that predominantly black schools are inferior and that black students cannot learn unless they are in a predominantly white milieu. Unhappily, in a country with a history of slavery and Jim Crow institutions, either a policy of mandatory racial dispersion or a policy of color blindness has racist overtones; that is the burden of the past.

When Americans urge one concept or the other on the public schools, they usually have in mind a certain kind of society that the schools are supposed to produce. Since American society is made up of hundreds, perhaps thousands, of different cultures and subcultures, the schools are incessantly torn between pressures to enforce unity and pressures to reinforce diversity.

The danger of extreme versions of either cultural separatism or monism must be recognized. A society in which pluralism reigns supreme verges on disintegration and anarchy, while a society that employs its schools to stamp out diversity moves toward totalitarianism. Reconciling these values is difficult but not impossible. Public schools should not become the vehicles for particular racial, religious, or ethnic groups. Those who want to teach the superiority of their cultural heritage should do so voluntarily. The public schools, as Robert Hutchins has written, "are dedicated to the maintenance and improvement of the public thing, the *res publica;* they are the common schools of the commonwealth, the political community." It is their primary task to prepare citizens who are capable of reading, thinking, discussing, participating, and voting.

The school can respect group differences while enabling its students to perceive the common concerns that transcend group and sectional barriers. The school will be better able to teach common understanding and shared values if it is not homogeneous. To the extent that it is demographically feasible, schools should bring children of different backgrounds together. This could come about if the education profession considered intercultural comity as vital a goal as small classes and good test scores, and if government agencies developed long-range policies to encourage and maintain stable, integrated neighborhoods. Ingenious educators, relying more on persuasion and incentives than on coercion, could devise a variety of special programs to connect public and private schools, city and suburban schools. No one should be made to feel, as a result of government action, that his school and his community are "no good."

In this murky period, while courts ponder and politicians quaver, there is a political consideration that has not escaped some black leaders. If blacks were distributed evenly across America and made up approximately 12 percent of every city, town, and hamlet, they would have little political power. Blacks, like the Irish and Italians before them, have won political office where there are sizable black concentrations. Blacks are aware that other groups have used political power to attain economic power. To be dispersed is to be placed in the role of a permanent dependent, a perpetual minority.

This realization, plus a growing awareness that desegregation is not necessarily linked to higher academic achievement, has caused many black politicians, leaders, and scholars to criticize the civil rights lawyers' single-minded pursuit of city–suburban mergers. Atlanta's black leadership, now in control of the city government and the school administration, has no interest in diluting its base of political power. Charles Hamilton, a professor of political science at Columbia and successor to integrationist Kenneth Clark as president of the Metropolitan Applied Research Center, testified against busing before a congressional committee; Hamilton believes that blacks need economic and political self-sufficiency more than they need racially balanced schools.

Derrick Bell, professor of law at Harvard and a former civil rights lawyer, has written that civil rights lawyers have not adjusted their tactics to take into account the demographic changes since 1954. While they press unswervingly for racial balance, the cities get blacker and the educational needs of black children are ignored. Ronald

Edmonds, director of the Center for Urban Studies at Harvard's Graduate School of Education, has complained that desegregation orders frequently deny black parents the right to make educational choices for their children. Howard University's Kenneth Tollett, while approving of desegregation initiatives in elementary and secondary schools, fears that the next legal onslaught will imperil black colleges and universities, which continue to serve important educational, psychological, and cultural functions for blacks. Economist Thomas Sowell holds that it is untrue that black schools are inherently unequal; he maintains that excellence has nothing to do with ethnicity.

Those blacks who are critical of the current thrust of the integration movement are not separatists; they are professionals who move in a racially mixed world and who value integration. They share a common fear that black institutions will be stigmatized by the implicit insult that whatever is black is inferior. They have been groping for language to express their views without giving aid and comfort to the George Wallaces and Louise Day Hickses of America. The idea that blacks should reject black institutions has been so deeply ingrained that most of the critics feel they must apologize for appearing to be disloyal to the spirit of *Brown*. Each in his own way has been trying to evolve a pluralist position for blacks that grants black institutions and organizations the same legitimacy accorded those of other ethnic groups, without in any way diminishing the opportunity for full interracial contact. "We will not be free," says Charles Hamilton, "until we have freed ourselves of the mentality of dependency. We must no longer be white America's permanent ward and favorite cause."

The emergence of thoughtful dissent among blacks is perhaps the healthiest trend in the evolution of race relations in America. So long as the question of assimilation is resolved by whites on behalf of blacks, then blacks remain in a subordinate, unequal position. It is blacks who must decide on what terms they wish to relate to other members of American society. The present debate among blacks about how, when, and whether to be integrated is likely to end not in unanimity but in a diversity of responses. Some will want to live in predominantly white worlds, others will not. The role of government must not be to choose a "right" answer, but to preserve the same options for blacks that are now available to everyone else.

16

Desegregation: Varieties of Meaning

(1980)

WHAT'S in a name? In social policy, the way a word is defined is far more than a semantic exercise. The definition of a strategic term such as "desegregation" is itself a statement of policy. Furthermore, embedded within a particular definition are assumptions, values, and policy goals. Thus, it becomes a matter of importance to make explicit, wherever possible, precisely which policies and goals are being advocated behind the neutral appearance of a definition.

Over the past twenty-five years, the words "segregation" and "desegregation" have shifted significantly in their meaning, and by examining these changes it may be possible to detect concurrent shifts in the direction of social policy. At certain times, these terms have had a meaning that then seemed clear. In the early 1950s, there was a general understanding of the meaning of these two words: "segregation" in school was a state-imposed policy of separating children solely on the basis of race; "desegregation," conversely, meant the elimination of state-imposed racial distinctions. These conventional definitions were repeated time and again in the record of the *Brown* v. *Board of Education* case. The way to end "segregation," as it was then defined, was to strike down all racial distinctions in the law as invidious and unconstitutional; a society freed of racial distinctions, it was then assumed, would be a desegregated society. These are no longer the definitions and the policies and the goals that are in common usage. "Segregation" today is a term that applies interchangeably both to discrimination against minorities and to racial concentrations of minorities in neighborhoods or in schools, and "desegregation" is commonly used to mean "racial balance." The change in meaning over a twenty-five-year period has been of a qualitative nature, with implications for policy. The policy implicit in these definitions is one of dispersion of racial minorities among the white majority in order to achieve desegregation, as it is presently defined.

What we must be concerned about in understanding the gradual redefinition of these terms is that the semantic discussion is merely the surface of larger issues. Beneath the surface are debates about how blacks ought to fit into American society; how to make amends for the injustices of the past; how various minorities have achieved success in American society; how blacks are similar to or different from other minorities; and what role the school plays in promoting the successful functioning of individuals and groups and in affecting the nature of community in modern America. We cannot understand the current arguments about the meaning of desegregation without directly considering these issues, examining their historical antecedents, their intellectual bases, and the choices implied for the future.

In the nineteenth century, one of the most fertile fields for speculation was, as it was then described, "the Negro question." What was to be done about the Negro? Here in these United States were millions of black people, brought to these shores in chains, held in bondage, and kept in a state of ignorance. Numerous books and articles were written about "the Negro problem" or "the Negro question," and various proposals were advanced. What the problem was depended on the viewer's perspective. From a modern perspective, the problem was that white Americans tolerated human slavery and treated blacks—slave and free—in ways that contradicted the expressed ideals of the nation. But to most white observers of the time, the problem was that blacks were different, so different that there could ultimately be no place in this country for them. This view, which had broad currency, stimulated a number of predictions about the destiny of the blacks. One of the most popular of these was the idea of colonization, either in Africa or some other warm climate. Advocates of colonization had many different motivations. Some felt that white prejudice against people of color was so intense that the departure of the latter from American shores was best for the sake of both. Thomas Jefferson repeatedly expressed the fear that blacks would rebel against their masters or that deep-rooted prejudice would lead to a disastrous race war after emancipation. Some colonizers were convinced of the essential inferiority of black people; others predicted that free blacks, handicapped by white prejudice, were bound to become a dangerous and degraded class. The supporters of the colonization movement saw it as an effective way to encourage gradual, voluntary manumission of slaves. While some colonizers truly believed in the equality of blacks, their cause was a capitulation to white prejudice. As an answer to the Negro question, it promised a racially homogeneous America, an all-white nation freed of the Negro problem.[1]

In the early 1830s, the star of the colonization movement began to fade when the cause was vehemently denounced by William Lloyd Garrison as a plot to bolster the institution of slavery by eliminating free blacks from the South. The abolitionists were not primarily concerned with whether the black was assimilable, but with the very existence of slavery as an immoral institution that crushed human potential and violated American and Christian ideals.

Yet even among the critics of slavery, there were different understandings of what would happen to black people after slavery ended. Some abolitionists were, in George M. Frederickson's term, "romantic racialists," who accepted the verdict of the crude social theorists of the day that the races were essentially different, each possessing special characteristics of mind and heart. Even in their defenses of blacks and their attacks against slavery, the romantic racialists succumbed to the fallacy of ascribing different human natures to different races. In the racial stereotyping that was popular at mid-century, the Anglo-Saxon was a conqueror, a man of enterprise and intellect, a restless and hardy pioneer, and America was assuredly an Anglo-Saxon country. Romantic racialists, instead of rejecting the stereotypes altogether, claimed that the stereotypical Negro had much to offer the tough, insensitive, domineering Anglo-Saxon. The Negroes, said the romantic racialists, were a docile, gentle, emotional, and affectionate people; so simple and childlike was the man of African descent, thought some, that he was potentially a better Christian than the haughty Anglo-Saxon. To the romantic racialist, the solution to the Negro problem was some form of amalgamation, either the physical absorption of the black race into the white majority or cultural amalgamation, in which the special gifts of the darker race would enrich and ennoble the national character. Such views, while intended to be humanitarian, were condescending, paternalistic, and patronizing; at times, they veered dangerously close to the idea of black inferiority. "It was never suggested," writes Frederickson, "that whites become literally like the black stereotype and sacrifice their alleged superiority in intellect and energy." In the proposed process of amalgamation, whether physical or cultural, there was never any question which race would remain dominant and which would eventually be submerged. It is in such views as these that it becomes clear that the *answers* arrived at were wrong because the *questions* and the underlying *assumptions* were fundamentally wrong.[2]

White supremacists had no trouble contemplating the future of the dark-skinned race; they were convinced that blacks were inferior and well suited to remain in slavery. Indeed, they maintained that slavery was a benevolent system in that it protected the slaves from a worse fate, that is, regression into barbarism. The doctrine of white superiority was bolstered by the work of the leading social theorists, whose ersatz "evidence" often included biblical references and whose theories amounted to a justification of racial subordination. Their main ideas, which received broad circulation, were that racial differences were permanent and inherent, that certain races were innately superior to others, and that racial hybrids were weak and sterile. All of their theories and cranial measurements and proofs boiled down to a single assumption: that race is a fixed determinant of human behavior and character.[3]

The popular racial theories of the day influenced the context within which opponents of slavery analyzed the prospects for the Negro. Some critics of slavery predicted that the blacks, once emancipated, would inevitably migrate southward to the tropics, a climate congenial to their racial inheritance. Others, anticipating the Darwinian concept of the survival of the fittest, held that the inferior black race would eventually die out in the competition with the white race. Not everyone was willing to wait until the brutal laws of nature took their course, and in the decade before the outbreak of the Civil War, the colonization idea regained adherents. In 1858, an effort was made in Congress to win federal support for American Negro colonies in Central America; even during the Civil War, President Lincoln negotiated with Panama and Haiti for colonies and endorsed a government-subsidized program of colonization. Virtually all who supported colonization implicitly conceded that the white and black races would not be able to live together amicably as equals. All of these various proposed solutions to the Negro problem had one common denominator: the eventual disappearance of the Negro as a disturbing presence in the American body politic. Whether by dispersion, migration, amalgamation, exclusion, or extinction, the anticipated result was the whitening of America.[4]

But none of these alternatives satisfied the radical abolitionists, who rejected all the conventional assumptions, all the popular wisdom, about the nature of race. It was the view of the radical abolitionists that black and white people were members of the same race, the human race, and that all were individuals of equal worth. The problem, as they saw it, was that black people were denied, by slavery and other human institutions, the freedom to develop their potential to the fullest. While others analyzed the Negro problem as a question of what to do about these people who were so different, the radical abolitionists understood that these people, because of the color of their skin, were *treated* differently. Given this analysis, the problem was not what to do about the Negro but how to change those laws, institutions, and attitudes that permitted blacks to be treated as less than human and less than equal citizens.

At the close of the Civil War, these views were advanced in the Congress by radical Republicans, who sought to protect the newly freed slaves from those who would restore slavery under another guise. Even though southern representatives were temporarily excluded from the Congress, there were still legislators who objected strenuously to civil rights bills and guarantees of equality; their argument, bluntly stated, was that this was "a white man's government." In the debates between the radical Republicans and their opposition, the question facing the nation was, again, what is to be done about the Negro? The answer of the radical Republicans was that the Negro should be guaranteed full citizenship and equality before the law, and that these guarantees should be backed up by the Constitution. To achieve these ends, the Republican-dominated Congress pushed through the Thirteenth, Fourteenth, and Fifteenth Amendments, as well as civil rights legislation. And the purpose of the sponsors was unmistakable: it was to bar henceforth any discrimination based on race or color. Senator Lot M. Morrill of Maine acknowledged that the Congress was doing nothing less than reversing the Dred Scott decision and recognizing the black man as a full-fledged citizen:

If there is anything with which the American people are troubled, and if there is anything with which the American statesman is perplexed and vexed, it is to what to do with the negro [sic], how to define him, what he is in American law, and to what rights he is entitled. Hitherto we have said that he was nondescript in our statutes; he had no *status;* he was ubiquitous; he was both man and thing; he was three-fifths of a person for representation and he was a thing for commerce and for use. In the highest sense, then, in which any definition can ever be held, this bill is important as a definition. It defines him to be a man and only a man in American politics and in American law; it puts him on the plane of manhood; it brings him within the pale of the Constitution. That is all it does as a definition, and there it leaves him.[5]

The idea of wiping out all racial distinctions was a revolutionary idea, and it was an idea whose time had not yet come. Despite the passage of constitutional amendments guaranteeing equality, the doctrine of white supremacy in the South eventually outlasted efforts at Reconstruction. By the end of the nineteenth century, black people were trapped in a state of peonage in the South, disenfranchised and powerless. The abandonment of the rights of blacks is a familiar story, whose major features include the political deal struck to end Reconstruction, the activity of white terrorist organizations to intimidate black voters, the Supreme Court's nullification of the Fourteenth Amendment as a shield against racially discriminatory laws, the spread of Jim Crow codes throughout the South, and the Court's 1896 endorsement of racial segregation. Once again, there was a "solution" to the Negro problem, and the solution now adopted was to exclude blacks from the rights of citizenship.[6]

The separate-but-equal doctrine of the *Plessy* v. *Ferguson* decision in 1896 was the law of the land for nearly six decades; it symbolized the evisceration of the Fourteenth Amendment. But, echoing across the decades was a lone dissent from Justice John Marshall Harlan, a dissent which would serve as a benchmark for those who objected to policies of racial differentiation:

... In respect of civil rights, common to all citizens, the Constitution of the United States does not, I think, permit any public authority to know the race of those entitled to be protected in the enjoyment of such rights . . . in view of the Constitution, in the eye of the law, there is in this country no superior, dominant, ruling-class of citizens. There is no caste here. Our Constitution is colorblind, and neither knows nor tolerates classes among citizens. In respect of civil rights, all citizens are equal before the law.

When, in the early 1950s, NAACP lawyers decided that the time was right for a full-scale, frontal attack on the "separate-but-equal" doctrine, their briefs and arguments made numerous references to the principles enunciated by Justice Harlan. The chief argument in the *Brown* case was that "the Fourteenth Amendment precludes a state from imposing distinctions or classifications based upon race and color alone. The State of Kansas has no power thereunder to use race as a factor in affording educational opportunities to its citizens." The civil rights lawyers sought to establish that there was no difference between white and black children and that state-imposed racial separation was arbitrary and injurious. The record built in Kansas was intended to show that black children in Topeka were assigned to public schools solely on the basis of their race, that these children had to travel past their neighborhood school in order to attend distant "colored" schools, that this arbitrary separation from others created within them a sense of stigma, and that long travel on school buses was detrimental to the healthy development of young children.[7]

The chief premise of the attack on segregation was that racial distinctions, for whatever reason, were unconstitutional and unreasonable. Robert Carter stated this succinctly:

Now we rest our case on the question of the power of the state. We feel, one, that the state has no authority and no power to make any distinction or any classification among its citizenry based upon race and color alone. We think that this has been settled by the Supreme Court of the United States in a long line of cases which hold that in order for a classification to be constitutional it must be based on a real difference. . . . The

Supreme Court has also held in a series of cases that race and ancestry and color are irrelevant differences and cannot form the basis for any legislative action.[8]

Within the appellants' brief to the Supreme Court, there was no question about the primacy of the principle of color blindness. The brief maintained that "the Fourteenth Amendment compels the states to be color blind in exercising their power and authority. . . . this Court has uniformly ruled that the Fourteenth Amendment prohibits a state from using race or color as the determinant of the quantum, quality or type of education and the place at which education is to be afforded." The brief quoted Justice Harlan's famous dissent at length and stated simply: "That the Constitution is color blind is our dedicated belief."[9]

While the demand for color-blind application of the laws was the central thesis of the case against school segregation, a secondary theme was that Negro children were psychologically injured by being compelled to go to segregated schools. This argument went in two directions: One was the testimony that state-imposed racial segregation was official sanction of the doctrine of Negro inferiority; the other was testimony that Negro children were injured by lack of contact with white children and thus deprived of experience with members of the majority group. In the first strand of social science testimony, the damage to the black child was caused by governmental policies that assigned children to different schools on the grounds of race; in the second, the damage was caused by the absence of interracial contact. The first strand suggested a color-blind remedy, the second suggested an integration remedy.

This ambiguity within the *Brown* case can be traced throughout the record, from the original trial in Kansas to the final decision itself. In essence, the civil rights lawyers were simultaneously advocating both color-blind legal equality and color-conscious school integration. This ambiguity evolved during the following quarter century as an outright contradiction, since color-blind policies became, in many places, an obstacle to school integration. The possibility of a conflict between these two principles was not anticipated when the *Brown* case was argued before the Supreme Court. Responding to a question from Justice Felix Frankfurter, Thurgood Marshall spelled out what he wanted: "The only thing that we ask for is that the state-imposed racial segregation be taken off...." If school officials were enjoined from enforcing segregation, Marshall argued, "then I think whatever district lines they draw, if it can be shown that those lines are drawn on the basis of race or color, then I think they would violate the injunction. If the lines are drawn on a natural basis, without regard to race or color, then I think that nobody would have any complaint." Similarly, Spottswood Robinson, representing black plaintiffs in Prince Edward County, replied to Chief Justice Fred Vinson: "Now, we submit that you cannot continue to discriminate against Negroes, or these Negro students; under the circumstances, what you do is, you simply make all the facilities in the county available to all the pupils, without restriction or assignment to particular schools on the basis of race."[10]

In light of this background, it is intriguing to realize that the central precept of the case against segregation—Justice Harlan's principle of color blindness—has since come under attack as a subterfuge for segregation. How is it that those who fought to remove from the states any power to make racial classifications now argue for school assignments based on race? These changes in meaning and purpose came about gradually but with significant effect.

There are several perspectives from which to assess these transformations of meaning. Clues can be found in, first, the political response of the South to the *Brown* decision; second, the attitudinal reaction of northern liberals; third, the population movements of the past quarter century; and fourth, the implications of the common school ideal.

Of primary importance in shaping judicial remedies for racial segregation was the massive resistance by the southern states, their concerted efforts to defy desegregation orders, and in some instances, their resolve to close public schools rather than permit white and black children to attend the same schools. When open defiance failed, southern districts shifted to evasive tactics to preserve dual school systems. By proposing "freedom of choice" plans in which community intimidation effectively maintained segregated schools, the southern intransigents discredited the principle of free choice itself. In time, judicial orders began to counter strategies of duplicity and defiance by setting standards that, in some districts, required racial balancing as proof of compliance. Once the standard setting began, the difference between de jure and de facto segregation became increasingly obscure.

In northern cities, the *Brown* decision was early viewed as a declaration that predominantly Negro schools were segregated and inferior. It was often said that such a school could *never* be a good school. The liberal president of the New York City Board of Education told a Harlem audience in the fall in 1954 that there was no *intentional* segregation in New York, but that the schools their children attended were segregated nonetheless and were causing "a psychological scarring." The board publicly promised to reexamine the racial composition of its schools and to eliminate de facto segregation because racially homogeneous schools "damage the personality of minority group children," "decrease their motivation," and "impair their ability to learn." Given these assumptions, color-blind policy was tantamount to official toleration for schools that were segregated, inferior, and harmful to minority children."

But what to do? White resistance to racial balancing

was tenacious, and demonstrations of the low quality of black schools simply confirmed white racist fears about black neighborhoods, black schools, and black children. And the possibility of bringing about extensive integration through any color-blind redistricting diminished rapidly during the 1950s and 1960s, as whites moved out of cities and nonwhite minorities moved in. The spread of dense, racially homogeneous neighborhoods of blacks and other nonwhite minorities meant that neighborhood districting or any other racially neutral scheme would not bring about the elimination of predominantly minority schools.

Yet another blow to the concept of color blindness was the fact that many, probably most, of those who advocated a color-blind approach wanted an integrated society as much as they wanted a society that was blind to color; there was certainly no desire on the part of racial liberals, black or white, to achieve judicial sanction for racially segregated neighborhoods or for racial discrimination that was disguised as something else. Thus, it was scarcely surprising that many of the same people who had fought most earnestly for the vindication of Justice Harlan's dissent soon began to search for policies that would bring about more interracial contact. Since there had been systematic exclusion of blacks from participation in various careers, institutions, and centers of power, the transition from a policy of racial subordination to one of racial neutrality was fated to be an inadequate response; it simply could not guarantee black entry into lily-white institutions. And yet, using race as the criterion by which to confer benefits or to impose restrictions has its inevitable cost. As the NAACP brief put it in 1953, "Any distinction based upon race was understood as constituting a badge of inferiority." And, as Thurgood Marshall argued, "racial distinctions in and of themselves are invidious."[12]

What ultimately undermined the full implementation

of the color-blind principle was not just political, demographic, or ideological factors, but conflicting conceptions of the purpose of public schooling in America. Just as they do today, people in the 1950s had differing ideas about what the public schools were supposed to accomplish on behalf of society. Perhaps the most generally held conception was that of the public school as the common school, a school in which all sectors of the community learn together as equals and overcome differences in social origins; this common school, as it was projected by Horace Mann and other reformers of the 1840s and 1850s, was to be a great social equalizer, a pillar of democracy, and an agency of social assimilation. To those who saw the *Brown* decision within the context of the common school ideal, the implications of the decision ran counter to color-blind policy. For if equality and democracy depend on a mixture of all races and classes in the same schools, then it becomes necessary to enumerate and sort and match the children to achieve the right mixture.

Educators had long believed that a major purpose of the public school was to hasten the assimilation of diverse minorities to American culture. The public school had been generally charged with the responsibility for creating a unified American community by teaching a common culture and introducing children to the language, literature, history, and hero tales of the majority. One persistent problem was that the common culture was usually defined as white, Protestant, Anglo-American culture and history, and the process of assimilation tended to mean giving up any culture or language that was different. Too often, "different" meant "inferior." For example, the mass arrival of millions of Italians and Jews at the end of the nineteenth century inspired fears that America was being overrun by inferior races and inferior cultures. One response was to cut off future immigration of these groups; another was to

239

place new emphasis on the public school as an agency of Americanization and assimilation.

The common school, in its ideal form, has proved difficult to achieve, and it has historically worked best in areas that were largely white Protestant, where there was little dissonance between the culture of the school and the culture of the students. Part of the problem is that the ideal itself is a small-town ideology, which presents the vision of a school bringing together all the elements of an entire community under a common roof to live and learn together as equals. Transferred to cities, the same ideology has been realized only sporadically, since most big cities have within them islands of homogeneous ethnic groups. Thus, while a city like New York has had considerable mixture of children of different ethnicity in its schools, it has also had over the years many schools in which a single group predominated, be it Irish, Italian, Jewish, black, or Hispanic.

Another impediment to the establishment of the common school ideal has been the fact that some minorities— ethnic, religious, or linguistic—did not want to be absorbed into the common culture. Some (but not all) Catholics stayed out of the public schools and created their own schools, where they could protect their religious values against the implicit Protestantism of the public school. Others supplemented the public school education with their own cultural maintenance programs. To the extent that the common school was an agency of the melting pot, it has stimulated alternative traditions of schooling, which represent resistance to the assimilationist view of American citizenship. Such an impulse has generated support for the idea of the community school, that is, a public school that reflects and serves its immediate community. In minority communities, pressure has often been applied to public schools to make them more responsive to the surrounding community, in ways such as maintaining a library of Italian books or serving ethnic foods or teaching ethnic group history or offering bilingual instruction. There are many instances of public schools that made accommodations to those with different cultures; when the public schools fail to bend, groups with strong feelings about their religion, their heritage, or their language sometimes opt out and create nonpublic schools.

And yet, the important point to recognize is that assimilation of all of these groups into American society did take place, whether they were in the public schools or not. The public school was not alone in teaching immigrants the language of the land, its traditions, and its values; assimilation was also promoted by other agencies, such as the military, the press, political parties, labor unions, and the mass media. Eventually, as one historian points out, even "the educational agencies maintained by immigrant communities for the perpetuation of their own unique cultures were themselves transformed by Americanization. More and more, they became agencies not only for the transmission of immigrant culture to immigrant children but also for the mediation of American culture to the immigrant community."[3]

This legacy of conflicting interpretations of the role of the public school entered into the debate about the implications of the *Brown* decision. Those who believed that the public schools had brought about the social advance of European immigrants by speeding their assimilation expected them to do the same for blacks. Those who saw the public school as an indispensable element in the successful functioning of the melting pot presumed that the school should play its customary role by contributing to the assimilation of blacks.

It was not long before the conflict between the goals of color-blind policy and of assimilationist ideology became apparent. In the 1950s, social scientists who testified against segregation assembled evidence to show that racial differences were inconsequential and that children of different races had the same capacity to learn. Their emphasis on the basic irrelevance of skin color supported the lawyers' appeal against racial classifications.

But a decade later, the work of social scientists emphasized the importance of assimilation as a remedy for "the Negro problem," and the way that assimilation was conceptualized was closely related to prevailing ideas about black culture. The literature of this period put heavy stress on cultural "deficiency" of blacks as a group and defined blacks as an inferior caste that had been culturally and psychologically damaged by historic discrimination. Gunnar Myrdal had made this point in his classic *An American Dilemma* in 1944:

> *In practically all its divergences, American Negro culture is not something independent of general American culture. It is a distorted development, or a pathological condition, of the general American culture.* The instability of the Negro family, the inadequacy of educational facilities for Negroes, the emotionalism in the Negro church, the insufficiency and unwholesomeness of Negro recreational activity, the plethora of Negro sociable organizations, the narrowness of interests of the average Negro, the provincialism of his political speculation, the high Negro crime rate, the cultivation of the arts to the neglect of other fields, superstition, personality difficulties, and other characteristics are mainly forms of social pathology which, for the most part, are created by caste pressures.[14]

By the early 1960s, many social scientists had incorporated this perspective into their work, so that black culture was viewed as a culture of poverty and the skin color of the black person was itself a badge of caste; as one study of the personality of "the Negro child" argued, "The stigma of his caste membership is inescapable and insurmountable.

It is inherent in his skin color, permanently ingrained in his body image." [15]

Most sociologists in the early 1960s seemed to agree that blacks were trapped in an inferior caste status; that they could escape only by becoming integrated into a predominantly white setting; that black culture was in various ways deficient for historical reasons; and that a predominantly black school could never be a good school because it was predominantly black. These ideas gave a cogency and moral force to the remedy of racial balancing. In accord with these assumptions, integration leaders often said that "real" integration could take place only with a white majority. New York State was the first to write this perspective into its educational policy: In 1963, the State Commissioner of Education declared that any school in which more than 50 percent of the students were Negro was racially imbalanced and therefore incapable of providing equal educational opportunity. In effect, once a school passed the 50 percent mark, the predominance of nonwhites gave the school a label of "inferior." By April 1965, the Massachusetts Advisory Committee on Racial Imbalance and Education issued a similar policy statement, and one of the reasons it offered for eliminating racial imbalance was forthrightly based on the view that blacks are a caste, not an ethnic group, and as such have no culture to preserve. This is how the difference between blacks and European immigrant groups was explained:

History teaches us clearly why the Negro has not achieved equality in America as have the Irish, the Italians, the Jews. Only Africans, among all groups, were deprived of their cultural heritage. Only they were legally forbidden to marry. Only their children were taken from their parents to be bought and sold. The other groups, possessing a cultural heritage of their own, wanted to preserve it. For them, separation often meant protection; for Negroes it signified oppression. [16]

Meanwhile, among historians, a great debate has occurred about the black experience in America. Histories by Stanley Elkins and Kenneth Stampp, both published in the late 1950s, argued that American slavery brutalized blacks and damaged their personalities and cultural identity. More recently, histories by Eugene Genovese (1974), Herbert Gutman (1976), and Thomas Webber (1978) maintain that the black family and black culture were far stronger even under the constraints of slavery than earlier historians realized; their works make the case that blacks created and sustained a viable culture, with its own values, traditions, social forms, and strengths. Each of these historical accounts treats a different facet of the black historical experience, and the later works add an enriching dimension to the earlier focus on the victimization of blacks.[7]

The emphasis in the earlier histories on the damage done to black culture and personality was an appropriate backdrop to the sociology of the 1960s, which analyzed blacks as a caste group seeking to escape the stigma of their group identity through assimilation. This was yet another answer to the age-old question of what to do about "the Negro problem." There is a long-standing tradition in our historiography and sociology which holds that extensive assimilation of minorities into "the melting pot" is inevitable and desirable; it is only in the past fifteen years that Americans have begun to admit the possibility that members of minority groups can be different and part of the mainstream at the same time. While it has been widely noted that white ethnicity has persisted as a strong source of self-identity, despite the lures of the melting pot, social scientists have generally rejected the possibility that black culture might serve as a positive source of identity. Writing in 1964, one social psychologist countered white fears of racial miscegenation with the following argument:

Curt Stern has demonstrated that if panmixis—completely random mating with no regard to racial differences—were to take place in the United States, the darker skin shades of Negroes would be virtually eliminated, but there would be little noticeable effect on the skin color of Caucasians. In other words, the Negro one-tenth of the nation would be "inundated by a white sea" in respect to skin color.

The author then quotes Curt Stern, with a prediction that echoes nineteenth-century ideas:

When complete fusion has occurred, there will probably be no more than a few thousand black people in each generation in the entire country, and these are likely to have straight hair, narrow noses and thin lips. I suppose that if some person now living could return at that distant time, he would ask in wonder, "What became of the Negro?"[18]

This, of course, is a statement of the melting pot ideology, which in its most ideal pronouncements prophesied a time when all Americans would blend together to form a new race, a new religion, and a new culture. What critics of the melting pot ideology argue is that many people are content to retain their culture, their noses, their lips, and their hair, so long as they can live in a society in which there are no restrictions placed on them for being different.

In assessing the meaning of the *Brown* decision today, we must recognize that it deals not just with the question of access to schools, but with the question of how to define black people, and what part blacks should play in defining their own purposes. If blacks are seen as a caste group that has been deprived of its culture and its history, then one set of remedies seems appropriate; if seen as a self-conscious group with a viable culture, then other remedies might be in order. But whichever perspective prevails, the role of government must be to provide blacks with the opportunity and the means to make choices for themselves, because it was precisely this power to make decisions that was denied to blacks in the past.

So, the issues which policymakers must settle are complex. What should be common about the public schools? What should all Americans share in order to be fully American? How much difference is tolerable from one group to the next? How much difference is desirable in order to maintain a healthy diversity among our people? In seeking answers to these questions, we also confront the meaning of community in modern America. While it is commonplace to say that the school should be closely related to the community, we should bear in mind that each of us is a member of many communities, because each of us has different interests and commitments. Person X is a member of a family, a neighborhood, a race, a religion, a regional community, a city, perhaps a nationality group, an occupation, a labor union, a political party, a sports group, a hobby club, a social group; some of these circles will overlap, others will not. The point is that none of us is one-dimensional, none of us is only a member of a racial group and nothing else. The more one participates in a variety of communities, the more democratic one's sense of community becomes. We tend to give conflicting signals to the school by asking both that it reinforce the values of a particular community and that it enable each individual to come into contact with a broader environment beyond his or her own group. The resolution of this seeming contradiction is to be found in the school's relationship to other educating agencies, some of which (like the family and church) teach the particular culture far better than the school, others of which (like the mass media and the political system) teach the universal far better than the school. Seen in this light, the school is the transitional agency between the particular and the universal. The problem is *e pluribus unum,* "out of many, one," and the question is a persistent American conflict between the legitimate demands of the many and the legitimate requirements of the society as a whole.

What, then, should desegregation mean today? Certainly, it should mean the removal of all barriers based on race, but it should not mean the dismantling of autonomous black institutions, like the black press, black political organizations, black churches, and black communal societies. It should mean a heightened consciousness of the value of interracial contact in every sphere of activity, but it should not mean that a stigma must be attached to any activities pursued by blacks without the participation of nonblacks. It should mean participation by blacks at every level of our political and economic structures, and it should therefore mean continued efforts to increase the level of black educational attainment and black occupational achievement until racial differences are insignificant. In light of the demographic changes of the past quarter century, it should also mean the implementation of policies to provide and protect racially integrated neighborhoods inside and outside the cities.

This brief exploration of the interplay between past and present is intended as a reexamination of the intellectual bases of social policy. As such, it raises questions instead of providing answers. When we inquire into the meaning of segregation and desegregation, we find ourselves defining not just words or individual policies but the nature of the relationship of black people to the rest of American society. And when we inquire whether blacks are a caste, a race, an ethnic group, or some combination, the answer tends to imply some policy, since the definition contains certain assumptions about the value and extent of assimilation and about the strengths or weaknesses of black culture. Questions necessarily arise as we explore definitions and policies: Is equality to be found only in the melting-pot ideology? Are the cultural differences between blacks and others a handicap or a source of diversity, to be eliminated or to be prized? What is the relation of the black experience to that of other minority groups in America? Which values, which policies will bring us to a time in which people of all backgrounds accord each other the respect due every human being?

17

Color-Blind or Color-Conscious?

(1979)

IN 1954 the Supreme Court declared that state-imposed school segregation was unconstitutional and invalidated state laws that assigned children to school on the basis of their race. Today that decision, *Brown* v. *Board of Education,* is cited as authority for a network of judicial decisions, laws, and administrative regulations that specifically require institutions to classify people on the basis of their group identity and to deal with them accordingly.

By denying states the power to differentiate among its citizens by race, the *Brown* decision provided a strong precedent to bar racial discrimination in every realm of civic and public activity. Its effect was strengthened and extended by the Civil Rights Act of 1964, which prohibited discrimination based on race, color, religion, sex, or national origin. The Civil Rights Act embodied the fundamental principle that everyone should be considered as an individual without regard to social origin. This idea attracted the support of a broad alliance composed of blacks, liberals, organized labor, Catholics, Jews, and others who perceived that the black cause was the common cause of everyone who wanted to eliminate group bias from American life. The particular genius of the civil rights movement was its successful forging of a coalition led by blacks but far more numerous than the black population alone; at the height of its power, in 1964–65, the coalition was potent enough to win passage of the Civil Rights Act, federal aid to education, the Voting Rights Act, and the antipoverty program.

The recent shift in focus from antidiscrimination to group preference has splintered the civil rights coalition of the 1960s and has changed the nature of civil rights issues. The issues of the late 1970s are far more complex than were those of the 1950s and 1960s, when the public could readily understand the denial of the civil and political rights of black people. Issues such as racial balancing, busing, affirmative action, and quotas are not nearly so clear-cut. People of good will of all races and both sexes can be found on different sides of these questions.

But these disagreements arise among one-time allies in the struggle for universalism and equal rights not just because the issues today are complicated, but also because there is an essential dilemma: The group-based concepts of the present are in conflict with the historic efforts of the civil rights movement to remove group classifications from public policy. And at the heart of this dilemma is the *Brown* decision.

The *Brown* case was one of several school segregation suits brought before the Supreme Court in the early 1950s by the NAACP Legal Defense Fund. The cases were intended to challenge the "separate but equal" doctrine of statutory racial segregation that was upheld in the *Plessy v. Ferguson* decision in 1896. The Supreme Court then held that a state law requiring the separation of the races in railway coaches was no violation of the Constitution as long as the races had equal facilities. The decision of the majority gave legal reinforcement to social customs and "black codes" based on the presumption of black inferiority.

Only Justice John Marshall Harlan dissented from the *Plessy* decision, and his dissent was for many decades a foundation stone of the civil rights movement. Harlan denied that the states had the power to regulate their citizens solely on the basis of race: "Our Constitution is color-blind, and neither knows nor tolerates classes among citizens. . . . The law regards man as man, and takes no account of his surroundings or of his color when his civil rights as guaranteed by the supreme law of the land are involved."

The city of Topeka, Kansas, where the *Brown* case originated in 1951, maintained racially segregated schools for the first six grades. The Topeka school district contained eighteen elementary schools for white students and four elementary schools for black students. White children attended their neighborhood school, but many black children were required to travel long distances by school bus to attend a designated "colored" school.

The arguments against racial segregation were of two kinds: those derived from constitutional objections, and those derived from social science. The constitutional arguments explicitly rejected the power of the state to recognize racial differences. The social science arguments were ambivalent, asserting both that color was irrelevant and that interracial experiences were valuable.

In building their case, the NAACP lawyers stressed the fact that blacks were denied the right to send their children to the nearest school. Segregation imposed on black children the handicap of spending extra time traveling to and from school, which was detrimental to the children's development. Oliver Brown, the named plaintiff, testified about the inconvenience and lack of safety that resulted from busing his daughter, Linda Carol Brown, to a "colored school" twenty-one blocks away, instead of the neighborhood school only seven blocks from his home.

Among the social scientists who testified, there were contradictory themes. Some held that blacks were deprived by lack of contact with whites. But others emphasized that segregation was wrong because it accorded different treatment to children on the basis of their ancestry. Thus the social scientists' testimony left unresolved a major dilemma: Should policy be color-blind or color-conscious? Were black parents suing for the right to gain admission to their neighborhood school or for the right to an integrated education? Was the constitutional wrong to blacks the denial of liberty or the denial of integration?

The constitutional argument contained no such ambivalence. Robert Carter, chief counsel for Topeka's black plaintiffs, rested the case against school segregation on two grounds: first, that "the state has no authority and no power to make any distinction or any classification among its citizenry based upon race and color alone"; and second, that "the rights under the Fourteenth Amendment are individual rights," not group rights.

When the unfavorable decision in Kansas was appealed to the Supreme Court in 1952, the chief argument in the appellants' brief was the unconstitutionality of racial classification by the state: "The Fourteenth Amendment precludes a state from imposing distinctions or classifications based upon race and color alone." The NAACP conceded that the state may "confer benefits or impose disabilities upon selected groups of citizens," but the selection of such groups must be related to real differences. Race, the NAACP said, is not a real difference.

Black organizations maintained in the 1970s that the Fourteenth Amendment bans legislation that discriminates against blacks but does not ban legislation intended to confer benefits on blacks. But this was not the position of the NAACP in its *Brown* brief. On the contrary, the appellants' brief was a cogent, tightly reasoned documentation of the view that the Fourteenth Amendment was written specifically to ensure that all state action would henceforth be color-blind. There was no suggestion in the brief that racial distinctions might, in some circumstances, be tolerable.

The NAACP said, "The evidence makes clear that it was the intent of the proponents of the Fourteenth Amendment, and the substantial understanding of its opponents, that it would, of its own force, prohibit all state action predicated upon race or color.... [A]s a matter of law, race is not an allowable basis of differentiation in government action."

In the oral arguments before the Supreme Court, Thurgood Marshall for the NAACP described the kind of remedy that he sought, and he was clear that race should play no part in school assignment. Marshall said the Court should forbid explicit segregation and segregation by gerrymandering of school district lines, but, "If the lines are drawn on a natural basis, without regard to race or color, then I think that nobody would have any complaint." Thurgood Marshall made the most conclusive and unambiguous statements about the constitutional issues before the Court. Marshall said that under the Constitution, "the state is deprived of any power to make any racial classification in any governmental field."

When the Brown decision was announced on May 17, 1954, it appeared that the grounds for it were more sociological than constitutional. In retrospect this seems surprising in light of the solidity of the constitutional argument and the controvertible nature of sociological evidence. The Court did not, in its *Brown* decision, declare the Constitution to be color-blind, which explains some of the present-day confusion about the meaning of the decision. The decision can be read, as it was then, as removing from the states the power to use race as a factor in assigning children to public schools. It can also be read, as it is now, as a mandate to bring about racial integration in the public schools by taking race into account in making assignments.

But it was the former interpretation that the NAACP lawyers used at the time. In 1955, Robert Carter asked for a decree from the Supreme Court that would order the Topeka school board "to cease and desist at once from basing school attendance and admission on the basis of race or color." James M. Nabrit, Jr., argued in the same vein for a Supreme Court decree for the District of Columbia public schools: "Do not deny any child the right to go to the school of his choice on the grounds of race or color within the normal limits of your districting system. . . . Do not assign them on the basis of race or color, and we have no complaint."

Today the *Brown* decision is considered the progenitor of a host of color-conscious and group-specific policies. The decision that was supposed to remove from the states the power to assign children to school on the basis of race has become the authority for assigning children to school solely on the basis of race, even where official segregation never existed. One western school district, which contains nineteen variants of the governmentally-designated minority groups, has voluntarily undertaken to maintain a racial-ethnic balance of these groups in its schools for both students and teachers.

For at least the first ten years after the *Brown* decision, belief in color-blind policy was the animating force behind the civil rights movement. In the hearings on the Civil Rights Act in 1963, Roy Wilkins denounced employment quotas as "evil" and predicted that they would be used to restrict the opportunities of black workers. In the same hearings, Attorney General Robert Kennedy, in a heated sparring match with Senator Sam Ervin, forced the senator to agree with him that the *Brown* decision established the right of the individual to attend his neighborhood school. The Civil Rights Act ultimately included an unequivocal definition of desegregation:

"Desegregation" means the assignment of students to public schools and within such schools without regard to their race, color, religion, or national origin, but "desegregation" shall not mean the assignment of students to public schools in order to overcome racial imbalance.

Not long after Congress passed into law the color-blind principle embodied in the Civil Rights Act of 1964, several trends converged to undermine it.

First, white southern intransigence had effectively preserved segregation despite the *Brown* decision. The dismantling of state-segregated school systems was occurring at a snail's pace; by 1964, only 2 percent of the black students in the deep South attended schools with white students. Southern politicians boasted of their success in frustrating the implementation of the *Brown* mandate, and southern legislatures devised numerous schemes to protect the dual school systems. In some cities, white students were allowed to transfer away from their neighborhood schools to avoid desegregation. Some districts were gerrymandered to conform to the racial division of neighborhoods. In some districts, blacks who applied to attend white schools were required to pass special tests to prove their fitness.

Second, the Civil Rights Act of 1964 authorized federal

officials to cut off federal funds from districts that failed to desegregate their schools. This meant little in 1964, when federal funds for elementary and secondary schools were minor, but it became a powerful weapon to compel desegregation after 1965, when federal aid to education was passed by the Congress. The United States Office of Education moved swiftly to establish guidelines by which it might determine whether a district was obeying the Civil Rights Act. For a year, the guidelines permitted free-choice plans. By 1966, unhappy with the slow pace of the first year, education officials promulgated new guidelines which set out in detail the numerical range of proportions of each race that had to be in integrated schools in each district in order to assure the flow of federal funds. The Fifth Circuit Court of Appeals rejected challenges to the federal guidelines, holding that freedom of choice was permissible only so long as it brought about integration. By 1968, the Supreme Court invalidated a free-choice plan that did not produce substantial integration. And by 1971, the high court directed the schools of Charlotte-Mecklenburg, North Carolina, to do whatever was necessary—including busing children away from their neighborhood schools, gerrymandering of districts, and creation of non-contiguous attendance zones—in order to bring about "truly non-discriminatory assignments."

Third, just as the federal bureaucracy and the federal judiciary began to abandon the color-blind principle, the Black Power movement emerged. Black Power spokesmen derided the leaders of the civil rights movement as Uncle Toms and accommodationists. It was not their rejection of integration that gave them mass appeal, however, but rather their open advocacy of black self-interest. While old-line civil rights leaders championed policies of nondiscrimination, the black advocacy movement demanded black principals, black teachers, specific jobs, here and now,

256

period. Even after the more flamboyant black activists passed from the national scene, many of their ideas and goals were absorbed into the programs of the traditional organizations of the civil rights movement.

Fourth, the color-blind principle lost much of its luster for the civil rights organizations as soon as it was established in law. Once it was a fact, it ceased to be a goal. Organizations either generate new goals or become defunct. One cannot keep a mass movement excited about goals that have already been attained. Nor can a revolution of rising expectations be satisfied by nondiscrimination policies alone.

Fifth, some of those who had led the fight against segregation came to believe that color blindness is an abstract principle with no power to alter the status quo and no possibility of making up for the effects of past discrimination, either in institutional or in personal terms. One of the early champions of color-blind policy, Robert Carter, now a federal district judge, believes that group preferences will in time cause the nation's institutions, professions, and work force to reflect the racial, ethnic, religious, and gender composition of the population. In his view, the color-conscious policy brings about by compulsion what the color-blind policy should have brought about if implemented in good faith.

Thus it was that the idea of a color-blind society fell out of fashion almost as soon as it was enacted into law and well before it became part of custom. This is a turn of events with consequence for American society. We do not have a broad-based civil rights movement in the United States today precisely because the only common purpose that could bind dozens of minorities together is the goal of preventing discrimination against *all* minorities. The fight to ban discrimination, which gathered to its banners a powerful coalition of diverse groups, has been replaced for now by groupism, or every interest group for itself. The idea of universalism is in retreat, an idea whose time came and went with amazing speed.

Black civil rights leaders fear that color blindness today means a willful refusal to recognize exclusionary practices that operate under the guise of racial neutrality. Opponents of group-conscious policies fear that to replace old-fashioned racism with well-intentioned racialism is divisive and wrong. Somewhere between total color blindness and extreme color consciousness, there must be a reconciliation of democratic values. Strict neutrality in admissions and hiring, with no effort to remedy the effects of past discrimination, will leave many blacks right where they are, at the bottom. The alternative to racial quotas is the kind of program that prepares blacks to succeed without racial preferences, such as special tutoring for college admission or for union apprenticeship tests. A remarkable example is the Recruitment and Training Program (RTP), a New York-based national organization that since 1965 recruited and trained more than 30,000 blacks for well-paid apprenticeships in construction trade unions. As a result of RTP's efforts, minority membership in the affected unions grew from 3 percent to 19 percent. Similarly, educational programs that upgrade academic skills have enabled black students not only to gain admission to colleges and graduate schools, but to complete their studies successfully. One noteworthy example is the ABC (A Better Chance) program, founded in the early 1960s. ABC identifies promising minority youngsters from economically disadvantaged backgrounds and helps them to get high-quality college preparation, either in their own communities or in boarding schools. Several thousand students have received financial aid from ABC for their secondary schooling, and more than 90 percent have entered college. Most ABC students are accepted in selective colleges, where their preparation enables them to compete as equals.

Such creative interweaving of color-conscious and racially neutral approaches recognizes the need to overcome the effects of past discrimination by supplying the skills and motivation to achieve without regard to race or social origins. In the long run, the ability of minorities to sustain the occupational and educational gains of the past fifteen years depends not only on those who enter higher education but on those who can hold their own academically, and not only on those who win union jobs but on those who can do the job well.

Whether it is possible to treat people as individuals rather than as group members is as uncertain today as it was in 1954. And whether it is possible to achieve an integrated society without distributing jobs and school places on the basis of group identity is equally uncertain. What does seem likely, though, is that the trend toward formalizing group distinctions in public policy has contributed to a sharpening of group consciousness and group conflict. As a people, we are still far from that sense of common humanity to which the civil rights movement appealed. We may yet find that just such a spirit is required to advance a generous and broad sense of the needs and purposes of American society as a whole.

18

Politicization and the Schools: The Case of Bilingual Education

(1984)

THERE has always been a politics of schools, and no doubt there always will be. Like any other organization populated by human beings, schools have their internal politics; for as long as there have been public schools, there have been political battles over their budget, their personnel policies, their curricula, and their purposes. Anyone who believes that there was once a time in which schools were untouched by political controversy is uninformed about the history of education. The decision-making processes that determine who will be chosen as principal or how the school board will be selected or whether to pass a school bond issue are simply political facts of life that are part and parcel of the administration, financing, and governance of schools. There is also a politics of the curriculum and of the profession, in which contending forces argue about programs and policies. It is hard to imagine a school, a school system, a university, a state board of education, or a national department of education in which these kinds of political conflicts do not exist. They are an intrinsic aspect of complex organizations in which people disagree about how to achieve their goals and about which goals to pursue; to the extent that we operate in a democratic manner, conflict over important and even unimportant issues is inevitable.

There is another kind of politics, however, in which educational institutions become entangled in crusades marked by passionate advocacy, intolerance of criticism, and unyielding dogmatism, and in which the education of children is a secondary rather than a primary consideration. Such crusades go beyond politics-as-usual; they represent the politicization of education. Schools and universities become targets for politicization for several reasons: First, they offer a large captive audience of presumably impressionable minds; second, they are expected to shape the opinions, knowledge, and values of the rising generation, which makes them attractive to those who want to influence the future; and third, since Americans have no strong educational philosophy or educational tradition, almost any claim—properly clothed in rhetorical appeals about the needs of children or of American society—can make its way into the course catalogue or the educational agenda.

Ever since Americans created public schools, financed by tax dollars and controlled by boards of laymen, the schools have been at the center of intermittent struggles over the values that they represent. The founders of the common school, and in particular Horace Mann, believed that the schools could be kept aloof from the religious and political controversies beyond their door, but it has not been easy to keep the crusaders outside the schoolhouse. In the nineteenth century, heated battles were fought over such issues as which Bible would be read in the classroom and whether public dollars might be used to subsidize religious schools. After the onset of World War I, anti-German hostility caused the German language to be routed from American schools, even though nearly a quarter of the high school population studied the language in 1915. Some of this same fervor, strengthened by zeal to hasten the process of assimilation, caused several states to outlaw parochial and private schools and to prohibit the teaching of foreign language in the first eight years of school. Such laws, obviously products of nationalism and xenophobia, were struck down as unconstitutional by the United States Supreme Court in the 1920s. The legislative efforts to abolish nonpublic schools and to bar the teaching of foreign languages were examples of politicization; their purpose was not to improve the education of any child, but to achieve certain social and political goals that the sponsors of these laws believed were of overwhelming importance.

Another example of politicization in education was the crusade to cleanse the schools of teachers and other employees who were suspected of being disloyal, subversive, or controversial. This crusade began in the years after World War I, gathered momentum during the 1930s, and came to full fruition during the loyalty investigations by state and national legislative committees in the 1950s. Fears for national security led to intrusive surveillance of the beliefs, friends, past associations, and political activities of teachers and professors. These inquiries did not improve anyone's education; they used the educational institutions as vehicles towards political goals that were extraneous to education.

A more recent example of politicization occurred on the campuses during the war in Vietnam. Those who had fought political intrusions into educational institutions during the McCarthy era did so on the ground of academic freedom. Academic freedom, they argued, protected the right of students and teachers to express their views, regardless of their content; because of academic freedom, the university served as a sanctuary for dissidents, heretics, and skeptics of all persuasions. During the war in Vietnam, those who tried to maintain the university as a privileged haven for conflicting views, an open marketplace of ideas, found themselves the object of attack by student radicals. Student (and sometimes faculty) radicals believed that opposition to the war was so important that those who did not agree with them should be harassed and even silenced.

Faced with a moral issue, the activists argued, the university could not stand above the battle, nor could it tolerate the expression of "immoral" views. In this spirit, young radicals tried to prevent those with whom they disagreed from speaking and teaching; towards this end, they heckled speakers, disrupted classes, and even planted bombs on campus. These actions were intended to politicize schools and campuses and, in some instances, they succeeded. They were advocated by sincere and zealous individuals who earnestly believed that education could not take place within a context of political neutrality. Their efforts at politicization stemmed not from any desire to improve education as such, but from the pursuit of political goals.

As significant as the student movement and the McCarthy era were as examples of the dangers of politicization, they were short-lived in comparison to the policy of racial segregation. Segregation of public school children by their race and ancestry was established by law in seventeen states and by custom in many communities beyond those states. The practice of assigning public school children and teachers on the basis of their race had no educational justification;

it was not intended to improve anyone's education. It was premised on the belief in the innate inferiority of people whose skin was of dark color. Racial segregation as policy and practice politicized the schools; it used them to buttress a racist social and political order. It limited the educational opportunities available to blacks. Racial segregation was socially and politically so effective in isolating blacks from opportunity for economic advancement and educationally so devastating in retarding their learning that our society continues to pay a heavy price to redress the cumulative deficits of generations of poor education.

The United States Supreme Court's 1954 decision, *Brown* v. *Board of Education,* started the process of ending state-imposed racial segregation. In those southern states where segregation was the cornerstone of a way of life, white resistance to desegregation was prolonged and intense. The drive to disestablish racial segregation and to uproot every last vestige of its effects was unquestionably necessary. The practice of assigning children to school by their race and of segregating other public facilities by race was a national disgrace. However, the process through which desegregation came about dramatically altered the politics of schools; courts and regulatory agencies at the federal and state level became accustomed to intervening in the internal affairs of educational institutions, and the potential for politicization of the schools was significantly enlarged.

The slow pace of desegregation in the decade after the *Brown* decision, concurrent with a period of rising expectations, contributed to a dramatic buildup of frustration and rage among blacks, culminating in the protests, civil disorders, and riots of the mid-1960s. In response, Congress enacted major civil rights laws in 1964 and 1965, and the federal courts became aggressive in telling school boards what to do to remedy their constitutional violations. Initially, these orders consisted of commands to produce racially mixed schools. However, some courts went beyond questions of racial mix. In Washington, D.C., a federal district judge in 1967 directed the school administration to abandon ability grouping, which he believed discriminated against black children. This was the first time that a federal court found a common pedagogical practice to be unconstitutional.[1]

In the nearly two decades since that decision, the active intervention of the federal judiciary into school affairs has ceased to be unusual. In Ann Arbor, Michigan, a federal judge ordered the school board to train teachers in "black English," a program subsequently found to be ineffectual in improving the education of black students. In California, a federal judge barred the use of intelligence tests for placement of students in special education classes, even though reputable psychologists defend their validity. In Boston, where the school board was found guilty of intentionally segregating children by race, the federal judge assumed full control over the school system for more than a decade; even reform superintendents who were committed to carrying out the judge's program for desegregation complained of the hundreds of court orders regulating every aspect of schooling, hiring, promotion, curriculum, and financing. In 1982, in a case unrelated to desegregation, a state judge in West Virginia ordered the state education department to do "no less than completely re-construct the entire system of education in West Virginia," and the judge started the process of reconstruction by setting down his own standards for facilities, administration, and curriculum, including what was to be taught and for how many minutes each week.[2]

Perhaps this is as good a way of bringing about school reform as any other. No doubt school officials are delighted when a judge orders the state legislature to raise taxes on behalf of the schools. But it does seem to be a repudiation of our democratic political structure when judges go beyond issues of constitutional rights, don the mantle of school superintendent, and use their authority to change promotional standards, to reconstruct the curriculum, or to impose their own pedagogical prescriptions.

Now, by the definition of politicization that I earlier offered—that is, when educational institutions become the focus of dogmatic crusaders whose purposes are primarily political and only incidentally related to children's education—these examples may not qualify as politicization, although they do suggest how thin is the line between politics and politicization. After all, the judges were doing what they thought would produce better education. The court decisions in places like Ann Arbor, Boston, California, and West Virginia may be thought of as a shift in the politics of schools, a shift that has brought the judiciary into the decision-making process as a full-fledged partner in shaping educational policy. Reasonable people differ about the appropriate role of the courts as mediators among conflicting parties in educational disputes, even those involving questions of pedagogy and curriculum.

The long struggle to desegregate American schools put them at the center of political battles for more than a generation and virtually destroyed the belief that schools could remain above politics. Having lost their apolitical shield, the schools also lost their capacity to resist efforts to politicize them. In the absence of resistance, demands by interest groups of varying ideologies escalated, each trying to impose its own agenda on the curriculum, the textbooks, the school library, or the teachers. Based on the activities of single-issue groups, any number of contemporary educational policies would serve equally well as examples of politicization. The example that I have chosen as illustrative of politicization is bilingual education. The history of this program exemplifies a campaign on behalf of social and political goals that are only tangentially related to education. I would like to sketch briefly the bilingual controversy, which provides an overview of the new politics of education and demonstrates the tendency within this new politics to use educational programs for noneducational ends.

Demands for bilingual education arose as an outgrowth of the civil rights movement. As it evolved, that movement contained complex, and occasionally contradictory, elements. One facet of the movement appealed for racial integration and assimilation, which led to court orders for busing and racial balance; but the dynamics of the movement also inspired appeals to racial solidarity, which led to demands for black studies, black control of black schools, and other race-conscious policies. Whether the plea was for integration or for separatism, advocates could always point to a body of social science as evidence for their goals.

Race consciousness became a necessary part of the remedies that courts fashioned, but its presence legitimized ethnocentrism as a force in American politics. In the late 1960s, the courts, Congress, and policymakers—having been told for years by spokesmen for the civil rights movement that all children should be treated equally without regard to their race or ancestry—frequently heard compelling testimony by political activists and social scientists about the value of ethnic particularism in the curriculum.

Congress first endorsed funding for bilingual education in 1968, at a time when ethnocentrism had become a powerful political current. In hearings on this legislation, proponents of bilingual education argued that non-English-speaking children did poorly in school because they had low self-esteem, and that this low self-esteem was caused by the absence of their native language from the classroom. They claimed that if the children were taught in their native tongue and about their native culture, they would have higher self-esteem, better attitudes toward school, and higher educational achievement. Bilingual educators also insisted that children would learn English more readily if they already knew another language.

In the congressional hearings, both advocates and congressmen seemed to agree that the purpose of bilingual education was to help non-English speakers succeed in school and in society. But the differences between them were not then obvious. The congressmen believed that bilingual education would serve as a temporary transition into the regular English language program. But the bilingual educators saw the program as an opportunity to maintain the language and culture of the non-English-speaking student, while he was learning English.[3]

What was extraordinary about the Bilingual Education Act of 1968, which has since been renewed several times, is that it was the first time that the Congress had ever legislated a given pedagogical method. In practice, bilingual education means a program in which children study the major school subjects in a language other than English. Funding of the program, although small within the context of the federal education budget, created strong constituencies for its continuation, both within the federal government and among recipient agencies. No different from other interest groups, these constituencies pressed for expansion and strengthening of their program. Just as lifelong vocational educators are unlikely to ask whether their program works, so career bilingual educators are committed to their method as a philosophy, not as a technique for language instruction. The difference is this: Techniques are subject to evaluation, which may cause them to be revised or discarded; philosophies are not.

In 1974, the Supreme Court's *Lau* v. *Nichols* decision reinforced demands for bilingual education. The Court ruled against the San Francisco public schools for their failure to provide English language instruction for 1,800 non-English-speaking Chinese students. The Court's decision was reasonable and appropriate. The Court said, "There is no equality of treatment merely by providing students with the same facilities, textbooks, teachers, and curriculum; for students who do not understand English are effectively foreclosed from any meaningful education." The decision did not endorse any particular remedy. It said, "Teaching English to the students of Chinese ancestry who do not speak the language is one choice. Giving instruction to the group in Chinese is another. There may be others."[4]

Despite the Court's prudent refusal to endorse any particular method of instruction, the bilingual educators interpreted the *Lau* decision as a mandate for bilingual programs. In the year after the decision, the United States Office of Education established a task force to fashion guidelines for the implementation of the *Lau* decision; the task force was composed of bilingual educators and representatives of language minority groups. The task force fashioned regulations that prescribed in exhaustive detail how school districts should prepare and carry out bilingual programs for non-English-speaking students. The districts were directed to identify the student's primary language, not by his proficiency in English, but by determining which language was most often spoken in the student's home, which language he had learned first, and which language he used most often. Thus a student would be eligible for a bilingual program even if he was entirely fluent in English.[5]

Furthermore, while the Supreme Court refused to endorse any given method, the task force directed that non-English-speaking students should receive bilingual education that emphasized instruction in their native language and culture. Districts were discouraged from using the "English as a Second Language" approach, which consists of intensive, supplemental English-only instruction, or immersion techniques, in which students are instructed in English within an English-only context.

Since the establishment of the bilingual education program, many millions of dollars have been spent to support bilingual programs in more than sixty different languages. Among those receiving funding to administer and staff such programs, bilingual education is obviously popular, but there are critics who think that it is educationally unsound. Proponents of desegregation have complained that bilingual education needlessly segregates non-English speakers from others of their age. At a congressional hearing in 1977, one desegregation specialist complained that bilingual programs had been funded "without any significant proof that they would work. . . . There is nothing in the research to suggest that children can effectively learn English without continuous interaction with other children who are native English speakers."[6]

The research on bilingual education has been contradictory, and studies that favor or criticize the bilingual approach have been attacked as biased. Researchers connected to bilingual institutes claim that their programs resulted in significant gains for non-English-speaking children. But a four-year study commissioned by the United States Office of Education concluded that students who learned bilingually did not achieve at a higher level than those in regular classes, nor were their attitudes towards school significantly different. What they seemed to learn best, the study found, was the language in which they were instructed.[7]

One of the few evidently unbiased, nonpolitical assessments of bilingual research was published in 1982 in the *Harvard Educational Review*. A survey of international findings, it concluded that "bilingual programs are neither better nor worse than other instructional methods." The author found that in the absence of compelling experimental support for this method, there was "no legal necessity or research basis for the federal government to advocate or require a specific educational approach."[8]

If the research is in fact inconclusive, then there is no justification for mandating the use of bilingual education or any other single pedagogy. The bilingual method may or may not be the best way to learn English. Language instruction programs that are generally regarded as outstanding, such as those provided for Foreign Service officers or by the nationally acclaimed center at Middlebury College, are immersion programs, in which students embark on a systematic program of intensive language learning without depending on their native tongue. Immersion programs may not be appropriate for all children, but then neither is any single pedagogical method. The method to be used should be determined by the school authorities and the professional staff, based on their resources and competence.

Despite the fact that the Supreme Court did not endorse bilingual education, the lower federal courts have tended to treat this pedagogy as a civil right, and more than a dozen states have mandated its use in their public schools. The path by which bilingual education came to be viewed as a civil right, rather than as one method of teaching language, demonstrates the politicization of the language issue in American education. The United States Commission on Civil Rights endorsed bilingual education as a civil right nearly a decade ago. Public interest lawyers and civil rights lawyers have also regarded bilingual education as a basic civil right. An article in 1983 in the *Columbia Journal of Law and Social Problems* contended that bilingual education "may be the most effective method of compensatory language instruction currently used to educate language-minority students." It based this conclusion not on a review of educational research but on statements made by various political agencies.[9]

The article states, for example, as a matter of fact rather than opinion: ". . . by offering subject matter instruction in a language understood by language-minority students, the bilingual-bicultural method maximizes achievement, and thus minimizes feelings of inferiority that might accompany a poor academic performance. By ridding the school environment of those features which may damage a language-minority child's self-image and thereby interfere with the educative process, bilingual-bicultural education creates the atmosphere most conducive to successful learning."[10]

If there were indeed conclusive evidence for these statements, then bilingual-bicultural education *should* be imposed on school districts throughout the country. However, the picture is complicated; there are good bilingual programs, and there are ineffective bilingual programs. In and of itself, bilingualism is one pedagogical method, as subject to variation and misuse as any other single method. To date, no school district has claimed that the bilingual method succeeded in sharply decreasing the dropout rate of Hispanic children or markedly raising their achievement scores in English and other subjects. The bilingual method is not necessarily inferior to other methods; its use should not be barred. There simply is no conclusive evidence that bilingualism should be preferred to all other ways of instructing non-English-speaking students. This being the case, there are no valid reasons for courts or federal agencies to impose this method on school districts for all non-English speakers, to the exclusion of other methods of language instruction.

Bilingual education exemplifies politicization because its

advocates press its adoption regardless of its educational effectiveness, and they insist that it must be made mandatory regardless of the wishes of the parents and children who are its presumed beneficiaries. It is a political program whose goals are implicit in the term "biculturalism." The aim is to use the public schools to promote the maintenance of distinct ethnic communities, each with its own cultural heritage and language. This in itself is a valid goal for a democratic nation as diverse and pluralistic as ours, but it is questionable whether this goal is appropriately pursued by the public schools, rather than by the freely chosen activities of individuals and groups.

Then there is the larger question of whether bilingual education actually promotes equality of educational opportunity. Unless it enables non-English-speaking children to learn English and to enter into the mainstream of American society, it may hinder equality of educational opportunity. The child who spends most of his instructional time learning in Croatian or Greek or Spanish is likely to learn Croatian, Greek, or Spanish. Fluency in these languages will be of little help to those who want to apply to American colleges, universities, graduate schools, or employers, unless they are also fluent in English.

Of course, our nation needs much more foreign language instruction. But we should not confuse our desire to promote foreign languages in general with the special educational needs of children who do not know how to speak and read English in an English-language society.

Will our educational institutions ever be insulated from the extremes of politicization? It seems highly unlikely, in view of the fact that our schools and colleges are deeply embedded in the social and political mainstream. What is notably different today is the vastly increased power of the federal government and the courts to intervene in educational institutions, because of the expansion of the laws and the dependence of almost all educational institutions on public funding. To avoid unwise and dangerous politicization, government agencies should strive to distinguish between their proper role as protectors of fundamental constitutional rights and inappropriate intrusion into complex issues of curriculum and pedagogy.

This kind of institutional restraint would be strongly abetted if judges and policymakers exercised caution and skepticism in their use of social science testimony. Before making social research the basis for constitutional edicts, judges and policymakers should understand that social science findings are usually divergent, limited, tentative, and partial.

We need the courts as vigilant guardians of our rights; we need federal agencies that respond promptly to any violations of those rights. But we also need educational institutions that are free to exercise their responsibilities without fear of pressure groups and political lobbies. Decisions about which textbooks to use, which theories to teach, which books to place in the school library, how to teach, and what to teach are educational issues. They should be made by appropriate lay and professional authorities on educational grounds. In a democratic society, all of us share the responsibility to protect schools, colleges, and universities against unwarranted political intrusion into educational affairs.

19

A Good School

(1984)

IN the not distant past, when attitudes toward public education were strongly positive, it rarely occurred to anyone to seek out examples of "effective" schools. The evident assumption was that most schools were good, and that the ineffectual school was an aberration. The first annual Gallup Poll about public schools in 1969 showed a strikingly high regard for schools and the teaching profession; three out of four persons responded that they would like to see their children take up teaching as a career. The level of public esteem for the schools at that time was even more remarkable in light of the overwhelmingly negative tone of the popular literature on schools in the mid-1960s.

After a decade of strident attacks on the schools, a decade in which public confidence waned, a small number of educational writers and researchers started looking for examples of good schools. There had long been a tradition of writing about a particular school as a way of trumpeting certain values that the school embodied, but the climate of the times tended to define the "good school." In the

Progressive era, certain schools were singled out because of their antitraditional features, such as their combination of work and play or their engagement in the social life of the surrounding community. In the 1960s, certain schools were lauded for their political activism or their success in "liberating" children from bourgeois values.

By the late 1970s and early 1980s, an "effective school" came to be identified with the characteristics set out in the writings of the late Ron Edmonds of the Harvard Graduate School of Education. Perhaps because Edmonds was black, he was able to assert values that would have sounded disturbingly traditional to the educational establishment if voiced by a white. Edmonds identified schools where academic achievement seemed to be independent of pupils' social class, and he concluded that such schools had an outstanding principal, high expectations for all children, an orderly atmosphere, a regular testing program, and an emphasis on academic learning.

Edmonds' conclusions may have seemed like a series of commonplace observations to most people, but they were received as stunning insights in the arcane world of educational policy. (Outsiders are repeatedly astonished by what passes for revelation in the education field; for instance, one of the great discoveries of recent years— though still not universally accepted—is that student achievement may be positively related to something called "time-on-task." In other words, what one learns is determined in part by the time spent learning it.) In fact, Edmonds was not alone in his interest in learning as the major measurement of school quality. Other studies reinforced his view that student achievement could be raised by sound educational practices. To appreciate the importance of this change in orientation, one must recall the many years in which academic achievement was treated with disdain in comparison to nonacademic goals.

A Good School

Writing about a single school is also a good way for a writer to test out his own educational ideals and to display them for public inspection. Now, in the interest of candor, I confess that I instinctually hew to John Dewey's admonition: "What the best and wisest parent wants for his own child, that must the community want for all of its children. Any other ideal for our schools is narrow and unlovely. . . ." The best and wisest parents, I expect, want their child to read and write fluently; to speak articulately; to listen carefully; to learn to participate in the give-and-take of group discussion; to learn self-discipline and to develop the capacity for deferred gratification; to read and appreciate good literature; to have a strong knowledge of history, both of our own nation and of others; to appreciate the values of a free, democratic society; to understand science, mathematics, technology, and the natural world; to become engaged in the arts, both as a participant and as one capable of appreciating aesthetic excellence. I expect such parents would also want a good program of physical education and perhaps even competence in a foreign language. Presumably, these mythical best and wisest parents want their child to have some sense of possible occupation or profession, but it seems doubtful that they would want their child to use school time for vocational training, at least in the precollegiate years.

That our public schools have long operated on contrary assumptions should be obvious. The program I have described is usually called the "academic track," and not more than 35 to 38 percent of American secondary students were receiving this kind of well-balanced preparation in the early 1980s. Acting not *in loco parentis* but on behalf of the state, educators have sorted children into vocational or general tracks, the former to prepare for a specific job, the latter being neither academic nor vocational. For reasons that are rooted largely in misplaced compassion—not in meanness or ignorance—our educational philosophy has dictated that academic learning is not for everyone; that it is too demanding for the average student; that its apparent inutility limits its value to the average student; that too much of it will cause students to drop out of high school in droves; and that such students should take courses that provide job skills, life skills, practical know-how, and immediate relevance to their own lives.

In public schools, curricular tracking has become a common practice. By tracking, I refer to the academic/vocational/general trichotomy, not to ability grouping. Ability grouping permits students to take different amounts of time to reach roughly similar goals; tracking offers students vastly different kinds of educational programs. The practice of tracking raises all sorts of questions: Who decides which students go into the academic track? At what age does the tracking begin? To what extent is the decision to funnel a student into a nonacademic track a response to his parents' occupations and social class? Should the public school—supported by taxes from all citizens—have the right to determine that some students will get an education of high quality while others will get a denatured version?

To such questions, which go to the core of our democratic ideology, the defender of the present system might well respond: "Such naiveté! Dreams of perfection! In a perfect world, where all children had the same genetic and cultural inheritance, such a scheme of high-quality education for all might make sense. But in reality, children differ dramatically. Some come to school already knowing how to read; others can barely decipher words after six years of trying. Some are brilliant; others struggle to master the rudiments of learning. The smart ones are clearly college bound and should have an academic curriculum. The others should have courses where the level of challenge is not too high, where they can get a feeling of success. And more than subject matter, what the majority needs most is vocational training to get them ready for the workplace. That is what they want, and they should get it. Let us not forget that the great achievement of modern educational research has been the recognition that the curriculum must be adjusted to meet the differing needs of children."

For years, such views have represented the conventional wisdom in public education. The school that I have selected as an example of an effective school—the Edward R. Murrow High School of Brooklyn, New York— explicitly rejects these views. Its principal, Saul Bruckner, is a product of the public schools as well as a twenty-seven-year veteran of the New York City public school system. I learned a great deal by spending time in his school; I changed some of the ideas I brought with me. I am not sure that I agree with every practice and program in the school, but I deeply admire its tone and its high academic aspirations for all pupils. I think what Bruckner is doing deserves attention, not because it is the only way or even the best way, but because it is one successful way of wedding traditional goals with nontraditional means.

Murrow was opened in 1974 and officially designated an experimental school by the New York City Board of Education. Its 3,000 students are drawn from the borough of Brooklyn. Half are white, and half are members of minority groups. One of the many unusual features of the school is that it treats all of its pupils as college bound. No one is tracked into a vocational or "general" program. Yet the school is purposely composed of children with a broad range of abilities. By board of education mandate, at least 25 percent of Murrow's entering students read below grade level; no more than 25 percent read above grade level; and the remaining 50 percent read at about grade level. There is no entrance examination, but competition for admission is vigorous; in 1983, there were some 9,500 applicants for 800 places in the entering class. Critics complain that special schools like Murrow "cream away" the best students from other public high schools, but about one-fourth of Murrow's enrollment consists of students from parochial and independent schools whose parents had previously rejected the public schools. Student morale is undoubtedly lifted by awareness of the difficulty of gaining entry into Murrow. The very process of applying makes every student a committed participant in his own education and eliminates the handful of unwilling students who otherwise make school life an ordeal for teachers and other students. Since Murrow has the luxury of not admitting those who have a well-established record of truancy, disruptive behavior, or criminal activity, it occasionally gets pilloried by detractors as "atypical," but it may instead demonstrate that mixing those who want to learn with those who don't want to learn is no favor to either group.

Even though the students at Murrow represent a wide ability range, all are expected and required to take a strong academic program in order to graduate, that is, a minimum of five academic courses throughout the school year. The academically gifted take more than five, and there are advanced placement courses in every subject area. The New York City school system requires one year of foreign language, but most students at Murrow take three or four (the school offers Spanish, French, Latin, Hebrew, and Italian). Similarly, most students take more than the required two years of science and mathematics. Advanced science students may enroll in a sequence that includes six years of science; weak science students may take astronomy or horticulture instead of the rigorous course in physics. All must take at least four years of English, including a year of writing instruction, and three and a half years of social studies. This level of academic engagement stands in stark contrast to the figures reported by national surveys. For example, only about 15 percent of American secondary students study *any* foreign language; only 6 percent of the nation's students finish a third year of foreign language study, but at Murrow at least 65 percent do. When compared to national enrollment rates in subjects like algebra, geometry, and the natural sciences, Murrow looks like a private school instead of a public school made up of a broad cross section of pupils.

The students who read two or more years below grade level receive intensive remedial instruction in reading and writing while enrolled in regular courses. The school does not exclude average or below-average students from any of its upper-level courses, as many schools do. Consequently, even advanced placement courses in English, social studies, mathematics, and science contain a diverse spectrum, and occasionally teachers complain about students in their advanced placement classes or the calculus class "who don't belong there." But the school's philosophy is that no student should be discouraged from taking on an academic challenge. Unlike teachers at many other public schools, most teachers at Murrow do not practice grade inflation (20 percent of all its grades last year were "no credit," the equivalent of not passing the course) or social promotion (no one graduates until all of the academic requirements are met, and some students take longer than four years to finish).

The results of the Murrow program have been impressive. The annual dropout rate is only 4 percent, compared to a citywide rate of 11 percent. Daily attendance averages 88 percent, far above that of other urban high schools. Disciplinary problems are negligible. Nearly 90 percent of its graduates continue to either a four-year or a two-year college program. The school urges even those who intend to be secretaries to take a degree at a community college in order to promote their occupational mobility later. The chairman of the social studies department, Mary Butz, explained to me on my first visit to the school, "The climate of the school is middle-class Jewish. These kids all believe that education will help them get ahead, move up into college and good jobs. They have bought the whole package. They believe in themselves, and they believe in us."

How can Murrow get away with its ambitious program? Well, for one thing, its students have been persuaded that Murrow is a very special school and that they are very special students. The school year and the day are organized somewhat differently from what is usually found in a typical school. Instead of two semesters, there are four cycles of ten weeks each. The principal believes that the advantage of four ten-week courses is that students are encouraged to take risks, knowing that they won't be stuck for an entire year (or semester) with a bad choice. Instead of every subject meeting daily, the time is divided into four weekly meetings; this gives the students some blocks of optional time which they can use as they wish, either to study, to do homework, or to socialize with friends. Unlike most other schools, Murrow permits the students to cluster in the halls during their optional time, and affinity groups have claimed different territories (none based on race). "Over there are my theater groupies," says Bruckner. "And those kids are the science groupies." As we walk through the hall, he sees a Hispanic girl curled up on the tile floor, deeply engrossed in a paperback book. "What's that you're reading?" She holds up the book, and he reads: *"Richard II."* In the English "resource center" (like a study hall), a group of youngsters work together on a project. In an otherwise empty classroom, half a dozen boys are setting up a videotape camera, part of a project for their literature course, "Detective Story." In the computer center, two or three students share a single machine, figuring out problems together, teaching each other.

Murrow represents an ingenious answer to the question: How do you enlist students' interest in their education without giving them control of the curriculum? Murrow does it by setting high requirements for graduation, but permits students to meet those requirements by choosing among a carefully designed mix of required and elective courses. The required sophomore course in American literature, for example, focuses on textual analysis of major poems, novels, and plays. Whether required or elective, all academic courses assign homework and writing exercises. The many ten-week elective courses have jazzy titles but fairly traditional readings; for example, students in "Youth and Identity" read Salinger's *The Catcher in the Rye,* Carson McCullers' *A Member of the Wedding,* Paul Zindel's *The Pigman,* and Elie Wiesel's *Night.* Students in "Novel into Film" read *The Great Gatsby* and *Great Expectations.* Many electives are unabashedly classical, like the Shakespeare class that reads *Romeo and Juliet, Richard II,* and *Othello,* or the advanced placement course that reads Milton, John Donne, Ben Jonson, Jane Austen, and other great writers of English literature.

In reviewing the literary offerings available to Murrow students, I could not help but contrast them to my own public school education in Texas. Although it is customary to lament the decline of public education, I believe that Murrow is a far better school than my alma mater in Houston. The literature curriculum of San Jacinto High School was uniform and limited. I recall a year of British fiction that never moved beyond *Silas Marner* and *Julius Caesar.* I have no idea why this selection was inviolate for so long, because I believe that such books as *Pride and*

Prejudice or *Emma* or *Great Expectations* are wonderfully appealing to adolescents, while few adolescents have the maturity to appreciate George Eliot's complex prose.

Wisely administered, electives enable a school to provide what I would call the illusion of choice. Students do, in fact, make choices, but "wisely administered" means that they should not be permitted to make bad choices, like junk courses without academic merit ("bachelor living" or "personal grooming"). The illusion of choice can be readily adapted to the English sequence because the traditional English I through English VIII (which I took in my four years of public education) can easily be rearranged and attractively packaged. Thus, a course called "The Woman Writer" appeals to the modern sensibility, but is a fine setting in which to teach the works of Jane Austen, George Eliot, and Charlotte Brontë, and "The Literature of Social Protest" turns out to be a good marketing tool for the works of writers like Orwell and Dickens.

While repackaging can work neatly for the English curriculum, it has proved to be nearly a disaster in the undisciplined realm of the "social studies." The field—once dominated by history—is now rootless and very nearly formless. Among social studies educators, the phrase "chronological history" is frequently used as a term of derision. Even courses entitled "American History" are likely to eschew the traditional narrative of events, leaders, ideas, and institutions in favor of themes, topics, and trends. A significant portion of the Murrow social studies curriculum reflects the political and social fragmentation of the past generation, as well as the disorganization of the social studies as a field. There is a required course in American government, focusing on political institutions, and a required course in American diplomatic history, relating the history of America's foreign policy, but most other courses are either specialized excursions into some

thematic "experience" (the word "history" is usually
avoided) or overly broad, like "the global experience."
While history is in retreat, psychology, economics, and
law studies are thriving: A student, for example, may
choose among eight different psychology courses (e.g.,
"Social Psychology," "Abnormal Psychology," "Developmental Psychology," "The Psychology of Aging," etc.).

Despite my reservations, the social studies program at
Murrow is far stronger than at most schools. For one
thing, there are no contentless courses in "values clarification," "process skills," or "decision making"; second,
while the catalogue contains the feminist "Herstory" and
"The Black Experience," there is otherwise no further
ethnic or group fragmentation of the curriculum. Perhaps
most important, the department includes some gifted
teachers, who have before them at all times the example
of their principal, Saul Bruckner, himself a master teacher
of American history. He is frequently in classrooms, observing, prodding, and instructing other members of the
staff to enliven their presentations and their teaching style.
Under his critical gaze, the course in "Origins of Western
Civilization" really is a treatment of Western civilization
from ancient Rome to the Renaissance, and the "Isms"
course turns out to be a history of eighteenth- and nineteenth-century Europe.

I have to explain how I happened to learn about this
school. I was involved in sponsoring a conference in
Minneapolis in the spring of 1984, on behalf of the
National Endowment for the Humanities, on improving
the teaching of the humanities in the high schools. The
opening speaker was a distinguished social historian, who
discussed the problem of integrating ethnic diversity into
the common culture. It has been my experience that public
discussions of ethnicity, especially among educators, invariably are pervaded by a sanctimonious tone. Everyone

speaks reverentially of the nobility and struggles of oppressed minority groups (who cumulatively add up to a large majority of the population), and the air gets heavy with guilt and piety.

During the coffee break, a young teacher grabbed me by the arm to tell me, in an unmistakably Brooklyn accent, that an American Indian woman—known in current bureaucratic jargon as a Native American person—had just assailed her in scatological language. "What?" I said. "What? How can this be?" "Well," she said, "this Indian woman asked me if she could use the bathroom, and I told her that the bathroom was reserved for conference participants. So, she used the bathroom anyway. When she came out a few moments later, she jabbed her finger in my chest, called me by an odious term, and warned, 'White woman, don't mess with me anymore!'"

Her name card said, "Mary Butz, Edward R. Murrow High School, Brooklyn, New York." Charmed by her indifference to the demands of ethnic piety, I asked her to tell me about her school. She said, with what I later learned was characteristic candor, that it was the best school in New York City, because it had the best principal and "the greatest kids." I was startled, because over the years, I have met so many embittered teachers in the New York City school system, who recall or have heard of the school system's reputation in another era, an era when the New York City public schools were widely recognized as pioneers and when their students were pressing hard for future greatness as literati or scientists.

Naturally, I wanted to see the best school in New York City, the best principal, and the greatest kids, particularly because I had been in so many high schools that seemed like armed camps and in so many subway cars at the end of the school day when high school students used their raw energy to intimidate everyone else. So, not many days later, I trekked out to the Midwood section of Brooklyn to find an undistinguished, nearly windowless modern brick building, set in the midst of an ethnically diverse middle-class neighborhood. In an example of incredibly stupid planning, the Murrow building abuts the subway tracks (the noise of passing trains regularly disrupts classes in progress) and has no surrounding campus, although the students are able to use another school's athletic field across the street.

As it happened, I arrived on the day that Bruckner teaches an advanced placement section of American history. There were about thirty youngsters in the class, and the question for the day was: "Was it moral for the United States to drop the atomic bomb on Japan?" Something inside me warned that I was in for a session of moralistic Truman bashing, but I was wrong. The students (some of whom were Oriental) had read the textbook description of the war. When I entered, the class was discussing the incidence of cancer in Hiroshima and Nagasaki. Then Bruckner used an overhead projector to display contemporary news stories from the *New York Times* and the *Herald Tribune.* One headline told the human cost of capturing Okinawa: 45,000 American casualties, 90,000 Japanese casualties. How many lives might be lost in an invasion of the mainland? A mimeographed handout discussed Japanese kamikaze raids and brutality towards American prisoners, which gave the students a flavor of Japanese and American wartime attitudes. A fair conclusion, which did not involve prejudice towards our Japanese adversaries, was that they would fight ferociously to the end. Lest anyone jump to the easy conclusion that the decision to drop the bomb was moral, the principal-teacher also displayed comments by generals and revisionist historians that dropping the bomb was not necessary to end the war.

THE SCHOOLS WE DESERVE

The lesson was taught in a Socratic manner. Bruckner did not lecture. He asked questions and kept up a rapid-fire dialogue among the students. "Why?" "How do you know?" "What does this mean?" "Do you really think so?" Sometimes he called on students who were desperately waving their arms; other times he solicited the views of those who were sitting quietly. By the time the class was finished, the students had covered a great deal of material about American foreign and domestic policies during World War II; they had argued heatedly; most of them had tried out different points of view, seeing the problem from different angles. It was a good lesson: It was well planned, utilizing a variety of materials and media; and the students were alert and responsive.

Bruckner's lesson was at odds with the usual characterization of American teaching. In the past year or two, most critics of the schools have complained about the quality of teaching. Educators like John Goodlad of UCLA and Theodore Sizer, former headmaster of Phillips Andover Academy, believe that there is too much "teacher telling," too much student passivity, and little if any thought-provoking activity in the typical classroom. A major study prepared for the National Institute of Education a few years ago contended that teaching in American schools has remained unchanged—that is, boring and teacher dominated—throughout the century. Well, I thought to myself, I have seen one great teacher; what happens in the other classrooms?

I visited many classrooms and observed teachers in every subject area. I saw some outstanding teaching, some passably good classes, and a few that failed, but in no instance did I see a teacher droning on to a class of bored students. The teaching style in the building was remarkably consistent, and every teacher used materials and experiences that were outside the textbook. In the best classes, the focus of the lesson was on the dialogue, the intellectual exchange sparked by the teacher and kept alive by student participation. In one literature class, the students debated O. Henry's use of language to establish the tone of a story; in a chemistry class, thirty-five students jointly figured out how a battery operates.

I later learned that Bruckner expects all his teachers to use what is called the "developmental lesson" or the "socialized recitation." If they do not know how to teach this way when they are assigned to Murrow, they are taught the method by the department chairman. At its best, it works magnificently: Students listen, speak out, think, disagree with each other, change their minds, make judgments. For this method to work, two things are necessary: One, the teacher has to be well prepared, having planned out the lesson in advance with an "aim" or problem to be solved, with pivotal questions to provoke student discussion, and with materials (a political cartoon, a newspaper headline, a quotation from a participant or critic, or an excerpt from a book) to stimulate new lines of inquiry; two, the students must bring something to the lesson in the way of reading or homework, so that they can respond to the teacher's questions with ideas and insights of their own. If the teacher does not prepare well and if the students are uninformed, the developmental lesson can dwindle into a vapid exchange of uninformed opinion, of less value than a traditional didactic lecture.

Bruckner's biggest problem is building a good teaching staff. Within the context of the public school bureaucracy, this requires consummate skill. When Bruckner opened Murrow in 1974, he was officially permitted to select only 35 percent of his staff. Because he was a veteran of "the system," he was able to play the teacher selection game like a Stradivarius, and he ended up with a staff in which about 70 percent of the teachers were of his choosing. He might encourage a skilled teacher to apply to join his staff, who would then not be counted as one of his "picks." Since the school opened in the midst of the city's fiscal crisis, Bruckner was able to hire many talented young teachers who had been laid off by other schools. Among the 30 percent or so that he did not choose were, inevitably, some lemons. It is possible, but not easy, to fire a probationary teacher (who has taught for less than three years); it is nearly impossible to oust a tenured teacher. "A principal can't fire a teacher simply because he is boring or incompetent or even when you know that he treats the kids like dirt," Bruckner says. "He must be grossly negligent, persistently late for class, drunk in class, something like that."

What a principal can do, however, is to lay off staff, but only in order of seniority. One principal, Bruckner says, wiped out most of his English department to get rid of a teacher with fifteen years of seniority; seven able young teachers were excessed in order to drop a bad senior teacher. Bruckner closed down his guidance department in order to remove the person assigned to Murrow. Eventually, the Brooklyn superintendent for high schools ordered him to hire guidance counselors, and he continued to hire and lay off until he got the people he wanted. Usually it is easier to lay off personnel than to go through the procedure of ousting them. Not only is it time-consuming, but if the principal wins, the teacher is stripped of his license. It is akin to having a lawyer disbarred, with this exception: The teacher can get a license in another area. For example, Bruckner had the licenses revoked from two probationary teachers: One was a teacher of the handicapped (special education); the other taught social studies. Before long, both were reinstated: The ex-special education teacher had become an elementary teacher, and the ex-social studies teacher had moved into special education. "Well," he says with resignation, "I didn't get them out of the system, but I got them out of this school."

Bruckner speaks with passion about how the structure of public education contributes to the "infantilization" of teachers. "Teachers," he complains, "have little responsibility for the conditions of their working lives. We call teaching a profession, but if so, it is the only profession in which there is no opportunity for growth while remaining in the profession." Teachers have lost a great deal of authority to make decisions, not only to supervisors but also to their own organizations and to federal, state, and local mandates. "For most of the important things in their day," Bruckner says, "teachers depend on someone else. Someone else assigns them a room, someone else gives them a daily schedule, someone else writes their lesson plan." Yet in the classroom they have total control, and no matter what the official course of study says, the teacher defines the curriculum every day. Outside the classroom, however, the teachers "are like students. They have very limited say over their life and that creates bitterness and hostility." To break through this "infantilization," Bruckner encourages teachers to design their own courses and to take more responsibility for school affairs. Perhaps the most promising innovation has sprung from the science department, where teachers visit one another's classrooms and discuss content and methodology; their professional critiques of one another take the place of an official observation by a supervisor. Bruckner hopes that other departments will follow suit: "Doctors observe each other practice and learn from one another; so do lawyers. Why shouldn't teachers?"

Like other big-city high schools in the 1980s, Murrow is constantly threatened by financial pressures. Average class size is now up to thirty-four in the city's high schools, the largest in many years. The library is funded at only one dollar per year per student; half of the library budget pays for the *New York Times* on microfilm and its index, leaving only $1,500 for books and magazine subscriptions. At today's prices, $1,500 does not buy much of either. In order to continue using a diversity of materials and media in the classroom, which is integral to the lively approach that Bruckner advocates, the school has heavy expenses for equipment, supplies, and repairs. Occasionally, he has traded in a teaching position (valued at $33,000) in order to maintain the school's duplicating machines, mimeograph machines, computers, overhead projectors, and audiovisual equipment.

The school has a climate that is relaxed and tension free. Teachers and students alike know that they are in a good school, and this sense of being special contributes to high morale. Yet the tenuousness of the authority structure of a big school was revealed to me one morning when the principal was away. Word spread through the building that the police bomb squad had closed off part of the second and third floors, and it was true. Students milled in the corridors, elaborating on the rumor. An assistant principal announced on the public address system, "Everyone return to your classroom. There is no danger at the present moment." Since the police had sealed off a major portion of the building, most students had no classroom to return to. In the absence of sensible adult instructions, nearly half of the students went home. The surprising thing, Mary Butz observed, was not that so many left, but that so many stayed, because the bomb scare had effectively ended the school day.

Schools cannot function as they once did. Teachers cannot presume to have the respect of the students. They have to win it in the classroom. Many New York City school teachers have found it difficult to adjust to the loss of authority over the past generation and the change in the pupil demography from predominantly white to pre-dominantly black and Hispanic. Some professionals in the New York City public schools labor with a sense of nostalgia for a lost golden age, a time when student motivation could be taken for granted and when teachers were respected figures in the community. This image of a lost golden age is a mixture of truth, misty memories, and historical accident. The Great Depression was a time when many overeducated teachers entered the school system because there were no jobs in higher education or the professions; when there was an unusual number of second- and third-generation Jewish students who were eager to use their education to get ahead; and when the less motivated students dropped out to work as elevator operators or messengers or in some other low-skill job.

Life was hard for most people during the depression, but in many ways it was not as complicated for school people as it is today. Many of the children at Murrow, who come from a broad mix of racial, religious, and ethnic backgrounds, bear the scars of social dissolution. While trying to educate them, the school cannot ignore the family crises, the broken homes, the child abuse, the parental negligence that cut across all socioeconomic lines. In other urban schools, the wounds that families inflict on their children are far worse. Sometimes the best that a school can do is to provide a sympathetic adult who will listen.

Bruckner knows that the school competes for children's attention with the pathology outside its doors, with the lure of television, drugs, sex, and the adolescent culture. He has not created a social service program; the school is not a social work agency. What he has tried to do is to make it a place where adolescents feel at home, a place that they might want to come to even if they didn't have to. He has done this, not by turning the school into a playing field with low hurdles, but by harnessing nontraditional means to traditional academic goals. The smart kids have no ceiling on their ambitions; they can go as far and as fast as their brains will take them. Not many public schools in the nation can match Murrow's advanced courses in science and mathematics. But this richness for the bright students is not achieved by pushing the average ones into nursing and automobile mechanics. All of them have available a strong basic curriculum and a diversity of learning opportunities that enable them to learn at their own pace, and all are accorded equal respect as students.

There are many different kinds of effective schools. Some of them, like Murrow's neighbor in Brooklyn, Midwood High School, are highly structured and traditional. Visiting Midwood is like stepping into a school in the early 1950s; it is quiet and orderly, and the students seem serious and purposeful. What effective schools have in common should be available to all American students: a strong academic curriculum, a principal with a vision and the courage to work for it, dedicated teachers, a commitment to learning, a mix of students from different backgrounds, and high expectations for all children.

20

On Thinking About
the Future

(1983)

IT is obvious that anyone who tries to predict what the future holds is foolhardy, brave, or both. Yet it is also true that those who devise policy and direct social institutions must try to plan ahead, both to anticipate what might happen and to affect what does happen. In trying to think about what American schools might look like in the year 2000, I found myself reflecting on earlier attempts to conjure up the school of the future.

I hold no brief for the idea that the future is to be discovered by searching the past, but it struck me that it would be instructive to see what could be learned from the past about the limitations of social forecasting and about what might be the enduring qualities of the schools. Anyone who has studied the past knows that history has a limited predictive value. Knowledge of the past is vital because it helps us to avoid reinventing the wheel, and it may enable us to learn from our failures and our successes. But it doesn't tell us what to do next. The more we know about the past, the more we realize that any significant change is the result of many different factors, some of which are beyond our control.

This is especially difficult to acknowledge in education, because of the settled belief that education is responsive to rational planning. In our society, it is impossible to find any comparable activity so directly controlled by government; the job market and such basic industries as housing, communications, and agriculture may be monitored or even regulated by government, but they are essentially planned and run by countless private individuals and corporations. Yet, because 90 percent of U.S. youths attend public elementary and secondary schools, the expectation that schools can and should be an instrument of the public intent encourages planners, critics, and visionaries to plot the future of the schools.

Still, even the most attractive plans are subject to the influence of the unpredictable. War, depression, economic stress, demographic flux, changing social mores, and other such phenomena that are beyond the reach of government planners affect the way schools function—and even their concept of how they are supposed to function. For example, when confronted by the social effects of the war in Vietnam, which fueled youthful revolt and challenges to adult authority, the parts of schooling that officials directly manipulated—such as curriculum, teachers' qualifications, schedules, and graduation requirements—seemed relatively insignificant to the cause of the unrest.

If plans are subject to disruption by the unforeseen and the uncontrollable, they are also subject to failure because of unintended consequences. It is not simply human error alone that causes plans to go astray; it is also true that the plans themselves sometimes fail to produce the intended results. Sometimes opposite results are obtained simply because the planners' assumptions were wrong. For example, several experiments in community control in the late 1960s were founded on the assumption that low-income parents would support radical reforms. However, contrary to the expectations of foundation and university reformers, the parents wanted orderly schools, well-prepared teachers, and a school climate that stressed traditional learning and discipline.

Despite the well-known dangers of prediction, the field of education is dependent on future thinking. By its very nature, education is a forecast, for in deciding what children (or adults) should learn, we are making a statement about what they will need to know in the future. School officials and curriculum makers are constantly involved in future thinking, because they must determine what children should study and because they must adapt to changing social and economic trends, for example, enrollment declines, shifts in the composition of the student population. We might call such planning everyday future thinking, and it is a basic administrative tool of school officials.

Usually, however, it is not school officials, but scholars, social critics, and blue-ribbon panels, who have the leisure to think about the long-range future. In order to think about what the school might look like in the year 2000, I have selected some well-known past attempts to predict the future of the school. A backward glance can tell us about the hazards of future thinking and about the nature of the school as well.

Probably the best-known effort to depict what we would call the "wave of the future" is John and Evelyn Dewey's *Schools of Tomorrow,* published in 1915. The Deweys described a wide variety of experimental programs, illustrating the differences between what was then customary in conventional public schools and what a handful of progressive educators were attempting. The typical public school of 1915, the reader learns, stressed order, physical immobility, obedience, silence, rote drill, and memorization of facts; subject matter in these schools bore no relation to the life of the child or the life of society.

In the several schools that the Deweys visited, children were busily engaged in physical education, handicrafts, industrial training, nature study, and dramatic play. One school was akin to a social settlement in its efforts to raise the standard of living of its students and to fit them for future employment; another trained students in shops to do the kind of industrial work needed by both the school and the community. "Learning by doing" was a central element in the progressive curriculum. In one school, the second graders set up a shoe shop, which provided a practical means to learn English and arithmetic as children wrote about a family visiting the shop; fifth graders ran a parcel post office, which gave them reason to count, measure, weigh, and make maps. The Deweys were especially interested in educational methods that discarded "the mere accumulation of knowledge" and made learning a part of each student's life, connected to his or her present situation and needs. These were schools of the future, John Dewey wrote, because they exhibited "tendencies toward greater freedom and an identification of the child's school life with his environment and outlook; and, even more important, the recognition of the role education must play in a democracy."

The Deweys argued that the conventional school, with its standardized curriculum, its recitation and drill methods, and its reliance on grades and punishments as motivating tools, trained children for "docility and obedience" and was ill suited to a democratic society. Thus they forecast that the school of the future would be one in which children were allowed freedom, were consciously engaged in the improvement of their neighborhood or city, were taught through methods that used their own experiences and activities, and were motivated by appeals to their interests.

With hindsight, we can see that the Deweys' predictions had a mixed fate. While some teachers may have continued to use rote methods, by the mid-1930s the education profession as a whole had accepted the importance of such things as physical health and recreation, vocational education, arts and crafts, and the use of activities and projects in the classroom. However, some of the Deweys' emphases produced unexpected, and sometimes undesirable, outcomes. The industrial program that they lauded in Gary, Indiana, seemed to other observers to be a narrowly vocational program, intended to create skilled workers for the mills and plants of the industrial Midwest, rather than a broad and progressive educational program for the future. The Rousseauean experiments in student freedom that impressed the Deweys held little appeal for the vast majority of public school teachers, in part because teachers were responsive to community values. Regardless of the Deweys' predictions, most schools continued to use textbooks, to give grades, to rely on a conventional curriculum organized along subject-matter lines, and to give greater weight to traditional in-school learning than to community-based activities.

Although many of those who called themselves followers of John Dewey refused to believe it, he was not opposed to the systematic organization of subject matter, nor did he scorn the learning that comes from books. In one school he praised in his 1915 book, children dramatized one of Cicero's orations against Catiline and wrote "prayers to Dionysius and stories such as they think Orpheus might have sung." Dewey repeatedly tried to explain that he did not think that all worthwhile knowledge necessarily flowed from the immediate needs and interests of pupils. In what must be considered a losing battle, he wrote *Experience and Education* in 1938 to explain to his followers that children's experiences were a means, and not the end of education.

In 1944 the Educational Policies Commission of the National Education Association (NEA) tried its hand at future thinking. The commission members forecast two different futures for American schools, depending on whether or not the federal government provided financial assistance. If such aid were not provided, they predicted that by 1950 secondary education would be directly administered by the federal government, because of the failure of the public schools to prepare for the vocational needs of the postwar era. This future could be avoided, they said, if the public schools received enough federal aid to provide vocational training, citizenship training, family-life education, and other developmental programs.

In the future that the commission members hoped would come to pass, the school would be reformulated by 1950 into a major social service agency for the entire community. The age of compulsory education would rise to eighteen, and communities would offer a thirteenth and a fourteenth year of free public education. No one would have to leave school for financial reasons, because the school would obtain part-time employment for students. Vocational preparation would become a central role of the school, and students could train there for any industrial or semi-professional work. The school would provide education and guidance not only for students but for everyone else as well; the counselors would be available to help everyone, not just the students. The curriculum of the school of the future would concentrate on vocational training, health and physical education, "common learnings" (a guidance course stressing "cooperative living in family, school, and community," merging English, social studies, family life, and various other aspects of becoming a good citizen), and "individual interests."

The school that the NEA envisioned would mold citizens and workers. School personnel would direct the adjustment between school and work and would guide youngsters' career choices. The school would take a more active role in determining the decisions traditionally made by families (sometimes based on faulty information) and in coordinating industrial and vocational planning. The cultural interests that the school had fostered historically—through the study of such subjects as literature, science, mathematics, foreign languages, and history—would survive, but as a relatively minor aspect of the school's overall function as a community service agency.

Neither of these predictions about the future of the school, offered by some of the keenest minds in American education, came close to realization. There was neither federal aid for schools by 1950 nor, in its absence, a federal takeover of secondary education. Nor did the schools, either in the postwar period or in the years since general federal aid was passed in 1965, become comprehensive social service agencies. We can see today that the first prediction was a bit of political propaganda, intended to abet the long and unsuccessful NEA campaign for federal aid. Since opponents claimed that federal aid would lead to federal control, the NEA countered with the charge that *failure* to pass federal aid would lead inexorably to a federal takeover because of local and state incapacity to run the schools. The second prediction—that schools would become the centerpiece of a planned society—reflected both the wartime mood, when centralized planning was widely accepted, and the ascendancy among educators of the idea that the most important function of the school was to adjust young people to society. After the war, this point of view was identified with the "life adjustment movement," which is now remembered principally for the attacks it inspired by critics who considered it anti-intellectual, manipulative, and mindlessly utilitarian.

Skip to the late 1960s. The future thinkers of this decade projected many different scenarios, but on one point they all agreed: The school as it was then constituted—that is, buildings with classrooms and teachers and textbooks—would not (and should not) long survive. One critic, the radical priest Ivan Illich, called for "deschooling society." His associate, Everett Reimer, proclaimed in the title of his book that *School Is Dead*. George Leonard, in *Education and Ecstasy,* predicted the withering away of the school as it was then known, to be replaced by "free-learning situations," "encounter groups," and computer-assisted instruction. By the year 2001, he prophesied, children would learn freely and ecstatically through dialogues with a magnificent computer console situated in a geodesic dome. Their environments would be characterized by sensory bombardment, and, in this wondrous setting, children would absorb all the "commonly agreed-upon cultural knowledge . . . in the four years from age 3 through age 6." In Leonard's fantasy school, three-year-olds master spelling and syntax, a four-year-old carries on a dialogue with her computer about primitive cultures, and a six-year-old "is deep into a simple calculus session." Here at last is the fulfillment of children's ancient end-of-term cry: "No more classes, no more books, no more teachers' dirty looks!"

The fifteen years that have passed since Leonard sketched the school of the future have given little encouragement to his prophecy of a fusion between the school and the human potential movement. To be sure, computers have begun to gain a secure place in schools, but they are still used only marginally as instruments of instruction. The "free schools" that Leonard saw as the trend setters of educational method have survived, but only as a small sector of U.S. private education. The wave of innovation that he believed was relentlessly crashing down on the school turned out to be not the wave of the future, but a prelude to and stimulus of the back-to-basics movement.

To reflect on the fate of predictions is a sobering experience. A teacher whose career began in 1960 has lived through an era of failed revolutions. One movement after another arrived, peaked, and dispersed. Having observed the curriculum reform movement, the technological revolution, the open education movement, the free school movement, the deschooling movement, the accountability movement, the minimum competency movement, and, more recently, the back-to-basics movement, a veteran teacher may be excused for secretly thinking, when confronted by the next campaign to "save" the schools, "This too shall pass."

Curiously, certain features of the school survive despite nearly unanimous condemnation by expert opinion. A teacher-in-training, for example, is likely to read numerous books denouncing the system of examinations and grading, the textbook, the recitation method, curricula that focus on discrete disciplines, and other hallmarks of the traditional school. Yet those features persist in the overwhelming majority of public and private schools, even though no pedagogical giant equivalent to Dewey exists to lend legitimacy to such means of managing the classroom. Classroom teachers must frequently feel a sense of inadequacy, knowing that the techniques they find necessary for teaching have been condemned by progressive pedagogical experts for most of the century. If so great a divergence between theory and practice existed in any other profession, it would most likely be considered a scandal.

Any future thinking about the school must take into account the history of efforts to change the school. We should begin by noting that the school has not withered away, despite predictions to the contrary over the years. Critics, scholars, and educational leaders have predicted time and again that the school was no longer relevant as a school—that it had to be turned instead into a social settlement or a vocational training agency or almost anything other than what it was. Yet the school as a school is still with us, which suggests that it serves social purposes that have enabled it to survive even the most vigorous attacks and outspoken criticisms.

Not all efforts to reform the schools have foundered. Although we have seen some spectacular failures, we have also seen many small but significant successes. Compared to twenty-five years ago, more students are in school today, more of them graduate from high schools and colleges, more teachers have college degrees, school buildings are more commodious, teaching materials are more diverse, and teaching methods are more varied. What we should have learned by now is that the reforms that take root are those that are limited, specific, and reasonably related to the concerns and capacities of those who must implement them. A proposal that tells teachers that everything they have done up to now has been wrong is likely to receive a cold reception. A reform that deals contemptuously with those who must implement it is not likely to take hold. To be effective, a proposal for change must appeal to teachers' educational ideals, respect their professionalism, and build on their strengths.

Bearing in mind the strengths and the limitations of the schools, we can then ask what a school should be in the year 2000—less than twenty years from now. Both past history and present reality suggest that there will still be schools in the year 2000. Today, about half of all women are in the workforce, a trend that seems likely to continue in the years ahead. This means that our society will need, more than ever, good institutions designed to nurture and to supervise young children during most of the day. This is and will continue to be one of the important roles of the school.

Because of the growth of professional, semiprofessional, and technical occupations and the decline of industrial and manufacturing jobs, schools have an important mission to perform in preparing youngsters to fill these new, more intellectual careers. Job training will be of less importance in the year 2000 because of the rapid pace of technological change. Because most work in the future will require people who can think, plan, work with others, adapt to changing conditions, and make decisions, we will look to the schools to nurture in the young such traits as initiative, reasoning skills, judgment, empathy, independence, and self-discipline. Instead of job training, young people will want to learn specific skills for such leisure activities as woodworking, cooking, bookbinding, weaving, and other handicrafts.

Because the social and political trends of our nation are increasingly egalitarian, we will want the school in the year 2000 to provide for all children the kind of education that is available today only to those in the best private and public schools. We will expect all children to become literate, able to read books and magazines without difficulty, and to use their literacy for further learning. Of course, all children will learn to use such tools as computers, which by the year 2000 will be as commonplace as television sets are now. We will want all children to study history in considerable depth—U.S., European, and non-Western—in order to have a secure sense of the past and to understand the great achievements and the awesome failures of human civilization. When they are old enough to grasp complex concepts, we will want them to discover how the various social sciences contribute to our understanding of society. And at all ages, from the time they are old enough to be read to, we will want all children to appreciate literature—to see how it can transport each of us across time and space and cultures and how it can evoke in each of us a sense of our common humanity. We will want all children not only to learn to read for knowledge and enjoyment, but also to learn to write in a variety of modes—sometimes trying out their creativity and imagination, other times organizing their thoughts carefully and constructing well-reasoned essays. Naturally, in the year 2000 we will expect every child to learn science and mathematics, so that scientific understanding is widely accessible and not merely the preserve of a scientific elite. We will expect in this school of the future that, once children have a firm understanding of their own language and culture, they will begin to study other cultures and languages. If our sights are high enough, every child in the United States will learn at least one language in addition to English, which will increase our ability to deal with other nations in the twenty-first century. Certainly, we will also insist that every school of the future have a comprehensive arts program, in which children learn both to appreciate great artistic accomplishment and to participate in creating music, drama, dance, painting, sculpture, film, and other forms of artistic expression.

In this school of the future, teachers will look on each student as a precious resource—a unique individual with talents to be discovered, skills to be developed, and a mind in need of challenges and nourishment. In this fantasy school, teachers will concern themselves with children's health, their character, their intellect, and their sensibilities.

In order to build a sense of community and mutual concern, the school of the future will be small, perhaps enrolling no more than 100 students per grade. (Several schools might share a resource center, where students could study foreign languages or advanced courses.) Unlike some present schools, which are as vast and impersonal as factories, the school of the future should be modeled on a family; here caring, knowledgeable adults would guide and instruct young people—and each person would be special.

This school would have ideals, and it would try to live by them. One ideal would be good citizenship; thus the school would prepare its students to take responsibility, to help their neighbors, to be good leaders and good followers, to do their part in making the community better for all of its members. Another ideal would be excellence, whether in the arts, in sports, or in academics. Students would learn to respect the excellence that results from hard work, persistence, and commitment. To inspire a love of excellence, teachers would share Matthew Arnold's ideal of making the best that has been thought and known in the world available to everyone.

Are we likely to have such a school in the year 2000? Probably not. Probability suggests that the schools in the year 2000 will bear the same relationship to schools of today as our current schools bear to the schools of seventeen years ago (1966). If we consider how little the schools have changed since the late 1960s, then it seems utopian indeed to predict that all schools might, in the foreseeable future, be as good as our very best schools of today.

The obstacles are many—but not insuperable, if the goal is one we wish to achieve. For many years, we have neglected the development of the teaching profession. Schools have been society's scapegoat for a long time. Teachers have been underpaid in relation to the importance of their profession. And teaching has been treated as a low-status profession. For all of these reasons, many excellent teachers have left teaching for more satisfying work, and uncounted others have chosen other careers from the start. In such vital fields as science, mathematics, and foreign languages, significant teacher shortages exist. Many of those who have remained in teaching have been demoralized by curricular chaos during the past twenty years. It will not be easy to improve the status of the teaching profession; nor will it be easy to persuade teachers and the public that the United States is serious about upgrading the quality of its schools and the importance of the teacher's role.

The distance between where we are now and where we might be in the year 2000 is great, but this distance is not beyond our capacities to span. Probably the greatest obstacle to achieving lasting reform is, paradoxically, the tendency of reformers to scoff at piecemeal change. Experience suggests that small changes are likely to be enduring changes. In many ways, the kind of school that I have described is very like the schools that now exist. I suggest that we take what is and develop it to its highest potential. This challenge may be more radical than the call for an entirely new institution to replace the school. Getting there—that is, achieving the highest potential—is first of all a matter of setting our sights and then of devising a series of small moves in the right direction. Better teachers, better teaching, better administration, better textbooks, better curricula, higher aspirations. The Tao says, "A journey of a thousand miles must begin with a single step." We know which steps to take; our problem will continue to be—as it has always been—reaching agreement on where we want to go.

21

Prospects

IF there is a single theme that I have tried to stress throughout these essays, it is this: What happens in the schools and to the schools is determined by our assumptions, our ideals, and our policies. As a society, we are responsible for the quality of our public schools because they are what we choose to make them. The policies that we adopt affect the preparation, selection, and retention of teachers; our beliefs about what is important to transmit to the next generation shape the curriculum, the graduation requirements, and the standards of accomplishment in the schools; the funding that is provided for them limits or expands their capabilities; the esteem in which we hold the work of the schools influences able people to teach in them or to shun them; the purposeful decisions made by courts, Congress, executive agencies, and legislatures may place unreasonable burdens on the schools, may assign to them duties that divert them from their proper ends, or may protect them from unwarranted political interference. There is nothing inevitable about the improvement or decline of our schools; the conditions that make schools better or worse are usually the result of our ideas and actions, not of impersonal economic or historical forces. Clearly, it is comforting to believe that events are beyond our control, because we are then relieved of responsibility for what happens. But this comfort must be denied us, for our schools reflect the kind of dedication and thought that we expend on them.

The effort to improve schools depends on the quality of our ideas, for ideas ultimately determine policies and actions. The best way to understand why certain policies were implemented is to examine the assumptions inherent in the conventional wisdom. Sometimes the conventional wisdom is in fact wise; but it is not necessarily so. Ideas must be judged by the policies and the actions that they inspire; policies and actions must be judged by their results; and results finally must be judged by our ideals. Good intentions do not validate an educational policy. In the end, we must judge the schools by whether they have fulfilled their mission as educational institutions, whether they have tried to educate children to the limits of their abilities, whether they have tried to prepare their students to think and act intelligently, rationally, and wisely. Given the limitations of human nature, we know that our ideals will never be entirely achieved. But we may justly ask whether our schools have tried to put into practice these aims and aspirations, and we may judge them harshly if they did not even make the effort.

As so many of our educational controversies have demonstrated, people differ about what they want from the schools, and heated battles have been fought in school districts, in the state capitols, and in the Congress over which purposes the schools should serve. Yet I would contend that such controversies mask the extent to which a genuine consensus exists on central questions of purpose. The battle lines get drawn and tempers flare over political problems like bilingual education, busing, tuition tax credits, school closings, bond issues, tax rates, teacher qualifications, textbook selection, and allocation of resources. But not one of these questions challenges the fundamental educational purpose of the schools, not one represents a refutation of the common expectations that parents and taxpayers have for their schools. Even when the disagreements seem to cut most deeply, even when neighbors glare across picket lines at one another, there remains a shared faith in the educative function of the school, in its power to develop fully their children's minds and talents. The frequency and intensity of these contretemps substantiate the importance that Americans attach to their schools; where their children are, there also are their hopes for the future.

The consensus is built around the idea that schools can make a difference in the lives of children, not by keeping them off the street through their adolescence, not by giving them marketable job skills, nor by training them to habits of docility, but by instilling in them the qualities of mind and character that will enable them to operate as self-governing citizens in a self-governing society. Most parents really do expect that the schools will provide their children with a good education; they hope that the quality of their children's education will depend on the youngsters' effort, not on the family's social status. Whether these expectations are justified depends entirely on the people who staff the schools, on the ideas and dedication that they bring to their work, and on the resources that the polity makes available for their efforts.

If one is to believe poll data, most people have fairly similar ideas about what children should learn in school. Large majorities regularly report that children should learn the basic skills and should study history, mathematics, science, literature, and the arts. For years, educators have disagreed about the elements that should be part of every student's education. This disagreement has contributed to the decline of high school graduation requirements. The public does not seem to share this uncertainty and confusion. Tracking of children into separate academic, voctional, and general programs did not occur because of public demand; nor did nonacademic electives proliferate in response to public taste. Regardless of their race, ethnicity, or social class, parents want their children to get a good education. Furthermore, they understand a good education to mean one in which the study of mathematics, English, history, and science is required of all students, because such studies build cultural and scientific literacy. Most parents want the same kind of education for their children that the best-educated, most-advantaged parents invariably select.

The poll data confirm that public support is strong for the provision of a broad liberal education to all children, a finding that coincides with the major recommendations of the many national reports of the early 1980s. The biggest impediment to the achievement of this ambitious goal is attitudinal: Many people, inside and outside the schools, do not believe that all children can or should be given the sort of education that is found in our most advantaged schools. Different arguments are offered against the idea: either that it is inefficient to educate so many people as we educate our best students; or that to do so would be too expensive; or that some children need only vocational training to make them happy and productive citizens; or that most children do not really "need" courses in subjects like science and history; or that to do so would be to impose elitist values on ordinary folks who want only job training from the schools; or that so much emphasis on a liberal education would remove from the schools their alleged duty to sort children into occupational roles; or that children from lower-class families will rebel against this kind of education by dropping out of school.

Each of these arguments is deficient. The reasoning behind them is snobbish, fallacious, or undemocratic. Vocational training is more expensive than a regular academic curriculum; in a democracy, all pay taxes and all should receive the same quality of schooling when it is provided at public expense; employers seem quite capable of sorting their employees on the basis of their ability to learn new skills; our instruments of assessment are far too crude to predict who will "need" science or history or literature in the future; there is no evidence that dropouts rise when poor students are in an academic curriculum, nor did the dropout rate fall during the long period when the academic curriculum was diluted and restricted to the talented; the people who argue for curricular differentiation never submit their own children to the prescriptions they think appropriate for other people's children.

Believing that we should provide a good liberal education for all children is a long way from being able to do it. The fact is that many of our current attitudes and practices undermine the prospects for change. I refer now not to the prevalent practice of educational tracking but to what has sometimes been called the "technicization" of the curriculum. Technicization occurs when teaching emphasizes abstract skills over course content, when children are taught procedures but not a common core of knowledge. This tendency has been particularly invidious in the teaching of literature and history and has produced students who have mastered the basic skills but have little knowledge of great literature or of the major events, ideas, and individuals that shaped history.

Technicization has been encouraged by overreliance on standardized tests. The verbal portion of the Scholastic Aptitude Test, for example, is supposed to be curriculum free; it tests vocabulary, reasoning skills, and grammar, all abstract skills. Since the nation's major college entrance test is curriculum free, students and teachers conclude that skills alone count, not knowledge of literature and history. When the National Assessment of Educational Progress, established with federal funding to monitor the status of education on a national basis, attempted to measure what American children knew about literature in 1970, it was quickly discovered that there were few books that all children had read; myths and stories once considered common knowledge were unknown to large numbers of children. In view of these significant gaps in exposure to basic literary works, the effort to assess knowledge of literature was abandoned. Recognizing the baneful influence of aptitude tests on the curriculum, some educators advocate greater use of achievement examinations rather than aptitude tests. The difference is this: An examination would test what had been taught, instead of testing abstract skills, in order to encourage greater emphasis on the quality and content of instruction. "Teaching to the test" is not nearly so dangerous to education as the spread of culture illiteracy.

Standardized tests are more a symptom of technicization than a cause of it. More important as a cause has been the fragmentation of our sense of a common culture. Within the education profession, there is widespread doubt about the existence of any such common culture, and this doubt has undermined the teaching of literature and history. Since the mid-1960s, one group after another has assailed the concept of a common culture as white, male-dominated, and Eurocentric. In response to complaints by blacks, women, Hispanics, and other groups, textbook writers and curriculum developers have shied away from acknowledging the authority of a central cultural tradition. In the absence of a coherent literary or historical tradition that is common to all Americans, students arrive in college with more skills than knowledge. Their professors' complaints about how little they know are unfair; even if they have read widely (which few have), the problem is that there is little common cultural ground among them, and there can be few allusions to writers, to seminal works, or to historical personages that will evoke general recognition.

Technicization and cultural fragmentation will continue to be a serious problem until the school curriculum is reconstructed along lines that are both common and pluralist. What we need are courses and textbooks incorporating the various strands that have forged the American culture. Students should study the development of Western civilization in order to understand where we got the ideals by which we judge ourselves. They must learn about the development of the institutions, the laws, and the democratic values that all Americans share. In studying American political, economic, and social history, they should understand that all of our ancestors—whatever their race, ethnic group, or gender—are part of the common story of the nation. In literature, students need a common foundation of readings. Unless they have read, as a minimum, the classical myths, the Bible, and some Shakespeare, they will be unable to comprehend the fundamental vocabulary of most Western literature. Teachers will surely have their own favorite works to add to this starting point, but a starting point there must be, a foundation consisting of the major works of our literary heritage.

The prospects for lasting educational improvement depend on our ability to liberate ourselves from the errant assumptions on which so much of present educational policy and practice is built. Do we really want to educate all children? Are we confident that children of all races and social classes are capable of learning? Do we believe that ethnic and racial heterogeneity in the classroom is no barrier to superior learning? Do we believe that a good education must include not just the basic skills, but also the study of history, literature, science, mathematics, foreign language, and the arts? Do we see each of these disciplines as a valuable way of understanding the world, without which students are deprived of knowledge and possibilities that would enrich their lives? Are we prepared to recognize the importance of good schools by amply rewarding dedicated teachers and educational leaders? Are we prepared to make the changes necessary to transform teaching from a civil service job to a real profession, analogous to college teaching, where adults work together as peers and colleagues? Will state and local school boards insist that all educators they hire—including elementary teachers—have a sound liberal education? Are we willing to relieve the schools of extraneous tasks that belong to other agencies in the community? Unless we can answer these questions affirmatively, then school reform is likely to remain locked in the familiar pendulum pattern, and we are likely to experience yet another cycle of fads as we veer from one pedagogical extreme to the other, perpetually dissatisfied with the results, disappointed in our schools and our teachers, not recognizing that the fault lies not in the institution but in our own inadequate thinking.

NOTES

Introduction

1. James P. Smith, "Race and Human Capital" (Santa Monica, Calif.: The Rand Corporation, 1984), p. 31.

2. John Dewey, *Freedom and Culture* (New York: Putnam, 1939), p. 42.

3. Diane Ravitch, *The Troubled Crusade: American Education 1945–1980* (New York: Basic Books, 1983).

4. Diane Ravitch, "Programs, Placebos, Panaceas," *The Urban Review,* April 1968, pp. 8–11.

5. Robert M. Hutchins, "The Democratic Dilemma," *Freedom, Education, and the Fund: Essays and Addresses, 1945–1956* (New York: Meridan Books, 1956).

Chapter 8: From History to Social Studies: Dilemmas and Problems

1. National Center for Education Statistics, Bulletin 83–223, "How Well Do High School Graduates of Today Meet the Curriculum Standards of the National Commission on Excellence?" (Washington, D.C.: U.S. Department of Education, September 1983).

2. Richard S. Kirkendall, "The Status of History in the Schools," *The Journal of American History* 62 (1975), pp. 557–570.

3. Telephone conversation, Office of Social Studies Director, New York City Board of Education, June 1984.

4. Bob L. Taylor and John D. Haas, *New Directions: Social Studies Curriculum for the 70's* (Boulder, Co.: Center for Education in the Social Sciences, University of Colorado, and Social Science Education Consortium, 1973).

5. Richard E. Gross, "The Status of the Social Studies in the Public Schools of the United States: Facts and Impressions of a National Survey," *Social Education* 41 (March 1977), pp. 194–200, 205. See also, Hazel Whitman Hertzberg, *Social Studies Reform, 1880–1980* (Boulder, Colo.: SSEC, 1981).

6. Kirkendall, "The Status of History in the Schools," pp. 563–564.

7. Edward A. Krug, *The Shaping of the American High School, 1880–1920* (New York: Harper & Row, 1964), pp. 4, 29; Rolla M. Tryon, *The Social Sciences as School Subjects* (New York: Charles Scribner's Sons, 1935), pp. 100–117.

8. Tryon, *Social Sciences as School Subjects,* p. 142.

9. National Education Association, *Report of the Committee on Secondary School Studies* (Washington, D.C.: U.S. Government Printing Office, 1893) hereafter cited as Committee of Ten Report.

10. Committee of Ten Report, p. 168.

Notes

11. Committee of Ten Report, p. 167.

12. Committee of Ten Report, pp. 167–168.

13. Committee of Seven, *The Study of History in Schools: Report to the American Historical Association* (New York: Macmillan, 1899), pp. 120, 122.

14. Committee of Seven Report, p. 113.

15. Committee of Seven Report, p. 17.

16. Tryon, *Social Sciences as School Subjects,* pp. 177, 187–189.

17. Tryon, *Social Sciences as School Subjects,* p. 182.

18. Commission on the Reorganization of Secondary Education, "Cardinal Principles of Secondary Education" (Washington, D.C.: U.S. Government Printing Office, 1918) Bulletin 35.

19. Committee on Social Studies of the Commission on the Reorganization of Secondary Education of the National Education Association, *The Social Studies in Secondary Education* (Washington, D.C.: U.S. Government Printing Office, 1916), Bulletin 28, p. 9.

20. Committee on the Social Studies Report, pp. 9, 40, 44; Krug, *Shaping the American High School,* p. 354.

21. American Historical Association, *A Charter for the Social Sciences in the Schools* (New York: Charles Scribner's Sons, 1932).

22. Henry Johnson, *An Introduction to the History of the Social Sciences* (New York: Charles Scribner's Sons, 1932), pp. 3, 21, 29, 30.

Chapter 9: Curriculum in Crisis: Connections Between Past and Present

1. National Science Board Commission on Precollege Education in Mathematics, Science and Technology, "Educating Americans for the 21st Century" (Washington, D.C.: Government Printing Office, 1983), pp. 1, 40; *On Further Examination: Report of the Advisory Panel on the Scholastic Aptitude Test Score Decline* (New York: College Entrance Examination Board, 1977); Annegret Harnischfeger and David E. Wiley, "Achievement Test Score Decline: Do We Need to Worry?" (St. Louis: CEMREL, 1976). See also, Ernest L. Boyer, *High School: A Report on Secondary Education in America* (New York: Harper & Row, 1983).

2. Education Week, December 7, 1983, pp. 6–17.

3. I.L. Kandel, *History of Secondary Education* (Boston: Houghton Mifflin, 1930), pp. 394–422.

4. Edward A. Krug, *The Shaping of the American High School, 1880–1920* (New York: Harper & Row, 1964), p. 34.

5. Krug, *American High School,* pp. 48–49; William Humm and Robert L. Buser, "High School Curriculum in Illinois," *Educational Leadership,* May 1980, pp. 670–672.

6. U.S. Bureau of Education, *Report of the Committee on Secondary School Studies* (Washington, D.C.: Government Printing Office, 1893), pp. 17, 51, 173–174.

7. Krug, *American High School,* pp. 68, 84–85.

8. Krug, *American High School,* p. 84.

9. National Education Association, *Report of the Committee on College-Entrance Requirements* (Washington, D.C.: NEA, 1899).

10. Krug, *American High School,* pp. 145, 192.

11. Krug, *American High School,* p. 225.

Notes

12. Krug, *American High School*, p. 240.
13. Krug, *American High School*, pp. 251, 276.
14. Krug, *American High School*, p. 282.
15. Krug, *American High School*, p. 354.
16. U.S. Office of Education, "Cardinal Principles of Secondary Education" (Washington, D.C.: Government Printing Office, 1918) Bulletin 35, p. 22.
17. Krug, *American High School*, pp. 398–399.
18. Daniel Tanner and Laurel N. Tanner, *Curriculum Development: Theory into Practice*, 2nd ed. (New York: Macmillan, 1980), pp. 103–114.
19. Krug, *American High School*, pp. 287, 341–342.
20. Diane Ravitch, *The Great School Wars: New York City, 1805–1973* (New York: Basic Books, 1974), pp. 224–225.

Chapter 12: The Case of Tuition Tax Credits

1. *Pierce* v. *Society of Sisters of the Holy Name*, 268 U.S. 510 (1925).
2. James Coleman, Sally Hoffer, and Thomas Kilgore, *Public and Private Schools* (New York: Basic Books, 1982); Nathan Glazer, "The Future Under Tuition Tax Credits," in *Public Dollars for Private Schools: The Case of Tuition Tax Credits*, ed. Thomas James and Henry M. Levin (Philadelphia: Temple University Press, 1983), p. 88.
3. David W. Breneman, "Where Would Tuition Tax Credits Take Us?," in Levin, *Public Dollars*, p. 108.
4. Dennis J. Encarnation, "Public Finance and Regulation of Nonpublic Education," in Levin, *Public Dollars*, pp. 175–195.

Chapter 13: The Uses and Misuses of Tests

1. Annegret Harnischfeger and David E. Wiley, "Achievement Test Score Decline: Do We Need to Worry?" (St. Louis: CEMREL, 1976).
2. *On Further Examination: Report of the Advisory Panel on the Scholastic Aptitude Test Score Decline* (New York: College Entrance Examination Board, 1977).
3. Jeanne S. Chall, "An Analysis of Textbooks in Relation to Declining SAT Scores" (New York: College Entrance Examination Board, 1977), p. 64.

Chapter 14: On the History of Minority Group Education in the United States

1. Among the leading contemporary revisionist histories are Michael Katz, *The Irony of Early School Reform* (Cambridge, Mass.: Harvard University Press, 1968); Michael Katz, *Class, Bureaucracy and Schools* (New York: Praeger, 1971); Stanley K. Schultz, *The Culture Factory: Boston Public Schools, 1789–1860* (New York: Oxford University Press, 1973); Joel H. Spring, *Education and the Rise of the Corporate State* (Boston: Beacon Press, 1972); Clarence J. Karier, Joel H. Spring, and Paul C. Violas, *Roots of Crisis* (Chicago: University of Illinois Press, 1973); and Colin Greer, *The Great School Legend* (New York: Basic Books, 1972).

2. Harold Isaacs, *Idols of the Tribe* (New York: Harper & Row, 1975), p. 3.

3. Diane Ravitch, *The Great School Wars: New York City, 1805–1973* (New York: Basic Books, 1974), pp. 7, 21.

4. James G. Carter, *Essays Upon Popular Education* (Boston: Bowles and Dearborn, 1826), p. 19.

5. Lloyd P. Jorgenson, *The Founding of Public Education in Wisconsin* (Madison: State Historical Society of Wisconsin, 1956), p. 7; Cornelius J. Heatwole, *A History of Education in Virginia* (New York: Macmillan, 1916), p. 102; Albert Fishlow, "The American Common School Revival: Fact or Fancy?" in *Industrialization in Two Systems: Essays in Honor of Alexander Gerschenkorn,* ed. Henry Rosovsky (New York: Wiley, 1966), pp. 40–67.

6. David Tyack, "The Perils of Pluralism: The Background of the Pierce Case," *American Historical Review,* vol. 74, October 1968, pp. 74–98.

7. *Pierce* v. *Society of the Sisters of the Holy Name,* 268 U.S. 510 (1925).

8. Jane Addams, *Newer Ideals of Peace* (Chautauqua, N.Y.: Chautauqua Press, 1907), p. 77.

9. Timothy L. Smith, "Immigrant Social Aspirations and American Education, 1880–1930," *American Quarterly,* vol. 21, no. 3, Fall 1969, pp. 523–543.

10. Mordecai Soltes, *The Yiddish Press: An Americanizing Agency* (New York: Bureau of Publications, Teachers College, Columbia University, 1925), pp. 151–152.

11. *Meyer* v. *Nebraska,* 262 US 390 (1923); and Arnold H. Leibowitz, "Educational Policy and Political Acceptance: The Imposition of English as the Language of Instruction in American Schools" (Washington, D.C.: Center for Applied Linguistics, ERIC Clearinghouse for Linguistics, March 1971), p. 34.

12. Leibowitz, "Educational Policy"; John B. Shotwell, *A History of the Schools of Cincinnati* (Cincinnati, Ohio: The School Life Co., 1902), pp. 289–301; Joshua A. Fishman, *Language Loyalty in the United States* (The Hague: Mouton & Co., 1966), p. 233; and Heinz Kloss, *Excerpts from the National Minority Laws of the United States of America* (Honolulu, Hawaii: East-West Center, 1966), pp. 48–55.

13. Kloss, *National Minority Laws,* p. 62.

14. Fishman, *Language Loyalty,* pp. 29–30.

15. Theodore Andersson and Mildred Boyer, *Bilingual Schooling in the United States* (Washington, D.C.: Government Printing Office, 1970), p. 211.

16. Robert F. Berkhofer, Jr., *Salvation and the Savage: An Analysis of Protestant Missions and American Indian Response, 1787–1862* (New York: Atheneum, 1972), pp. 16–43.

17. Leibowitz, "Educational Policy," pp. 67–78.

18. U.S. Senate Committee on Labor and Public Welfare, Special Subcommittee on Indian Education, *Indian Education: A National Tragedy—A National Challenge* (Washington, D.C.: Government Printing Office, 1969), pp. 147–148.

19. G.E.E. Linquist, *The Red Man in the United States* (New York: George H. Doran, 1923), pp. 40–41.

20. Institute for Government Research, *The Problems of Indian Administration* (Baltimore: Johns Hopkins University Press, 1928), pp. 22, 403, 408, 412.

21. U.S. Senate Committee on Labor and Public Welfare, Special Subcommittee on Indian Education, *Indian Education,* pp. 186–189.

22. Carter G. Woodson, *The Education of the Negro Prior to 1861* (Washington, D.C.: Associated Publishers, 1919), p. 1.

23. Henry Allen Bullock, *A History of Negro Education in the South: From 1619 to the Present* (Cambridge, Mass.: Harvard University Press, 1967), pp. 5–15; and Woodson, *Education of the Negro,* pp. 205–208.

24. Bullock, *Negro Education*, pp. 10–13, 21–26; and Woodson, *Education of the Negro*, pp. 128–144, 205–208.

25. Woodson, *Education of the Negro*, p. 317; and Schultz, *The Culture Factory*, pp. 160–162.

26. Horace Mann Bond, *Black American Scholars: A Study of Their Beginnings* (Detroit: Balamp Publishing, 1972), pp. 23, 53.

27. Bullock, *Negro Education*, pp. 23–25, 57–58.

28. Bullock, *Negro Education*, pp. 77–78; on the role of northern philanthropists, see Louis R. Harlan, *Separate and Unequal: Public School Campaigns and Racism in the Southern Seaboard States, 1902–1915* (Chapel Hill, N.C.: University of North Carolina Press, 1958).

29. Bond, *Black American Scholars*.

30. Fishman, *Language Loyalty*, p. 92.

Chapter 16: Desegregation: Varieties of Meaning

1. Thomas Jefferson, "Notes on Virginia," *The Writings of Thomas Jefferson*, ed. Paul Leicester Ford, vol. 3 (New York: Putnam, 1894), pp. 243–244.

2. George M. Fredrickson, *The Black Image in the White Mind: The Debate on Afro-American Character and Destiny, 1817–1914* (New York: Harper & Row, 1971), pp. 125, 97–129.

3. For the racial theories of the period, see Thomas F. Gossett, *Race: The History of an Idea in America* (Dallas: SMU Press, 1963), and Fredrickson, *The Black Image*.

4. Fredrickson, *The Black Image*, pp. 149–150.

5. *Great Debates in American History*, ed. Marion Mills Miller (New York: Current Literature, 1913) vol. 7, "Civil Rights," part 1, p. 392.

6. C. Vann Woodward, *The Strange Career of Jim Crow* (New York: Oxford University Press, 1957); Kenneth M. Stampp, *The Era of Reconstruction, 1865–1877* (New York: Knopf, 1966).

7. Brief for Appellants, *Brown* v. *Board of Education of Topeka*, United States Supreme Court, October Term, 1952, p. 5.

8. Appeal from the U.S. District Court for the District of Kansas, Transcript of Proceedings, *Brown* v. *Board of Education of Topeka*, 1952, p. 217.

9. Brief for Appellants, *Brown* v. *Board of Education* et al., October Term, 1953, pp. 22, 40–41, 65.

10. *Argument: The Oral Argument Before the Supreme Court in Brown v. Board of Education of Topeka, 1952–1955*, ed. Leon Friedman (New York: Chelsea House, 1969), pp. 47–49, 71–72.

11. Diane Ravitch, *The Great School Wars: New York City, 1805–1973* (New York: Basic Books, 1974), pp. 252–253.

12. Brief for Appellants, *Brown* v. *Board of Education* et al., October Term, 1953, p. 34; Friedman, *Argument*, p. 45.

13. Lawrence A. Cremin, "Americanization: A Perspective," *UCLA Educator*, vol. 19, no. 1, December, 1976, p. 9.

14. Gunnar Myrdal, *An American Dilemma* (New York: Harper & Row, 1944), pp. 928–929.

15. David P. Ausubel, "Ego Development Among Segregated Negro Children," *Mental Hygiene*, vol. 42, 1956, pp. 362–369.

16. *Report of the Advisory Committee on Racial Imbalance and Education*, Commonwealth of Massachusetts (1965), p. 3.

17. Stanley Elkins, *Slavery: A Problem in American Institutional and Intellectual Life* (Chicago: University of Chicago Press, 1959); Kenneth M. Stampp, *The Peculiar Institution: Slavery in the Ante-Bellum South* (New York: Knopf, 1956); Eugene D. Genovese, *Roll, Jordan, Roll: The World the Slaves Made* (New York: Random House, 1974); Herbert G. Gutman, *The Black Family in Slavery and Freedom, 1750–1925* (New York: Pantheon, 1976); Thomas L. Webber, *Deep Like the Rivers: Education in the Slave Quarter Community, 1831–1865* (New York: Norton, 1978).

18. Thomas F. Pettigrew, *A Profile of the Negro American* (Princeton: Van Nostrand, 1964), pp. 27–55, 62–63. For critiques of assimilation in American sociology and historiography, see Paul Metzger, "American Sociology and Black Assimilation: Conflicting Perspectives," *American Journal of Sociology*, vol. 76, January 1971; and Rudolph J. Vecoli, "Ethnicity: A Neglected Dimension of American History," *The State of American History*, ed. Herbert J. Bass (Chicago: Quadrangle, 1970).

Chapter 18: Politicization and the Schools: The Case of Bilingual Education

1. *Hobson* v. *Hansen*, 269 F. Supp. 401 (D.D.C., 1967); Alexander Bickel, "Skelly Wright's Sweeping Decision," *New Republic*, July 8, 1967, pp. 11–12.

2. Nathan Glazer, "Black English and Reluctant Judges," *Public Interest*, vol. 62, Winter 1980, pp. 40–54; *Larry P.* v. *Wilson Riles*, 495 F. Supp. 1926 (N.D. Calif., 1979); Nathan Glazer, "IQ on Trial," *Commentary*, June 1981, pp. 51–59; *Morgan* v. *Hennigan*, 379 F. Supp. 410 (D. Mass., 1974); Robert Wood, "The Disassembling of American Education," *Daedalus*, vol. 109, no. 3, Summer 1980, pp. 99–113; *Education Week*, May 12, 1982, p. 5.

3. U.S. Congress, Senate, Committee on Labor and Public Welfare, Special Subcommittee on Bilingual Education, 90th Cong., 1st sess., 1967.

4. *Lau* v. *Nichols*, 414 U.S. 563 (1974).

5. U.S. Department of Health, Education, and Welfare, "Task Force Findings Specifying Remedies Available for Eliminating Past Educational Practices Ruled Unlawful under *Lau* v. *Nichols*" (Washington, D.C., Summer 1975).

6. U.S. Congress, House, Subcommittee on Elementary, Secondary, and Vocational Education of the Committee on Education and Labor, Bilingual Education, 95th Cong., 1st sess., 1977, pp. 335–336. The speaker was Gary Orfield.

7. Malcolm N. Danoff, "Evaluation of the Impact of ESEA Title VII Spanish/English Bilingual Education Programs" (Palo Alto, Calif.: American Institutes for Research, 1978).

8. Iris Rotberg, "Some Legal and Research Considerations in Establishing Federal Policy in Bilingual Education," *Harvard Educational Review*, vol. 52, May 1982, pp. 148–168.

9. Jonathan D. Haft, "Assuring Equal Educational Opportunity for Language-Minority Students: Bilingual Education and the Equal Educational Opportunity Act of 1974," *Columbia Journal of Law and Social Problems*, vol. 18, no. 2, 1983, pp. 209–293.

10. Ibid., p. 253.

ACKNOWLEDGMENTS

"Forgetting the Questions: The Problem of Educational Reform" appeared originally in *The American Scholar*, vol. 50, no. 3, Summer 1981. Copyright © 1981 Diane Ravitch.

"The Schools We Deserve" appeared originally in *The New Republic*, April 18, 1981. Reprinted by permission of *The New Republic*. Copyright © 1982, The New Republic, Inc.

"The Continuing Crisis: Fashions in Education" appeared originally in *The American Scholar*, vol. 53, no. 2, Spring 1984. Copyright © 1984 Diane Ravitch.

"Bring Literature and History Back to Elementary Schools" appeared originally in *Education Week*, vol. 3, no. 16, January 11, 1984. Reprinted by permission of *Education Week*.

"American Education: Has the Pendulum Swung Once Too Often?" appeared originally in *Humanities*, November 1982. Reprinted by permission of *Humanities*, the bimonthly publication of the National Endowment for the Humanities.

"Scapegoating the Teachers" appeared originally in *The New Republic*, November 7, 1983. Reprinted by permission of *The New Republic*. Copyright © 1983 The New Republic, Inc.

"The Meaning of the New Coleman Report" appeared originally in *Phi Delta Kappan*, June 1981. Reprinted by permission of *Phi Delta Kappan*.

"From History to Social Studies" was originally delivered as a lecture at the Clio Conference, University of California at Berkeley, August 21, 1984. Copyright © 1984 Diane Ravitch.

"Curriculum in Crisis: Connections Between Past and Present" appeared originally in *Challenge to American Schools: The Case for Standards and Values*, ed. John H. Bunzel. Reprinted by permission of Oxford University Press. Copyright © 1985 Oxford University Press, Inc.

"Is Education Really a Federal Issue?" appeared originally in *The Washington Post*, June 5, 1983. Reprinted by permission of *The Washington Post*.

"'60s Education, '70s Benefits" appeared originally in *The New York Times*, June 29, 1978. Copyright © 1978 by The New York Times Company. Reprinted by permission.

"The Case of Tuition Tax Credits" appeared originally in *The New Republic*, December 3, 1984. Reprinted by permission of The New Republic, Inc.

"The Uses and Misuses of Tests" appeared originally in the *College Board Review*, No. 130, Winter 1983–1984. Reprinted by permission of the publisher of *The Uses and Misuses of Tests: Examining Current Issues in Educational and Psychological Testing*, ed. Charles W. Daves. Copyright © 1984 Jossey-Bass.

"On the History of Minority Group Education in the United States" appeared originally in the *Teachers College Record,* December 1976. Reprinted by permission of the *Teachers College Record.*

"Integration, Segregation, Pluralism" appeared originally in *The American Scholar,* vol. 45, no. 2, Spring 1976. Copyright © 1976 Diane Ravitch.

"Desegregation: Varieties of Meaning" appeared originally in *Shades of Brown: New Perspectives on School Desegregation.* Reprinted by permission of the publisher from Derrick Bell, editor, *Shades of Brown: New Perspectives on School Desegregation.* (New York: Teachers College Press, © 1980 by Teachers College, Columbia University.) All rights reserved.

"Color-Blind or Color-Conscious?" appeared originally in *The New Republic,* May 5, 1979. Reprinted by permission of *The New Republic.* Copyright © 1979 The New Republic, Inc.

"Politicization and the Schools: The Case of Bilingual Education" was originally delivered as a lecture to the American Philosophical Society, April 21, 1984, and published in the *Proceedings* of the Society for 1984. Reprinted by permission of the American Philosophical Society.

"A Good School" appeared originally in *The American Scholar,* vol. 53, no. 4, Fall 1984. Copyright © 1984 Diane Ravitch.

"On Thinking About the Future" appeared originally in *Phi Delta Kappan,* January 1983. Reprinted by permission of *Phi Delta Kappan.*

INDEX

ABC (A Better Chance) program, 258
Ability grouping, 14, 55, 265, 278
Abolitionist movement, 198, 199, 229, 231
Absenteeism, 49, 61, 176; in private schools, 107, 111
Academic freedom, 263
Academies, 135–36, 185
Accountability movement, 303
Accreditation standards, 169
"Achievement Test Score Decline: Do We Need to Worry?" (Harnisch-feger and Wiley), 176
Addams, Jane, 188, 320n8
Advanced placement courses, 280, 281, 287
Affirmative action, 250
American College Test, 49
American Dilemma, An (Myrdal), 242
American Historical Association, 121, 130
American Indians, *see* Indians
Americanization, 124, 140–41, 184, 188–92, 240–41; and Oregon ban on private schools, 187
Amherst College, 11–13
Andersen, Hans Christian, 77
Andersson, Theodore, 320n15
Ann Arbor, Michigan, teacher training in "black English" in, 265, 266
Anti-intellectualism, 35–36, 46, 85; of busywork, 180; of life-adjustment education, 82, 302
Antipoverty program, 250; *see also* Great Society
Arizona, minimum competency tests in, 47, 48
Arkansas, integration in, 113
Armstrong, General S. C., 201
Arnold, Matthew, 307

Arts, 155, 311, 316; in school of future, 306
Atlanta, Georgia, black population of, 210
Austen, Jane, 180, 283, 284
Ausubel, David P., 321n15
Authority, attitudes toward, 67–69, 85

Baby boom generation, 45, 94
Back-to-basics movement, 60, 177, 303
Baltimore, Maryland: bilingual schools in, 191; black high schools in, 202; black population of, 210
Bard College, 51–52
Barnard, Henry, 21, 186
Basal readers, 76–78
Basic Educational Opportunity Grants, 168
Bass, Herbert J., 322n18
Baum, L. Frank, 77
Bell, Derrick, 223
Bennett, William, 153
Berkeley, University of California at, 115
Berkhofer, Robert F., Jr., 320n16
Bestor, Arthur, 82, 94
Bible, 115, 315; Protestant, 162
Bickel, Alexander, 322n1
Biculturalism, 273
Bilingual education, 154, 266–73; in mission schools, 193–94; nineteenth-century, 191
Bilingual Education Act (1968), 268
Birmingham, Alabama, black population of, 210
Black American Scholars (Bond), 202
Black Power movement, 256
Blacks, 135, 197–205; achievement levels

Blacks *(continued)*
of, 105; in Catholic schools, 103, 104;
college enrollment of, 46, 158; and
cultural tradition, 314; dissent among,
223–25; doctorates received by, 202–
3; and higher education, 31; illiteracy
among, 47; industrial education for,
201–2; job training for, 258; in New
York City schools, 293; political
power of, 223; during Reconstruction
period, 199–200, 232–33; under slavery, 197–99, 228–32; strategy of dispersion of, 205; urban concentration
of, 210–11; violence against, 84; voting
rights denied to, 200–201, 233; *see
also* Desegregation; Integration; Racial discrimination; Segregation
Boarding schools for Indians, 195, 196
Bode, Boyd, 45
Bond, Horace Mann, 199, 202, 321*n*26
Boston, Massachusetts: assignment of
black teachers in, 217; high schools
in, 142; segregation in, 199, 217–18,
265
Bourne, Randolph, 149
Boyer, Ernest, 59, 134, 318*n*1
Boyer, Mildred, 320*n*15
Breneman, David W., 167, 319*n*3
Brontë, Charlotte, 284
Brookings Institution, 195
Brothers Grimm, 77
Brown, Linda Carol, 252
Brown, Oliver, 252
Brown v. Board of Education (1954), 10,
46, 166, 204, 209, 213, 214, 224, 227,
234–37, 239, 241, 245, 249–55, 264
Bruckner, Saul, 279, 282, 285, 287–93
Bullock, Henry Allen, 198, 320*n*23,
321*n*24
Bureau of Indian Affairs, 196
Burke, Edmund, 137
Buser, Robert L., 318*n*5
Businesses, basic skills programs run
by, 91
Busing, 223, 250, 256, 267
Butz, Mary, 282, 286, 292

Calhoun, John C., 199
California: bilingual schools in, 191;
high schools in, 65; intelligence test-
ing barred in, 265, 266; social studies
curriculum in, 116
California Roundtable, 65
Cameron, J. M., 44
"Cardinal Principles of Secondary Ed-
ucation" (Commission on the Re-
organization of Secondary Educa-
tion), 72–73, 126, 128, 146–47, 149
Career ladder programs, 4
Carlisle Indian School, 194–95, 201
Carnegie Council on Children, 106
Carter, James G., 185, 186, 320*n*4
Carter, Jimmy, 59, 164
Carter, Robert, 234–35, 252, 254, 257
Catcher in the Rye (Salinger), 283
Catholic schools, 103, 104, 108–10, 240;
declining enrollment in, 165; nine-
teenth-century, 162; Oregon ban on,
187; subsidization of, 187
Catholics, 250
Census Bureau, U.S., 210
Certification of teachers, 94, 97
Chall, Jeanne, 176, 180, 319*n*3
Charlotte-Mecklenburg, North Caro-
lina, school system, 214, 256
Chaucer, Geoffrey, 137
Cherokees, 194, 197
Chicago, University of, 102
Chinese, 191, 269
Choctaws, 194
Christian day schools, 165, 166
Christian missionaries, 193; *see also*
Mission schools
Church schools, *see* Catholic schools;
Religious schools
Cicero, 299
Cincinnati, bilingual schools in, 191
Civil disorders, 48
Civil Rights Act (1964), 104, 249–50,
255–56
Civil Rights Commission, U.S., 271
Civil rights movement, 11, 209, 251;
and bilingual education, 267, 271;
and Black Power, 256–57; coalition
forming, 250; and color-blind poli-
cies, 255, 257–58; and demographic
changes, 223; violence against, 84
Civil War, 117, 194, 199, 231, 232
Civilian Conservation Corps, 16

Index

"Civilization fund", 193
Clark, Kenneth, 223
Classical curriculum, 136–37, 139, 142
Cleveland, Ohio, black population of, 210
Cold War, 84
Coleman, James S., 54, 100–111, 167, 319*n*2
College, *see* Higher education
College Board, 47, 48, 60, 88, 174–76, 179
College Entrance Examinations, 179
Collier, John, 196
Colonization movement, 228–29, 231
Color-blind policies, 215, 217, 221, 235–39, 241, 249–59
Columbia Journal of Law and Social Problems, 271
Columbia University, 223; Teachers College, 97, 131
Commission on the Reorganization of Secondary Education, 72–73, 145–46; Committee on Social Studies of, 126–29
Committee of Eight, 124
Committee of Fifteen, 124
Committee of Five, 124
Committee of Seven, 121–23, 125, 127
Committee of Ten on Secondary School Studies, 71–72, 119–21, 125, 137–41, 143, 146
Committee on College-Entrance Requirements, 141–42
"Common learnings" courses, 82
Common schools, 21, 55, 185–86, 261; Catholic schools and, 104; desegregation and, 239–40; nineteenth-century, 185–86; segregation of, 199
Commonweal, 44
Community: meaning of, 246; sense of, 306
Community control, 106, 297
Community service agencies, schools as, 300–301
Compensatory education, 20–21, 86
Competency tests: for teachers, 90; *see also* Minimum competency tests
Compulsory education, 148, 300
Computer-assisted instruction, 302
Computer science, 64, 305

Conant, James B., 91
Congress, U.S., 4, 104, 154, 264, 309, 310; bilingual education funded by, 267–68; federal aid to education passed by, 255; Indian policies of, 193, 196; and Negro colonization, 231, 232; nineteenth-century civil rights legislation in, 232; and tuition tax credits, 164
Connecticut, social studies curriculum in, 116
Conrad, Joseph, 44
Constitution, U.S., 10, 209, 213, 251; Fourteenth Amendment to, 232–35, 252–53
Consumerism, 69
Council for Basic Education, 37
Counterculture, 85, 86
Counts, George, 182
Courts: politicization of education and, 265–66; schools' ability to maintain order eroded by, 92, 93; *see also* Supreme Court
Cremin, Lawrence A., 81, 321*n*13
Crisis in the Classroom (Silberman), 85
Cultural fragmentation, 314–15
cummings, e. e., 53
Curriculum, 41–43, 133–50; court-imposed, 265, 266; and cultural fragmentation, 314, 315; dilution of, 50, 52–53; disarray in, 43–44; early twentieth-century, 140–49; elementary, 55, 62, 75; fragmentation of, 70; functionalist, 67, 69, 72–73, 81, 82, 125; at Murrow High School, 283, 294; NEA predictions on, 300–301; nineteenth-century, 71–72, 135–40; of private schools, state regulation of, 169, 170; progressive, 208, 299; reflecting different needs, 279; required, 63–67; and SAT, 61, 62, 176–77, 179–80; strengthening, 155; technicization of, 313–15; *see also specific subjects*
Curriculum reform movement, 303
Curti, Merle, 182

Danoff, Malcolm N., 322*n*7
Declaration of Independence, 10

327

Dennison, George, 84
Denver, Colorado, segregated schools in, 215
Deschooling, 35, 46, 302
Desegregation, 213–14, 217, 220, 224, 226–48; Civil Rights Act definition of, 255; color-blind policies for, 235–39; and common school, 239–40; defiance of, 237; and federal aid to education, 256; and politicization, 264–66; and racial balance, 218; shift in meaning of term, 226–27, 247; *see also* Integration
Detroit, Michigan: black population of, 210; segregated schools in, 216, 218, 219
"Developmental lesson", 289
Dewey, Evelyn, 297–99
Dewey, John, 11, 72, 149, 220, 277, 297–99, 303, 317n2
Dickens, Charles, 44, 180, 284
Discipline, 13, 53; in private schools, 107, 110
Discrimination: against immigrants, 192; and political powerlessness, 206; *see also* Racial discrimination
Donne, John, 283
Dred Scott decision, 232
Dress codes, 110
Dropout rates, 67, 71, 135, 148, 150, 272, 278, 313; at Murrow High School, 281
Drugs, 48, 85, 88
Dubois, W. E. B., 201

Economic Opportunity Act (1964), 196
Edmonds, Ronald, 223–24, 276
Education, U.S. Department of, 51, 64, 101
Education and Ecstasy (Leonard), 302
Education for All American Youth (National Education Association), 83
Education of American Teachers, The (Conant), 91
Education of Black Philadelphia, The (Franklin), 203
Education Week, 76
Educational opportunity: and bilingual education, 273; equality of, 104; expansion of, 157; and standardized tests, 173
Educational Testing Service, 180
Educational vouchers, 100, 102, 104
Edward R. Murrow High School (Brooklyn), 279–94
Eisenhower, Dwight D., 113
Elementary and Secondary Education Act (1965), 196; Title I of, 158–59
Elementary schools: busywork in, 180; curriculum of, 55, 62, 75; instructional time in, 50; literature and history in, 75–79; mathematics and science requirements in, 64; private, 169; progressive, 298; segregated, 251; social studies in, 129; teacher training for, 94, 95; teachers in, 316
Eliot, Charles W., 71, 119, 137–40, 143
Eliot, George, 284
Elkins, Stanley, 244, 322n17
Emerson, Ralph Waldo, 68, 219
Emma (Austen), 284
Encarnation, Dennis J., 169, 319n4
English, 312; declining enrollment in, 50, 61; dissolution of curriculum for, 152; electives in, 52, 69; literacy in, bilingual education and, 154; at Murrow High School, 280, 284; in nineteenth-century schools, 136–39; remedial courses in, 65; required courses in, 64–66, 150; *see also* Literature
Ervin, Sam, 255
Ethnic associations, 189
Ethnicity, 207, 244
Ethnocentrism, 267
Experience and Education (Dewey), 300

Family, decline of, 48, 61
Faubus, Orval, 113
Featherstone, Joseph, 85
Federal aid to education, 31; and civil rights movement, 250; and desegregation, 256; and NEA predictions, 300, 301; recommended increase in, 59–60

Federal policies, 153–55; on Indians, 193–96
Fifth Circuit Court of Appeals, 256
Fishlow, Albert, 186, 320n5
Fishman, Joshua A., 192, 206, 320n12
Ford, Paul Leicester, 321n1
Foreign languages, 5, 6, 24, 42, 45, 316; and "Cardinal Principles", 146, 147, 149; classical, 136, 139, 148–49; declining enrollment in, 88, 152; early sixties enrollment in, 83; and global change, 83; at Murrow High School, 280, 281; in nineteenth-century schools, 136–39; percentage of students studying, 50–51; post-World War I ban on teaching, 163, 190, 262; in private schools, 109; required courses in, 52, 54, 64–66, 135, 155; in school of future, 306; shortage of teachers of, 153, 308; social utility of, 150; *see also* Bilingual education
Foreign Service, 271
France, quality of education in, 56–57
Frankfurter, Felix, 236
Franklin, Vincent P., 203
Frederick Douglass High School (Baltimore), 202
Frederickson, George M., 220, 230, 321n2
"Free" schools, 35, 302, 303
Freedmen's Bureau, 199
Freedom-of-choice desegregation plans, 213, 237, 256
Freud, Sigmund, 44
Friedenberg, Edgar Z., 84
Fundamental skills, 41

Gagnon, Paul, 56
Gallup Poll, 13, 275
Gannett newspapers, 50
Garrison, William Lloyd, 228
Garrity, Arthur, 217
Gary, Indiana: black population of, 210; vocational education in, 299
Gary plan, 149–50
Genovese, Eugene, 244, 322n17
Geography, 76

Germans, 189, 191
Gerrymandering, 253, 255, 256
GI Bill, 31
Glazer, Nathan, 167, 322n1
Goodlad, John, 288
Goodman, Paul, 84
Gossett, Thomas F., 321n3
Government regulation of private schools, 168–70
Grade inflation, 49, 61, 174, 176, 281
Graduate schools of education, 96–97
Great Britain, informal education in, 85, 87
Great Depression, 130, 293
Great Expectations (Dickens), 283, 284
Great Gatsby, The (Fitzgerald), 283
Great Society, 157–59
Greek immigrants, 188–89
Greeks, ancient, 53, 79, 115, 118
Green v. County School Board (1968), 213, 214
Greer, Colin, 319n1
Grey, Lady Jane, 145
Gross, Richard E., 116, 317n5
Grove City College, 170
Gutman, Herbert, 244, 322n17

Haas, John D., 115, 317n4
Haft, Jonathan D., 322n9
Haiti, proposed American Negro colony in, 231
Hall, G. Stanley, 139
Hamilton, Charles, 223, 224
Hampton Normal and Agricultural Institute, 201
Harlan, John Marshall, 233–34, 236, 238, 251
Harlan, Louis R., 321n28
Harnischfeger, Annegret, 49–50, 88, 176, 318n1, 319n1
Harris, W. T., 201
Hartford, Connecticut, segregation in, 199
Harvard Educational Review, 106, 270
Harvard University, 71, 96, 119, 176, 223; Business School, 169; Graduate School of Education, 224, 276

Index

Hawaii: Japanese private schools in, 190; social studies curriculum in, 116

Health, Education, and Welfare, U.S. Department of (HEW), 217

Heatwole, Cornelius J., 320n5

Henry, O., 289

Herndon, James, 84

Hertzberg, Hazel Whitman, 317n5

"High-performance" schools, 108-9, 110

High School (Boyer), 59

"High School and Beyond" (Coleman study), 101–102

High schools, 4, 14–17, 61–63, 76; anti-intellectualism and changes in, 36; black, 202; and "Cardinal Principles", 72–73; competency tests in, *see* Minimum competency tests; curriculum of, *see* Curriculum; early twentieth-century, 140–49; educational malpractice suits against, 37; grade inflation in, 173–74; graduation rates of, 30, 46; graduation requirements of, 4, 14, 15, 32–33, 63–69, 91, 92, 134, 135, 150, 152, 177, 312; history courses in, 78, 112–32; nineteenth-century, 71–72, 135–40; and open education, 87; and progressivism, 81; public v. private, 100–111; student radicalism in, 85; teacher training for, 94

Higher education, 6–7; access to, 29, 31, 47; admission requirements for, 4, 52, 68, 69, 91, 117–18, 152, 155, 177; anti-intellectualism and changes in, 36; black, 224; curricula in, 43; education majors, 90, 93–97; enrollment rates in, 46, 157–58; and government regulations, 170; grant programs in, 168; nineteenth-century 136–40; percent of Murrow graduates attending, 281–82; politicization of, 261, 263; proportion of young people entering, 30; and remedial courses, 36–37, 51–52, 63, 65; standardized tests for admission to, 173–75 *and see* Scholastic Aptitude Test; student protests in, 84; vocational education and, 147

Hispanics, 135; bilingual education for, 272; in Catholic schools, 104; and cultural tradition, 314; in New York City schools, 293; and racial balance, 218

History, 24, 42–44, 112–32, 311, 312, 316; declining enrollment in, 50, 61; dilution and fragmentation in teaching of, 116–17, 152; electives in, 52, 69; in elementary schools, 75–79; and growth of mass society, 83; at Murrow High School, 285, 287; and progressivism, 124–25; required courses in, 150, 155; rote memorization of, 118–21; in school of future, 305–306; social benefits of courses in, 121–23; social utility of, 150; values taught through, 23; *see also* Social studies

Hoffer, Thomas, 102, 319n2

Holt, John, 84

Homework, 49, 53–54, 61, 63, 65, 152, 155, 176; in private schools, 107, 108

House of Representatives, U.S., 164; *see also* Congress, U.S.

Houston, Texas, competency test for teachers in, 90; San Jacinto high school, 283

Howard University, 224

Human potential movement, 302

Humm, William, 318n5

Hurd, Paul DeHart, 69–70

Hutchins, Robert, 26, 82, 222, 317n5

Illich, Ivan, 84, 302

Illinois: nonacademic courses in, 138; released time for religious education in, 163–64; social studies curriculum in, 116

Illiteracy, 37, 47, 62; among blacks, 198, 200; among Indians, 195; as instrument of social control, 206; scientific, 51

Immersion programs, 271

Immigrants, 8–9, 239, 243; Americanization of, 124, 140–41, 188–92, 240–41; "impact aid" program for, 154; industrial education for, 143–44; and Oregon ban on private schools, 187; vocational education for, 149

"Impact aid" program, 154

Index

Indiana, history teachers in, 115
Indians, 192–97, 201
Industrial education, 143, 299; for blacks, 201–202
Inequality (Jencks), 106
Institute for Government Research, 195
Integration, 204–205, 217; and achievement levels, 105; and color-blind policies, 235–37, 252, 254; establishment of conscious policy of, 214–15; and freedom-of-choice plans, 256; and neighborhood schools, 216; and pluralism, 211–13, 220–25; in public v. private schools, 101, 102; and racial balance, 217–19, 243, 267; and teacher assignment, 217; *see also* Desegregation
Intelligence tests, 265
Introduction to the History of the Social Sciences, An (Johnson), 131
Iowa: history teachers in, 115; social studies curriculum in, 116
Iowa testing program, 49
Irish, 189, 207, 211, 223, 240, 243
Isaacs, Harold, 320n2
Italians, 189, 207, 211, 223, 239, 240, 243

James, Thomas, 319n2
Japan, quality of education in, 56
Japan as Number One (Vogel), 56
Japanese, 190, 191
Jefferson, Thomas, 228, 321n1
Jencks, Christopher, 106
Jessup, Georgia, black high school in, 203
Jews, 207, 243; in civil rights movement, 250; immigrant, 189–90, 211, 239; in New York City schools, 240, 293; private schools for, 191
Jim Crow laws, 221, 223
Johnson, Henry, 131, 318n22
Johnson, Lyndon, 31, 196
Jonson, Ben, 283
Jorgenson, Lloyd P., 320n5
Julius Caesar (Shakespeare), 283
Junior high schools, 62, 76; history in, 78; instructional time in, 50; mathematics and science requirements in, 64; science electives in, 70; social studies in, 116

Kandel, I. L., 318n3
Kansas, school segregation in, 234, 235, 252
Karier, Clarence J., 319n1
Katz, Michael, 319n1
Kennedy, John F., 83, 84, 113, 183, 196
Kennedy, Robert, 183, 255
Keyes v. Denver School District No. 1 (1973), 215
Kilgore, Sally, 102, 319n2
King, Martin Luther, Jr., 183
Kirkendall, Richard S., 317n2
Kloss, Heinz, 191–92, 320n12
Koerner, James, 91
Kohl, Herbert, 84
Kozol, Jonathan, 84
Krug, Edward A., 137, 140, 317n7, 318n4
Ku Klux Klan, 187

Lau v. Nichols, 268–69
"Learning by doing", 298
Leibowitz, Arnold H., 320n11
Leonard, George, 302–303
Levin, Henry M., 319n2
Life-adjustment education, 45, 82, 302
Lifelong education, 158
Lincoln, Abraham, 231
Linquist, G. E. E., 320n19
Lippincott (publisher), 77
Literature, 24, 42–44, 311, 316; assessment of knowledge of, 313; common foundation of readings in, 315; in elementary schools, 75–79; and growth of mass society, 83; at Murrow High School, 283–84; in nineteenth-century schools, 137; required courses in, 155; in school of future, 306; social utility of, 150; values taught through, 23
Loyalty investigations, 262

M. Street School (Washington, D.C.), 202

McCarthy era, 263

McCullers, Carson, 283

McDonough 25 High School (New Orleans), 202

Magnet schools, 167

Malpractice, educational, 37

Mann, Horace, 21, 186, 238, 261

Marshall, Thurgood, 236, 238, 253

Maryland, social studies curriculum in, 116

Massachusetts: Advisory Committee on Racial Imbalance and Education, 243; high school curriculum in, 61; racially imbalanced schools in, 218; University of, 56

Massachusetts Institute of Technology (MIT), 8

Master teachers, 90

Mathematics, 5, 6, 24, 42, 45, 311, 312, 316; and "Cardinal Principles", 146, 147; declining enrollment in, 50, 152; at Murrow High School, 280, 281, 294; in nineteenth-century schools, 136, 138, 139; in private schools, 110; remedial college courses in, 63, 65; required courses in, 52, 64–67, 69, 134, 135, 150, 155; in school of future, 306; shortage of teachers of, 153, 308; social utility of, 150; Sputnik and renewed emphasis on, 82, 83

Melting pot philosophy, 214, 219–21, 241, 244–45, 247

Melville, Herman, 44, 53

Member of the Wedding, A (McCullers), 283

Memphis, Tennessee, black population of, 210

Mental discipline, 118

Meriam, Lewis, 195

Merit pay, 4, 90, 177

Metropolitan Applied Research Center, 223

Metzger, Paul, 322n18

Meyer v. Nebraska (1923), 163, 190

Middlebury College, 271

Midwood High School, 294

Miller, Marion Mills, 321n5

Milliken v. Bradley (1976), 218

Milton, John, 53, 137, 283

Minimum competency tests, 37, 48, 60, 177, 303

Mini-schools, 167

Minnesota: social studies curriculum in, 116; tax deductions for educational expenses in, 164

Minnesota Scholastic Aptitude Test, 49

Minorities, 182–207; achievement levels of, 104, 105; and community schools, 240–41; and declining SAT scores, 48, 60, 176; dropout rate among, 67; and Great Society programs, 159; illiteracy among, 62; at Murrow High School, 279; and nineteenth-century schools, 185–87; occupational and educational programs for, 258–59; private schools for, 184, 187–88; special needs of, 150; writing ability of, 51; *see also specific groups*

Miseducation of American Teachers, The (Koerner), 91

Mission schools: for blacks, 198–200, 202; for Indians, 193–95

Missouri, social studies curriculum in, 116

Moral education, 22

Morrill, Lot M., 232–33

Moynihan, Daniel Patrick, 164, 168

Myer, Dillon S., 196

Myrdal, Gunnar, 10, 242, 321n14

Nabrit, James M., 254

Nader, Ralph, 37

"Nation at Risk, A" (National Commission on Excellence in Education), 75

National Assessment of Educational Progress, 47, 314

National Association for the Advancement of Colored People (NAACP), 218, 220, 221, 234, 238, 251–54; Legal Defense Fund of, 250

National Center for Educational Statistics, 64, 101, 154

National Commission on Excellence in Education, 4, 58, 59, 62, 69, 70, 75, 117, 133, 134, 151, 153

National Education Association (NEA), 37, 83, 119, 121, 126, 137, 141, 144, 147; Department of Superintendence of, 144; Educational Policies Commissions of, 300–301
National Endowment for the Humanities, 153, 285
National Institute of Education, 97, 288
National Opinion Research Center, 102
National Science Board, 64; Commission on Precollege Education in Mathematics, Science, and Technology of, 59, 134
National Science Foundation, 51, 86, 109, 153
Nebraska: foreign-language courses banned in, 190; social studies curriculum in, 116
Neighborhood school policies, 214–16
Neill, A. S., 68, 84
New Deal, 196
New Jersey: integration in, 199; Supreme Court of, 92
New Kent County, Virginia, school system, 213–14
New Mexico: bilingual schools in, 191; social studies curriculum in, 116
New Orleans: black high schools in, 202; black population of, 210
New Republic, 45, 84
New York City: Board of Education, 237, 279; Catholic schools in, 162; church schools in, 185; community control in, 106; ethnic minorities in, 240; Gary plan in, 149; high schools in, 279–94; history teachers in, 115
New York Herald Tribune, 287
New York State: graduation requirements in, 66; history teachers in, 115; open education in, 85; racially imbalanced schools in, 218, 243; social studies curriculum in, 116; Supreme Court decisions affecting, 164
New York Times, 287, 292
Newark, New Jersey, black population of, 210
Night (Wiesel), 283
Night school movement, 189
Nixon, Richard M., 113

North Carolina, social studies curriculum in, 116
Nursery schools, increased enrollment in, 157

Office of Education, U.S., 82, 256, 269, 270
Oklahoma: history teachers in, 115; social studies curriculum in, 116
Open Court (publishers), 77
Open education, 46, 68, 85–88, 303
Open enrollment, 167
Operation Head Start, 31, 158–59
Oregon: history teachers in, 115; public school attendance required in, 163, 187–88
Organization of American Historians (OAH), 115, 116
Orwell, George, 284
Othello (Shakespeare), 283

Packwood, Robert, 164
Panama, proposed American Negro colony in, 231
Parental involvement, 167
Parochial schools, 163; and Americanization, 189; ban on, 262; foreign language courses in, 190; *see also* Catholic schools
Paul Laurence Dunbar High School (Washington, D.C.), 202
Pennsylvania, Indian school in, 194
Pettigrew, Thomas F., 322m18
Philips Andover Academy, 288
Pierce v. Society of Sisters (1925), 163, 188
Pigman, The (Zindel), 283
"Platoon system", 149
Plessy v. Ferguson (1896), 233, 251
Pluralism, 207; and bilingual education, 273; in Indian education policies, 195, 197; and integration, 211–13, 220–25
Poles, 189, 191, 207
Political participation: decline in, 33–34; and values, 41

Politicization of education, 261–74; and bilingual education, 266–73; and desegregation, 264–66; McCarthy era, 262, 263; and segregation, 263–64; and student radicalism, 262–63

Poverty: culture of, 242; education as weapon against, 31–32; and industrial education, 143–44; rediscovery of, 84

Pratt, General R. H., 194, 201

Preliminary Scholastic Aptitude Test (PSAT), 175

Preschool education, 158

President's Commission on Foreign Language and International Studies, 50, 88, 109

Pride and Prejudice (Austen), 283–84

Prince Edward County, 236

Princeton University, 119

Private schools, 54, 100–111; ban on, 262; history courses in, 112–13; innovative, 303; for minorities, 184, 187–88, 190, 191, 205; nineteenth-century, 136, 185; see also Tuition tax credits

Progressive education, 45, 80–84, 144, 298–300, 303; curriculum in, 139, 143; examples of good schools according to, 276; history in, 124–25; and social efficiency, 144–45, 147

Promotion: automatic, 47, 49, 61, 176; court-imposed standards for, 266; at Murrow High School, 281; standards for, 68–69

"Public and Private Schools" (Coleman), 100–111

Pursuit of Excellence, The (Rockefeller Brothers Fund), 83

Quotas, racial, 250, 255, 258

Racial balancing, 217–19, 243, 267

Racial discrimination, 227; and ability grouping, 55; cultural and psychological damage inflicted by, 242–44; post-Civil War laws against, 232–33;

struggle against, 46 *and see* Integration; *see also* Segregation

Rand Corporation, 10

Reading, programs for teaching, 76–78

Reagan, Ronald, 59, 62, 64

Reconstruction, 200, 233

Recruitment and Training Program (RTP), 258

Reimer, Everett, 302

Released time for religious instruction, 163–64

Religious schools, 162–64, 166, 171; nineteenth-century, 185, 187; subsidization of, 261; *see also* Catholic schools

Remedial education: in college, 36–37, 51–52, 63, 65; at Murrow High School, 281

Republicans, post-Civil War, 232

Rhode Island, social studies curriculum in, 116

Richard II (Shakespeare), 282, 283

Riis, Jacob, 31

Robinson, Spottswood, 236

Rockefeller Brothers Fund, 83

Romantic racialists, 229

Romeo and Juliet (Shakespeare), 283

Roosevelt, Theodore, 143

Rosovsky, Henry, 320n5

Rotberg, Iris, 322n8

Rote memorization, 118–21

Rousseau, Jean-Jacques, 68

St. Louis, Missouri, black population of, 210

Salinger, J. D., 283

San Francisco, bilingual education in, 269

Scholastic Aptitude Test (SAT), 36, 37, 47–49, 60–63, 88, 90, 175–80, 313

School finance reforms, 166, 167

School Is Dead (Reimer), 35, 302

School prayer, banning of, 166

Schools of Tomorrow (Dewey), 297

Schools-without-walls, 46

Schultz, Stanley K., 319n1

Index

Science, 5, 6, 24, 42, 46, 311, 312, 316; and "Cardinal Principles", 146, 147; declining achievement scores in, 63; declining enrollment in, 50, 152; electives in, 69–70; illiteracy in, 51; at Murrow High School, 280, 281, 294; in nineteenth-century schools, 136–39; in private schools, 110; reduced requirements in, 52, 53; required courses in, 64–67, 69, 134, 135, 150, 155; in school of future, 306; shortage of teachers of, 153, 308; social utility of, 150; Sputnik and renewed emphasis on, 82, 83; values taught through, 22–23

Scott, Dred, 232

Sectarian schools, *see* Catholic schools; Religious schools

Segregation, 10, 105, 200–203, 208–9, 212, 217; in antebellum North, 199; in bilingual education, 270; *de jure* v. *de facto*, 214–16, 237; and politicization, 263–64; and separate-but-equal doctrine, 233–34; shift in meaning of term, 226–27, 247; Supreme Court ruling against, 208 *and see Brown v. Board of Education*

Senate, U.S., 164; *see also* Congress

Separate-but-equal doctrine, 233–34, 250–51

Sex-role stereotyping, 48

Shakespeare, William, 115, 137, 283, 315

Shotwell, John B., 320*n*11

Silas Marner (Eliot), 283

Silberman, Charles, 85

Sizer, Theodore, 288

Slavery, 197–99, 228–32, 244

Smith, James P., 10, 317*n*1

Smith, Mortimer, 82, 94

Smith, Timothy L., 189, 320*n*9

Social change, schools as instruments of, 31–35, 39, 86, 144, 147, 186

Social determinism, 104–106

Social efficiency, ideology of, 129–30, 144–45

Social services, schools as providers of, 21–22

Social studies, 112–32; and "Cardinal Principles", 126–28, 146, 147; at Murrow High School, 281, 284–85; required courses in, 64–66; *see also* History

Sociological perspective, 38–40

Soltes, Mordecai, 190, 320*n*10

Soviet Union, 84; *see also* Sputnik

Sowell, Thomas, 224

Special education, 265

Spring, Joel H., 319*n*1

Sputnik, 4, 46, 62, 73, 82–83, 113, 130, 151, 152

Stampp, Kenneth, 244, 322*n*17

Standardized tests, 114, 172–81; and college admissions, 173–75; curriculum-free, 179–80; declining scores on, 36–37, 48–50, 88, 152, 175–77; and "pursuit of excellence," 84; and quality of classwork, 180–81; of reading, 76; simplistic thinking promoted by, 178–79; and technicization, 313–14

Stanford University, 70, 96, 116

State education departments, 92

State legislatures, and high school graduation requirements, 92

Stern, Curt, 244, 245

Student radicalism, 46, 84, 85, 263

Subversion, fear of, 188, 262

Summerhill (Neill), 68, 84

Supreme Court, U.S.: bilingual education decision, 268–69, 271; college aid decision, 170; desegregation decisions, 208, 213–15, 217–19, 221, 234–36, 249–54, 256, 264; foreign language instruction decision, 190, 262; private school decisions, 163, 164, 188; separate-but-equal doctrine, 233

Swann v. Charlotte-Mecklenburg, 214–15, 217, 219, 221

Sykes, Gary, 97

Tammany Hall, 149

Tanner, Daniel, 319*n*18

Tanner, Laurel N., 319*n*18

Taylor, Bob L., 115, 317*n*4

Teachers, 90–99; authority of, 68; black, 217; "black English" training for, 265; competence of, 90, 91, 93; education of, 28, 93–98, 177; and

335

Teachers *(continued)*
educational fashions, 80, 89, 303, 304; and educational reformers, 19–20; federal programs for, 153–54; of history, 115, 120, 122, 123; and improvement in achievement, 155; lower expectations of, 53; loyalty investigations of, 262; minority, 216; at Murrow High School, 281, 288–92; poor conditions for, 152; in private schools, 164, 169, 170; professionalism of, 93, 98, 181, 316; and progressive education, 81, 299, 303; public attitudes toward, 275; qualification tests for, 4; quality of, 105, 133–34; salaries of, 4, 45, 90, 94, 98, 307; in school of future, 306; shortage of, 45, 94, 135, 308; status of, 65, 307–308; "subversive," 45, 262; testing of, 62, 90; training in open education for, 85, 87; unionization of, 29, 98; vocational, 17
Team teaching, 86
Technicization, 313–15
Television, 33, 54; and test score declines, 48, 61, 88
Textbooks: and cultural fragmentation, 314, 315; declining quality of, 61–62; emphasis on "objective answers" in, 180; grade level of verbal content of, 176; history, 118–20, 123; provided to nonpublic schools, 164; "subversive," 45
Therapeutic community, school as, 86
"Time-on-task", 54, 276
Tollett, Kenneth, 224
Tolstoy, Leo, 44
Topeka, Kansas, school segregation in, 234, 251, 252, 254
Tracking, 14, 63, 67, 73, 277–78, 312; and "Cardinal Principles", 126; and electives, 70; in public v. private schools, 107–08
Transformation of the School, The (Cremin), 81
Truancy, 53; *see also* Absenteeism
"Truth-in-testing" laws, 37
Tryon, Rolla M., 317n7
Tuition tax credits, 100, 102, 103, 161–71

Turner, Frederick Jackson, 219
Tuskegee Institute, 201
Twentieth Century Fund, 154
Tyack, David, 187, 320n6

UCLA, 288
Ungraded classrooms, 86
Unionization of teachers, 28–29, 98
Upper Arlington, Ohio, reading experiment, 76

Values; conflicting, 46; and politicization, 261; teaching of, 22–24; traditional, 276; widely-shared, 41
Vecoli, Rudolph J., 322n18
Vermont: open education in, 85; social studies curriculum in, 116
Vietnam war, 36, 48, 84, 88, 183, 262, 263
Vinson, Fred, 236
Violas, Paul C., 319n1
Virginia, nineteenth-century schools in, 186
Vives, Juan Luis, 131
Vocational education, 17, 69, 279, 301, 313; and academic requirements, 66, 135; and "Cardinal Principles", 126; and college admission, 147; declining enrollment in, 50; and federal aid to education, 300; for immigrants, 149; and tracking, 14, 67, 70, 277
Vogel, Ezra, 56
Voting rights, blacks' loss of, 200–201
Voting Rights Act (1965), 250

Washington, Booker T., 201
Washington, D.C.: ability grouping in, 265; black high schools in, 202; black population of, 210; segregated schools in, 254
Watergate, 48, 88, 183
Wayne County Training School (Jessup, Georgia), 202–203
Webber, Thomas, 244, 322n17

Index

West Virginia: reconstruction of system of education in, 265, 266; social studies curriculum in, 116

Western Michigan University, 8

White flight, 210

White supremacy, doctrine of, 197, 208–209, 230, 233

Whites: achievement levels of, 105; in Catholic schools, 104; illiteracy among, 47; percentage completing college, 158; *see also* Desegregation; Integration; Segregation

Wiesel, Elie, 283

Wiley, David E., 49–50, 88, 176, 318n1, 319n21

Wilkins, Roy, 255

Wilson, Woodrow, 119

Wirtz, Willard, 60–62, 69, 176, 180

Wisconsin: nineteenth-century schools in, 186; social studies curriculum in, 116

Women: college enrollment rates for, 46; and cultural tradition, 314; declining interest in teaching profession among, 94; in workforce, 48, 88, 305

Wood, Robert, 322n2

Woodson, Carter G., 198, 320n22, 321n25

Woodward, C. Vann, 321n6

Work ethic: contempt for, 85; and Indians, 193

World War I, 126, 143, 145, 149, 188, 190, 262

World War II, 81, 288; relocation of Japanese-Americans during, 196

Xenophon, 137

Yiddish press, 190

Zindel, Paul, 283